Fifteenth-Century Lives

ReFormations: Medieval and Early Modern

SERIES EDITORS: DAVID AERS, SARAH BECKWITH, AND JAMES SIMPSON

RECENT TITLES IN THE SERIES

Unwritten Verities: The Making of England's Vernacular Legal Culture, 1463–1549 (2015)
Sebastian Sobecki

Mysticism and Reform, 1400–1750 (2015)
Sara S. Poor and Nigel Smith, eds.

The Civic Cycles: Artisan Drama and Identity in Premodern England (2015)
Nicole R. Rice and Margaret Aziza Pappano

Tropologies: Ethics and Invention in England, c. 1350–1600 (2016)
Ryan McDermott

Volition's Face: Personification and the Will in Renaissance Literature (2017)
Andrew Escobedo

Shadow and Substance: Eucharistic Controversy and English Drama across the Reformation Divide (2017)
Jay Zysk

Queen of Heaven: The Assumption and Coronation of the Virgin in Early Modern English Writing (2018)
Lilla Grindlay

Performance and Religion in Early Modern England: Stage, Cathedral, Wagon, Street (2019)
Matthew J. Smith

Theater of the Word: Selfhood in the English Morality Play (2019)
Julie Paulson

Chaucer and Religious Controversies in the Medieval and Modern Eras (2019)
Nancy Bradley Warren

Versions of Election: From Langland and Aquinas to Calvin and Milton (2020)
David Aers

Saint Petronilla, Queen's College Manuscript 349, fol. 56 v. By permission of the provost and fellows of the Queen's College, Oxford.

Fifteenth-Century Lives

Writing Sainthood in England

KAREN A. WINSTEAD

University of Notre Dame Press
Notre Dame, Indiana

University of Notre Dame Press
Notre Dame, Indiana 46556
undpress.nd.edu

All Rights Reserved

Copyright © 2020 by the University of Notre Dame

Published in the United States of America

Library of Congress Control Number: 2020946985

ISBN: 978-0-268-10853-3 (Hardback)
ISBN: 978-0-268-10854-0 (Paperback)
ISBN: 978-0-268-10856-4 (WebPDF)
ISBN: 978-0-268-10855-7 (Epub)

FOR CARL

*With love and thanks
for everything.
Always.*

CONTENTS

Acknowledgments xi

Introduction 1

ONE   New Directions: The Hagiography of John Lydgate   11
TWO   Osbern Bokenham's Holy Women   41
THREE Holy Educators and "Teaching Hagiographies"   75
FOUR   Holiness and the Modern Woman   101
FIVE   Golden Legends and Foxe's *Acts and Monuments*:   125
       Rethinking the Hagiographical Anthology

Afterword: Afterlives   147

Notes   161
Bibliography   179
Index   193

ACKNOWLEDGMENTS

I thank the National Endowment for the Humanities for the year-long fellowship that supported my foundational research and initial writing for *Fifteenth-Century Lives*.

I thank James Simpson, David Aers, and Sarah Beckwith, who read chapters and encouraged me to submit the manuscript to their ReFormations series at the University of Notre Dame Press.

I thank Nancy Warren and the anonymous readers for UNDP for their careful readings and astute advice.

I thank Stephen Little of UNDP for his patient support.

I thank my husband, Carl, always my first reader, interlocutor, critic, and best friend. *Fifteenth-Century Lives* is for him.

INTRODUCTION

The fifteenth century was a golden age of Middle English hagiography.

From the early 1400s, English authors were celebrating vulnerable, even fallible saints whom readers could aspire to emulate, not just admire. Family-oriented, or at least family-tolerant, hagiography was in clear vogue by the middle of the century, when hagiographers were composing some of the first Middle English lives of wives and mothers and displaying marked attention to family relations in the legends of diverse saints. Fifteenth-century hagiographers were rewriting lives of virgins to stress their humility, piety, and gentility as much as, or more than, their unwavering commitment to celibacy; that is, they were emphasizing qualities that would be appropriate in lay readers.[1] At the same time, hagiographers increasingly celebrated teachers and pastors—men and women who prized the welfare of others and who aimed to foster an informed and intellectualized Christianity within their communities.

Formal experimentation abounded as authors tried out new approaches to telling lives and turned to new sources. John Lydgate's saints' lives, with their aureate rhetoric, are flamboyantly literary. The scope and intricacy of his "epic" five-book lives of saints Edmund and Fremund and of Alban and Amphibalus were unprecedented in Middle English hagiography. Other "firsts" were Lydgate's compact life of Austin, which focuses on a single incident, and his life of Giles, told in the second person. Jerome's *Life of Malchus*, translated into Middle English for the first time during the 1430s, is the first life of a saint told in the first person. John Capgrave relays his *Life of Saint Katherine* from the perspective of an opinionated narrator whose enthusiasm for his subject is unmistakable but whose reliability is suspect.² Not least of the experiments is the strongly hagiographical *Book of Margery Kempe*, a generic hybrid considered by many to be the first autobiography (or, as some call it, "autohagiography") in English.³

During the fifteenth century, lives of time-honored saints such as Katherine of Alexandria received new spins, and lives were translated that had never before been told in Middle English, from that of the wishy-washy desert father Malchus to those of the thirteenth-century beguines of Liège. Jacobus de Voragine's *Legenda aurea*, that hagiographical classic from the thirteenth century, was translated into English for the first time, and in the process it was updated to suit the literary tastes and religious sensibilities of a new age. Moreover, new kinds of specialized collections were assembled, including lives of teachers, lives of Continental holy women, and lives centered on parent–child relations.⁴ These collections contrast sharply with the traditional anthologies of lives of virgins or passions of martyrs, and they captured the new ideals of holiness that were being embraced by clergy and laity.

Various factors encouraged such inventiveness. During the fifteenth century, English replaced French as the preferred language of the cultural elite.⁵ Many of the "new" approaches to hagiography that first appear in English during the fifteenth century can be found in French and Latin hagiographies of the thirteenth and fourteenth centuries.⁶ Osbern Bokenham's exemplary holy women resemble in many respects Nicholas Bozon's; John Lydgate's lives have the historical and political complexity of Matthew Paris's; the narrator of Capgrave's *Life of Saint Katherine* is as obtrusive as that of Garnier of Pont-Sainte-Maxence's life of Thomas Becket.⁷ The values enshrined in fifteenth-century hagiography are consonant with those of a confident, socially conservative reading public that was intellectually inquisitive, widely read, and receptive to literary experimentation.

Many of these readers were women. Wealthy women had, from the twelfth century, been the intended or presumed readers for some of the most inventive hagiography written in the French of England, from Garnier's life of Thomas Becket to Matthew Paris's life of Edmund of Abingdon.⁸ Their savvy intellectual descendants in the fifteenth century—Ann Mortimer, Lady March; Elizabeth Vere, Countess of Oxford; Isabella Bourchier, Countess of Eu; Margaret, Duchess of Clarence, among others—were seeking reading material in English.⁹ Many enjoyed warm relationships with members of the clergy, who encouraged their spiritual development by providing books and also spiritual comfort and direction. These women encouraged and inspired the production of more, and more varied, lives of female saints. They also requested lives of Christian scholars and teachers of both sexes, from Mary Magdalene (considered an apostle to the apostles and missionary to Gaul) to Augustine of Hippo.[10] Freestanding lives of three Church Fathers—Augustine, Ambrose, and Jerome—were composed in Middle English for the first time during the fifteenth century, and at least two of them were written for particular women (the intended recipient of the third is unknown).[11] Simon Horobin hypothesizes that Cecily, Duchess of York, was the recipient of Bokenham's ambitious anthology of almost two hundred saints' legends.[12] An anonymous account of Cecily's pious practices attests that she listened to readings from the "legenda aurea," which may designate Bokenham's translation of Jacobus de Voragine's massive collection by that name.[13] As we will see, some of the most theologically sophisticated and intellectually demanding lives were written for and/or about women.

Paradoxically, creative and intellectually daring hagiography appears to have arisen from the climate of repression and censorship that prevailed during the first decades of the fifteenth century. Towards the end of the fourteenth century, antiheretical rhetoric escalated, paving the way, as Paul Strohm has shown, for the emergence of a "persecuting society" that was willing to kill its dissidents.[14] Shortly after the statute *De heretico comburendo*, passed by Parliament in 1401, made heresy a capital crime, the first Englishman, the Norfolk priest William Sawtry, was executed under it. John Badby became the first layman burned for heresy in 1410. Thomas Arundel, archbishop of Canterbury from 1397 to 1414, launched a vigorous campaign against Wycliffism and the "lollard" heresy. His "Constitutions," promulgated in 1409, aimed to stamp out error by prohibiting unauthorized translation of scripture and strictly regulating the oral or written transmission of religious thought.[15] They promoted what Rita Copeland has described as "a systematized pedagogy of infantilization, an 'education' structured around conserving ignorance."[16]

Since 1995, when Nicholas Watson famously labeled the "Constitutions" "one of the most draconian pieces of censorship in English history," scholars have vigorously debated exactly what its effect was.[17]

The general consensus, as Andrew Cole put it, is that the program envisioned by Arundel did not produce "a dampening down of ideas, a disinterest in vernacularity, and a quashing of experimentation in theology and literary form."[18] Kathryn Kerby-Fulton has called the fifteenth century "an age of *failed* censorship," while Jeremy Catto finds not a closing but an "opening of the English mind" in the generation following Arundel.[19] Though heresy continued to be persecuted, Arundel's successor, Henry Chichile, adopted a subtler, less strident approach.[20] His broadly "humanistic" archiepiscopate (1414–43) encouraged preaching and sought to dissociate itself from Arundelian extremism.[21] Chichile's successor, John Stafford, likewise promoted religious education. Though "Stafford's advocacy of vernacular religious learning may have been a minority position in the middle years of the fifteenth century," as Shannon McSheffrey notes, the situation changed drastically by the turn of the century, when the printing presses of William Caxton, Wynkyn de Worde, and Richard Pynson "were producing a deluge of editions of vernacular religious treatises," some advancing ambitious programs of lay religious education.[22]

Certain orthodox thinkers were promoting their own reformist agendas, and positions embraced by Wycliffites and by those who considered themselves orthodox commingled productively both in the minds of the faithful and in the literature they owned and read.[23] This is not to say that all post-Arundelian clergy embraced more capacious definitions of orthodoxy. Watson observes that "hospitality" to new ways of thinking competed with "hostility": "Chichile's church may have been more constructive than Arundel's; it was just as anxious."[24] From 1428 to 1431, sixty suspected heretics appeared before Bishop Alnwick of Norwich.[25] Through the century, heretics continued to be tried, condemned, and burned, and in some instances their consumption and ownership of books figured in their prosecution.[26] Opposition to vernacular "theologizing," at least in some quarters, remained strong. In 1457, Reginald Pecock, author of a series of books that aimed to combat lollardy through a rigorous program of religious instruction, was accused of heresy; though he recanted his "erroneous" beliefs, he was stripped of his bishopric and died in confinement at Thorney Abbey.[27]

The hagiography I will be examining in this book expresses the anxious reformist impulses of its time. Intellectually enterprising clergy who came of age when the intellectual climate was most toxic were perhaps more prone to value and to promote the efficacy of teaching and study over censorship and violence. For many of them, hagiography was an ideal vehicle for reform. In any case, hagiography that expressed liberal, reformist views proliferated through the fifteenth century and beyond. Some saints depicted in these fifteenth-century lives study scripture or self-consciously model their lives on the Gospels; martyrs routinely denounce the veneration of images and statues; saints of all kinds encourage a personal relationship with Jesus and a sound knowledge of the faith. Lollard readers experiencing what Fiona Somerset describes as "fraught personal and social tensions" would find kindred spirits in Middle English hagiography, from the epic lives of Lydgate to English translations of Jacobus's *Legenda aurea*.[28] Lollards were not the only ones to use stories to "show their readers how to feel like saints."[29] Such feeling was encouraged routinely by orthodox fifteenth-century hagiographers. The stories of lollards and orthodox alike, then, worked to promote an empowered, confident laity on the eve of the Reformation.

Fifteenth-Century Lives examines the promotion in fifteenth-century hagiography of an intellectualized, strongly feminized piety that is all too commonly assumed to be a product of the Renaissance. The first two chapters are devoted to two of the most prolific and innovative Middle English hagiographers: John Lydgate and Osbern Bokenham. Many of Lydgate's innovations would come to characterize fifteenth-century saints' lives. In chapter 1, I focus particularly on his lives of George, Giles, Austin, and his *Life of Saints Alban and Amphibalus*. These four lives exhibit tremendous formal variation, but they all celebrate saints who value education and service to community above a single-minded pursuit of heaven. Lydgate, I argue, invested his considerable capital as a monk, a court poet, and a Lancastrian propagandist to champion a humane Christianity and an informed orthodoxy. His stature and popularity contributed much to the establishment of a capacious, world-affirming paradigm of hagiography during the fifteenth century and beyond. Chapter 2 examines the lives of female saints by Osbern Bokenham, the century's most prolific and creative biographer of holy women. I argue that, throughout his oeuvre, Bokenham presents holy women that readers might identify with and emulate; however, in his later hagiography, Bokenham turns from proffering models of normative femininity to extolling heroines whose activities as scholars, teachers, and even preachers transgressed the norm and therefore promoted a broader definition of "femininity."

The proliferation of lives of scholars and of what I call "teaching hagiographies" is the subject of chapter 3. The fifteenth century witnessed a boom in lives of holy scholars and educators, both as freestanding narratives and within anthologies. Saints who were not especially known as teachers were represented as such, while the lives of celebrated scholars such as Katherine of Alexandria were written in ways that magnify the saint's training and scholarship. Hagiographers' attention to scholarship is further manifest in their inclusion of sometimes lengthy didactic passages. Saints' lives were becoming vehicles not just for edifying biography but for explicit moral and doctrinal lessons. These teaching hagiographies do not shy away from challenging material, as I will illustrate by comparing the expositions on the Trinity undertaken in fifteenth-century lives of Barbara and of Katherine of Alexandria.

Medieval England lacked the wealth of writings about modern holy women that proliferated throughout Western Europe.[30] Whereas thirteenth-century Continental clergymen were celebrating the lives of urban anchoresses by writing their biographies, their English counterparts were writing conduct guides to regulate anchoresses' lives.[31] Even English noblewomen known for their saintliness—Joan of Acre, for example—did not inspire hagiography. In the fifteenth century, however, lives of Continental holy women, including Elizabeth of Hungary, Bridget of Sweden, Catherine of Siena, and the holy women of women of Liège (Christina Mirabilis, Marie d'Oignies, and Elizabeth Spalbeek) were translated from Latin into Middle English for the first time. Moreover, during the first half of the century, an English holy woman, Margery Kempe of Lynn, undertook to tell her own story, in the process producing what many literary historians consider the first autobiography in English. Chapter 4 examines the portrayal of modern holy women in Middle English, moving from the brief mentions of holy women such as Jewet Metles ("Without Food") and Joan of Acre to the translated lives of Continental holy women to Margery Kempe's "autohagiography." Though Kempe's piety seems tame compared to that of her Continental sisters, I argue that her *Book* proffers an insular alternative to the radical asceticism of Bridget and her ilk, while preserving the saint's intellectual and spiritual precocity. In its own way, it is as audacious as any sacred biography written on the Continent. The "virtual piety" promoted in Kempe's *Book* makes sainthood available to anybody by dissociating it from radical asceticism. In that respect, the *Book of Margery Kempe* is closely aligned with the mass of Middle English hagiography discussed in the previous three chapters.

Chapter 5 treats the translation of Jacobus de Voragine's *Legenda aurea* during the fifteenth century and John Foxe's replacement of it with a legendary that purportedly replaces Catholic superstition with Protestant faith. I argue that the medieval translators of the *Legenda aurea* are, to varying degrees, transforming their source as they translate it through a process of embellishment, elision, and rewriting. In his *Acts and Monuments*, Foxe extols saints and martyrs whose virtues are similar to those celebrated by Bokenham, Lydgate, and Caxton. Though he inveighs against wonder-laden Catholic legends, he does not wholly banish the wonders he denounces. His legends, moreover, preserve the opposition between good and evil that many fifteenth-century hagiographers were eschewing for a more complex moral universe. Foxe, like his fifteenth-century predecessors, was not so much discarding the Catholic tradition of hagiography as reshaping it.

Many of the lives examined in chapters 1 through 5 circulated into the sixteenth century, either in manuscript or in print, including extracts from the *Book of Margery Kempe*, Wynter's *Life of Saint Jerome*, and, of course, Caxton's *Legenda aurea sanctorum*. It is hardly surprising that much of the new hagiography produced in post-Reformation England should show a high degree of continuity with the hagiography of the past century. That continuity is abundantly apparent in Henry Bradshaw's *Life of Saint Werburge* and George Barclay's *Life of Saint George*, as I discuss in the afterword. The Reformation, of course, complicated the situation. Though Catholic and Protestant reformers actually had much in common ideologically, Protestants naturally sought to emphasize—and, thus, often exaggerated—the differences between themselves and Catholics steeped in what they construed as the superstitions of a Dark Ages.[32] Post-Reformation Catholics, too, sought to distance themselves from medieval "superstitions." Yet the reformers, Catholic and Protestant, professed the values enshrined in the hagiography of Lydgate, Capgrave, Bokenham, and a myriad of anonymous hagiographers. And when, after a long hiatus, the lives of early Christian and medieval saints enjoyed a renewed popularity among English

Catholics in the first half of the seventeenth century, they looked very much like the lives written in the fifteenth century—inwardly oriented though richly contextualized, strongly female, committed to family and community, and supportive of Christian intellectualism. Seventeenth-century hagiography has been characterized as promoting obedience to authority, but I see a strong commitment to an activist, intellectual Christianity that had its roots in the late medieval past.

As my summary suggests, the valuing of social and family life, the attention to female spirituality, and the privileging of Christian education and intellectualism that I reckon among the hallmarks of fifteenth-century hagiography are not always found together, but they very often are. Whether they are encountered separately or together, the pervasiveness of these features worked to produce a more inclusive, democratic vision of sainthood than that which obtained in past generations. The saints were congenial mentors, not just lofty intercessors; the ordinary men and women who loved them were their heirs, their soulmates, their colleagues in pursuit of the common goal of spreading the Word, through word and deed, within the world. The work of the earliest saints and martyrs would continue *in saecula saeculorum*.

As we would expect, the adaptation of saints' lives in Middle English hagiography did not occur in isolation. A comparable process may be seen, for example, in the adaptation of monastic services in Books of Hours. Just as the makers of saints' lives were transforming martyrs, desert mothers, and Church Fathers into appropriate models for lay Christians, the makers of prayer books were generating versions of the Divine Office that busy laypeople could incorporate into their routines. Books of Hours, which one art historian dubbed books "for everybody," proliferated in England at the same time as what we might style saints for everybody.[33] Their illuminations imagine the saints, Holy Family, and patriarchs much as hagiographers were imagining their protagonists: as citizens of the world, often fashionably dressed, and often engaged in such worldly activities as reading, teaching, and ruling. The portrait of Petronilla in Queen's College, Oxford (MS 349) is a superb example of the approach to holiness favored by fifteenth-century English (see the frontispiece to this book): tending a cauldron as she pores over a book, ladle in hand, broom propped against the wall behind her, Petronilla exemplifies a busy, bookish womanhood, a mirror reflecting the kind of life that Christian education might produce and embodying the ideal of quotidian lay piety that fifteenth-century hagiography birthed and bequeathed to early modernity.[34]

Fifteenth-Century Lives is the culmination of my own passion for the literature and spirituality of fifteenth-century England, the book I have been edging towards ever since I began the research that led to my first monograph, *Virgin Martyrs*, during the mid-1980s. It represents my fuller understanding and appreciation of patterns I perceived only partially in *Virgin Martyrs* and *John Capgrave's Fifteenth Century*. I feel fortunate to have researched and written this book at a time when it is no longer necessary to argue that hagiography is a complex and subtle literary form or to apologize for studying the literature of fifteenth-century England, and at a time when those of us who love this period can focus on the nuances and resonances of its varied forms.

The study of late medieval and early Renaissance hagiography in English has truly blossomed over the past two decades. In *Her Life Historical*, Catherine Sanok has examined the preoccupation with exemplarity in the vernacular lives of female saints, exploring how hagiographers used those lives to think about history and community. Sanok and Cynthia Turner Camp have explored the representation of community and history in fifteenth- and sixteenth-century lives of British and Anglo-Saxon saints. Attention to history, politics, and exemplarity also figures prominently in studies of fifteenth-century lives of individual saints, from Audrey to George to Catherine of Siena.[35] *Fifteenth-Century Lives* offers a broader vision of what is happening in the hagiography of fifteenth-century England, as preoccupations with exemplarity, community, and history intersect and commingle with other themes: celebration of Christian intellectualism, narrative attention to nuances of emotion, and exploration of moral complexity. The result is a rich spirituality that could—and did—challenge social and religious norms.

Hagiography is one of the most enduring literary genres. Its popularity persisted from late antiquity through early modernity; indeed, vestiges of it are evident even in postmodernity.[36] This longevity makes it an ideal vehicle for reassessing the relationship between the late Middle Ages and the early modern era, a project that has lately been embraced by scholars of both periods.[37] Less obviously, hagiography's reputation as a static and conservative religious genre also makes it pertinent. The inventiveness and diversity of hagiography from the fifteenth through the seventeenth centuries embodies the variety and richness of orthodox spirituality, both before and after the Reformation, and it was precisely the assumption that hagiography was a tame, bland genre that liberated its practitioners to indulge in theological audacities and social critique.

I have entitled this book *Fifteenth-Century Lives* not only because it deals with the extraordinary life stories that were written during that century, but also because I suspect that those stories register, far more than did earlier Middle English hagiography, the lives of their creators and consumers. Presenting the saint as an imitable figure meant, in large part, refashioning the saint in the image of the fifteenth-century author and reader. Whether Bokenham's Barbara, Lydgate's Alban, or Capgrave's Katherine, the saint embodied impulses and aspirations that fifteenth-century men or women might recognize as their own.

CHAPTER ONE

New Directions

The Hagiography of John Lydgate

The single most influential figure in the development of Middle English hagiography was John Lydgate, a Benedictine monk from the ancient and wealthy Suffolk monastery of Bury St. Edmunds.[1] The breadth of Lydgate's taste, acquaintance, and experience informed and enriched his vast and diverse oeuvre, which comprised two books of prose and 150,000 lines of verse, including satires, complaints, debates, hymns, ballades, visions, fables, allegories, mummings, histories, romances, and saints' legends. Though he wrote mostly for an elite readership of kings, aristocrats, and civic leaders, his works circulated widely and were admired and imitated into the sixteenth century.

Lydgate's experience as a Lancastrian court poet inflected his writings, both secular and devotional.[2] His association with England's ruling house dated from his days as a student at Oxford during the first decade of the fifteenth century. In a letter written between 1406 and 1408, Prince Henry, the future Henry V, requested Bury's abbot to allow Lydgate to continue his studies in theology and canon law, for he is "de bonne conversacion et diligent pour apprendre."[3] Before long, Lydgate was diligently applying his talents in the prince's service. In 1412, he undertook one of his most ambitious narratives, a 30,000-line epic of the Trojan War, at Henry's request. Lydgate may also have composed his elaborate, multibook *Life of Our Lady* for Henry: an introductory colophon found in eleven of the forty-two surviving manuscripts of the *Life* states that Lydgate wrote "at the excitacion and styrryng of our worshipfull prince, kyng Harry the fifthe," but Lydgate does not allude to Henry within the text itself.[4]

There was much about Henry for Lydgate to admire. "The first king since Henry III to have shown more than conventional piety," he spurred ecclesiastical reform, encouraged liturgical innovation, and fostered the development of both private and public forms of religious expression.[5] Though deeply pious, Henry was also a savvy and conscientious politician determined to restore stability to the realm and to expunge the doubts about the legitimacy of Lancastrian rule that lingered throughout his father's troubled reign.[6] Lydgate represents Henry as a sovereign at once devout and valiant, loved and feared, an embodiment of the ideals he enshrined both in his secular poetry and in his hagiography.[7] Following the king's premature death in 1422, Lydgate's writings, as Maura Nolan observes, "betray a deep level of anxiety about sovereignty and are characterized by a sense of profound loss."[8]

For the remainder of the 1420s and into the 1430s, Lydgate served young King Henry VI and his guardians. He spent time at court and traveled to France on royal business. He wrote poems asserting the young king's right to the "rewmys twyne" of England and France; he provided Christmas entertainments for the royal household; and he wrote poetry to celebrate various state occasions, including Henry's French and English coronations. His first multibook saint's life, recounting the lives and martyrdoms of saints Edmund and Fremund, was written to honor Henry VI's extended stay at Bury St. Edmunds Abbey in 1433–34. Lydgate's monumental *Fall of Princes* was undertaken in 1431 at the request of the king's uncle Humphrey, Duke of Gloucester, and that project occupied much of his time during the 1430s. Yet, as scholars have come to appreciate, Lydgate was hardly a Lancastrian mouthpiece.[9] He finds ways, even in his most laudatory pieces, to register reservations about such subjects as the ongoing war with France. In accommodating the competing claims of duty and conscience in the charged political environment of the 1420s and 30s, he developed strategies that added nuance and complexity to his writings.

Lydgate's hagiography is substantial and diverse. He wrote two multibook epics, the *Life of Saints Edmund and Fremund* and the *Life of Saints Alban and Amphibalus*, and also shorter lives of saints George, Margaret, Petronilla, Giles, and Augustine of Canterbury. In addition, he composed numerous hymns to the saints and to the Virgin Mary and also the *Life of Our Lady* mentioned above. He invokes Saint Louis and Saint Edward the Confessor as Henry VI's heavenly sponsors in various occasional poems, and his "Mumming at Windsor" recounts Saint Clothilda's conversion of Clovis.[10] Lydgate's romance *Guy of Warwick* has distinct hagiographical overtones, as does his *Testament*, which recounts his own religious awakening in the manner of Augustine's *Confessions*.[11]

The high style and rhyme royal of Lydgate's saints' lives are reminiscent of Chaucer's rhetorically elaborate legend of Saint Cecilia, also composed in rhyme royal. Indeed, Lydgate was probably imitating Chaucer in producing a self-consciously literary hagiography. But Lydgate's saintly ideal is wholly unlike Chaucer's.[12] He replaces the social and religious radicals who populate Chaucer's Cecilia story—and other saints' lives of Chaucer's day—with sober citizens, paragons of chivalry and decorum who defer to secular authority until it directly conflicts with their faith. Lydgate tones down, and where possible eliminates, political, social, and religious conflict, celebrating those who wish to reconcile spiritual aspirations and worldly responsibilities and evincing what Anthony Bale has described as a characteristic "engagement with statecraft, class and political expedience."[13] His approach to hagiography is consonant with his peculiar situation as both monk and court poet. But even as he uses the saint's legend to support, in the main, the social, religious, and political agenda of the ruling elite he serves, he also uses it to criticize and offer alternatives to facets of that agenda.

I have elsewhere discussed at length Lydgate's transformation of Margaret and Petronilla into less confrontational and more exemplary saints and his representation of Saint Edmund as an exemplar of kingship.[14] In this chapter, I focus on Lydgate's lives of George, Giles, and Austin of Canterbury, and also his dual life of Alban and Amphibalus. These lives demonstrate Lydgate's range as an author of "sacred biography," for each represents a different type of experimentation with the genre of the saint's legend. Though apparently written to be inscribed on a tapestry, "George" is the most conventional saint's life in structure, length, and scope; "Giles" employs the second-person voice of prayer to narrate the saint's life, as it were, to the saint himself; "Austin" epitomizes the saint's career through an extended narration of a single miracle. Whereas "Austin" zeroes in on a particular episode of a saint's life, *Alban and Amphibalus* folds the lives of two saints into a vast epic of a Britain's religious awakening. Though these four saints' lives differ greatly in form, they promote a model of holiness informed by compassion and predicated on decorum and civility, even in dissent. They praise those who sacrifice their personal desires for the common good, especially as governors and educators. Through these exemplars of holiness, Lydgate prompts his readers to think beyond self-interest, towards the greater good that he indicates is an essential part of the pursuit of heaven.

Saint George: "Hooly martir, of knighthood loodsterre"

Lydgate composed his life of Saint George circa 1430 at the request of the London armorers. According to John Shirley's headnote, the poem was the "devyse of a steyned halle," or tapestry, depicting the life of Saint George, that the armorers commissioned for their new guildhall.[15] The tapestry no longer survives, but the success of Lydgate's "George" as freestanding hagiography is indicated by its preservation in three fifteenth-century manuscripts.

The armorers' was one of numerous guilds throughout England to have taken George as their patron. The saint's popularity in England surged after King Edward III established the Order of the Garter, with George as patron, in 1348.[16] George became enshrined in the national consciousness as a paragon of chivalry and an emblem of sovereignty, order, and national unity. His cult enjoyed even greater prestige during the reign of Henry V, for whom the chivalrous saint embodied the image he wished to project of himself as a warrior king and *miles Christi*. Contemporary sources report that Henry invoked George as he exhorted his troops at Agincourt in 1415 and that his army bore the saint's distinctive red cross banner into the battle.[17] The following year, Archbishop Chichele elevated George's feast to a *festum duplex*, calling him the patron and protector of England.[18]

An eloquent expression of George's status as (to quote Lydgate) "protectour and patroun" of "Englisshe men booþe in pees and were" occurs in the Bedford Hours, completed circa 1423 to honor the marriage of Henry's brother John of Bedford to Anne of Burgundy. The manuscript includes a full-page miniature of the duke kneeling before

George, who is decked out in full armor and attended by a squire carrying his lance and shield. This militant George, so favored by the late king, was a fitting patron for John, who, as regent of France, was charged with protecting and defending Henry's conquest.

Lydgate recast his source, Jacobus de Voragine's *Legenda aurea*, making it more consistent with the English association of George with social order, though perhaps less consistent with a militant George eager to advance the English cause in France. This is especially conspicuous in his rendition of George's fight with a dragon, the most famous episode of the legend and one depicted in many Books of Hours.[19] Rife with social and political tension, Jacobus's account is hardly a celebration of national unity or sovereignty. To appease a plague-bearing dragon that is threatening their town, the people of Silena agree to offer it one child each day, drawing lots to select the victim. When at last the lot falls to the king's only daughter, the king balks, offering his people his wealth and half his kingdom in exchange for her life. Jacobus relates: "The people were furious and shouted: 'You yourself issued this decree, O king, and now that all our children are dead, you want to save your own daughter! Carry out for your daughter what you ordained for the rest, or we will burn you alive with your whole household!'" (Jacobus de Voragine, *Golden Legend*, 1:239). When the king tries to stall, "they came back in a rage, crying: 'Why are you letting your people perish to save your daughter? Don't you see that we are all dying from the breath of the dragon?'" Powerless against his angry subjects, he sends his child to her fate.

Jacobus thus reminds sovereigns of the power of the people in their wrath and warns them not to suppose themselves above the law.[20] He does show that *God* privileges rank—after many children have been devoured, George arrives in time to save the princess—but God's agent is in his own way just as menacing as the citizens of Silena and perhaps even the dragon. Indeed, once George has wounded the dragon, he uses the beast to inflict his own form of terror on both king and town. George has the princess lead the wounded beast towards Silena. At the sight of it, the people "ran for the mountains and the hills, crying out: 'Now we will all be eaten alive!'" (*Golden Legend*, 1:239). George, however, tells them: "Believe in Christ and be baptized, every one of you, and I shall slay the dragon!" (240–41). Only after everybody is baptized—twenty thousand, not counting women and children—does

George kill the dragon. Spurning the riches that the king offers in gratitude, he then departs, admonishing the king to be a faithful servant of the Church. Here, as in so many of his legends, Jacobus asserts the authority of the Church and its agents over the hapless secular state, with his saint displaying the *contemptio mundi* that is a hallmark of his *Legenda aurea*.[21]

Lydgate altogether eliminates the conflict between sovereign and town. Silena is again united in terror: "Þe kyng, þe queene, þe lordes taken heed / Of þis sodeyne wooful aventure, / And þe people fellen in gret dreed" ("George," lines 43–45). But the city is also united in its horrifying strategy of appeasement: the king does not try to save his daughter from the fate that has befallen her "of necessytee" (71). Silena is united in its grief over the sacrifice of the princess: "Hir fadir wepte, hir moder, booþe tweyne, / And al þe Cytee in teerys did so reyne" (76–77). And it is united in exultation and ultimately in the Christian faith. In Lydgate's version, king and subjects cheer when the princess leads the wounded dragon towards town, knowing that they have been saved. After the king has inspected the beast and thanked George for having "delyverd" his city "out of dreed" (121), George kills it. Only after the carcass has been hauled away does he preach Christianity, converting king and town through persuasion rather than fear:

And affter þat he taught hem Crystes lawe,
By his doctryne and predicacyoun,
And frome þerrour by conuersyoun,
He made hem tourne, þe kyng and þe cyte,
And of oon hert baptysed for to be.
                        (127–33)

When George departs, he leaves a city united in faith. Lydgate omits altogether the king's offer of a reward and, with it, what might be taken as George's arrogant rejection of the king's generosity. Just as Lydgate has eliminated any suggestion of conflict between town and crown, he has also eliminated any suggestion of conflict between Church and state, represented, respectively, by saint and king.

Lydgate even diminishes political conflict in his account of George's martyrdom. In Jacobus's *Legenda aurea*, the saint sets out to make trouble and to undermine the prefect's authority. He casts off his military garb to dress as a Christian, an ostentatious act of defiance. Pushing his way into the crowd surrounding the prefect Dacian, he shouts: "All *your* gods are demons, and *our* God alone is the Creator of the Heavens" (Jacobus, *Golden Legend*, line 240; my emphasis). Asked to identify himself, George flaunts his pedigree and rank: "My name is George, I come of noble forebears in Cappadocia. With the help of Christ I have conquered Palestine" (240). The ensuing clash of wills between Christian martyr and pagan persecutor is typical of the *Legenda aurea*. Dacian racks, torches, and boils George, but the saint, protected by God, feels no pain, nor do poisons and knives harm him. Dacian then tries flattery, promising great honors if George will only sacrifice to the gods; George plays along and accompanies the prefect to the temple, whereupon he destroys both the building and its deities through his prayers. "Trickster!" charges Dacian. "Miserable man!" retorts George. The saint's defiance is contagious. When the prefect turns to his wife for sympathy, she declares: "Cruel, bloodthirsty tyrant! Did I not tell you not to go on mistreating the Christians.... I want to become a Christian" (241).

Lydgate replaces this colorful conflict with a more sober encounter between George and Dacian. The opposition between "you" and "us" is left implicit, as George declares: "Oon God þer is, fy on ydolatrye" ("George," line 161). Lydgate's self-effacing George sets aside his military attire to dress "pourely" (158), and he neither discloses his pedigree nor boasts of his conquests. The sizzling exchange between saint and persecutor is wholly absent in Lydgate's account, as George affirms his faith without taunting his adversary:

> Þe false Thyraunt by gret vyolence
> Commaunded haþe anoon þat he be taake,
> And to be brought vnto his presence;
> Bade þat he shoulde Crystes feyth forsake,
> But he ne liste noo delayes maake,
> Aunswerd pleynly, his lyff by deth to fyne,
> Frome Crystes lawe no thing shall him declyne.
> (162–68)

In the same spirit, Lydgate reports the conversion of the prefect's wife without having her scold her husband:

> Thorugh Goddes might and gracyous purveyaunce
> ... Alexandrea of Dacyan þe wyff
> Forsooke ydolles and al hir fals creaunce
> And became crysten with humble attendaunce.
> (219–22)

As in Jacobus's *Legenda aurea*, George endures awful tortures—he's scourged, torched, and cut open—but Lydgate does not attempt to minimize the saint's pain: "Were not hes peynes strong?" ("George," 174) he demands. In Lydgate's legend, heroism consists in steadfastness and a willingness to suffer rather than in simple defiance of authority.

Lydgate's George is the "loodsterre" of knighthood ("George," line 6), full of "manhoode and prowesse" (19). As we would expect in a work written for the armorers, Lydgate takes every opportunity to mention George's armor—"an armed knight" (82), "in steel armed bright" (21), "armed seet vpon a ryal steed" (86). Lydgate touts ability rather than divine aid, thus making George a figure with whom contemporary knights might more readily identify. In describing George's fight with the dragon, Jacobus wrote: "George, mounting his horse and arming himself with the sign of the cross, set bravely upon the approaching dragon and, commending himself to God, brandished his lance, dealt the beast a grievous wound, and forced him to the ground" (*Golden Legend*, p. 239). Lydgate's version is slightly longer, but it omits Jacobus's references to George making the sign of the cross and commending himself to God:

> Hooly Saint George his hors smote on þe syde
> Whane he þe dragoun sawe lyfft vp his hede,
> And towardes him he proudely gan to ryde
> Ful lyche a knight with outen fere or dreede;
> Avysyly of witt he tooke goode heed,
> With his spere sharp and kene egrounde
> Thoroughe þe body he gaf þe feonde a wownde.
> ("George," lines 99–105)

Though we can infer that "hooly" George is also armed with God's favor, Lydgate directly attributes his victory to the intelligence, skill, and bravery that inhere in being a good knight.

Although Lydgate's George is perhaps more "lyche a knight" than Jacobus's, he is *not*, I think, the knight who appeared above the English troops on the eve of Agincourt. Nor is he the militant George of the Bedford Hours. Lydgate pays much attention to the causes George fights for. He enumerates several not mentioned in the *Legenda aurea*: for example, sustaining truth, defending the Church, and upholding the rights of widows and virgins ("George," lines 32–35). However, he omits the one cause that Jacobus does mention: George's effort on behalf of the expansionist Roman Empire. Jacobus identifies George as having "the military rank of tribune" (*Golden Legend*, p. 238), and he has George boast to the prefect about his conquest of Palestine. By contrast, Lydgate says nothing about George having had a military career. When he meets the princess, he had already "forsooke" "his cuntree" ("George," line 30) to serve Christ and Our Lady (20, 85). His conquests were spiritual—over the world, the flesh, and the devil (19–20)—and his physical battles defensive rather than offensive. Lydgate even omits the miracle recounted in the *Legenda aurea* that has George leading the Crusaders to retake Jerusalem from the Saracens, the miracle that may have inspired the story of George's appearance at Agincourt.

Like the knights-errant of romance, Lydgate's George travels about, righting wrongs "with swerd of equytee" ("George," line 34). His rescue of the princess evinces a selfless heroism, sparked by "pytee and eeke compassyoun," a willingness to risk all for her sake: "For lyff nor deeth frome hir not to depart / But in hir quarell his body to Iupart" (92–98). Instead of reproaching her when she thanks the gods for his victory, he gently invites her to assume the role of "conqueresse" (113). When he abandons his "knightly weede" (157), he nonetheless remains "knightly" (214). What Lydgate's George would have thought of the war with France is by no means clear; however, Lydgate reminds his readers that George, the lodestar of knighthood, is England's patron "in pees" as well as in war, and he clearly shows that, in the last analysis, armor does not make a knight.

Saint Giles: "Comoun Profyght" and "Prudent Gouernaunce"

Lydgate claims to have composed his 368-line life of Saint Giles at the request of an unnamed "cryature" (line 28), who "of greet devossionn" sent him a "lytell bylle" containing the saint's life, along with a request that he do his "besy Cure" to translate it from the Latin.[22] Lydgate uncharacteristically avoids mentioning the patron's name, rank, or even gender, nor does he indicate why this patron was eager for the life. Although many English churches were dedicated to Saint Giles, Lydgate's is the first and only freestanding Middle English life; other accounts appear only within legendaries.[23]

Lydgate's "Giles," like his "George," is a formal hybrid. Just as "George," in its original incarnation, combined word and image, "Giles" combines *vita* with prayer. Lydgate was a master of both genres. His oeuvre includes numerous and diverse verse prayers. In some, Lydgate, following convention, says little about the saint's life or character; only a fleeting allusion to an incident or two from their lives distinguishes, say, Saint Katherine from Saint Margaret or Saint Christopher from Saint George. These plot references—Michael 'venquysshed the dragoun,' Katherine "brak the strong[e] wheel," Christopher "bar Iesu over the sterne fflood," and so forth—are like the emblems that in art distinguish one attractive haloed figure from another.[24] In other prayers, Lydgate incorporates rather more information about his subject's life, character, and most praiseworthy virtues.[25] He also particularizes the saints' supplicants, from the pilgrims who arrive in Canterbury "shod or bare" (Lydgate, "Thomas," line 83), to the women who "travaille" from "ache of bonys," spreading "gontes," and "veynes, wich sese nat to bleede" ("Leonard," lines 19–21), to those who misplace household items ("Ositha," lines 20–22). Some of these prayers look rather like miniature *vitae*. Conversely, Lydgate's life of Giles looks rather like an elaborated prayer.

Saints' lives and prayers to the saints are of course closely related literary forms. Some authors explicitly construe writing a saint's life as an act of devotion, as Chaucer does in the prologue to his life of Cecilia. Medieval saints' lives typically include prayer. They usually begin and end with prayers to their subjects; they often report the saints' sometimes lengthy prayers verbatim. Passages of prayer, whether the author's addresses to the saint, or the saint's to God, are naturally in the second person, set apart from the conventional third-person narration of the *vita* proper. Lydgate follows convention, beginning by beseeching that Giles guide his efforts and concluding by beseeching Giles's favor for all those who honor him. But the life that these prayers bookend also addresses the saint, marking the *vita* itself as prayer. As we will see, Lydgate invests his work with descriptions of the saint's many acts of kindness and vivid portraits of those helped by his kindness, thus magnifying his bona fides as an intercessor. As in Lydgate's more elaborate prayers, the saint is a benevolent helper, whose benevolence makes him not only a congenial patron but a fitting model for his devotees.

Previous hagiographers identified Giles as an early medieval hermit and abbot. His story, as told in the *Legenda aurea* and retold in Middle English legendaries, is a tissue of miracles, as is obvious from its first sentences. Jacobus writes:

> Giles, or Aegidius, was born in Athens of royal stock and was instructed in the sacred writings from childhood. One day as he was on his way to church, he came upon a sick man lying beside the road and asking for alms. He gave the sick man his coat, and as soon as the man put it on, he was cured of his illness. Another time, as he was returning home from church, he met a man who had been bitten by a snake, but Giles prayed for him and drove out the poison. Then a man possessed of the devil was in church with the rest of the people, disturbing the faithful with his clamor, but Giles drove the devil out and cured the man. (*Golden Legend*, 2:147)[26]

So holy that he can't help performing wonders, Giles quickly becomes a local celebrity. Fearing vainglory, he flees to a new location where the heal-and-run cycle begins again. At last Giles forsakes society altogether to live as a hermit, nourished daily from the milk of a doe.

As is typical of Jacobus's legends, the saint is contemptuous of princes and their gifts. A king out hunting who accidentally shoots Giles (he was aiming at the saint's doe) offers reparation, but Giles "refused medical care and spurned the gifts" (*Golden Legend*, 2:148). In fact, he prays that his wound never heal so that he might be perfected through illness (*sciens virtutem in infirmitate perfici*; Jacobus, *Legenda aurea*, p. 583). Though the king becomes a regular visitor at Giles's hermitage, gladly receiving the "food of salvation" there, Giles refuses gifts from the king, until at last, after much royal begging and weeping, he consents to take charge of an abbey built in his honor. As abbot, he continues to work miracles and to receive the homage of princes until his death.

Lydgate acknowledges Giles's reputation as a miracle-worker, but he transforms the saint into an exemplar of compassion and service to others. Lydgate's changed focus is evident early on, as he amplifies the brief reference to Giles being "instructed in the sacred writings from childhood" to praise Giles's "dyllygence vertu for to lere, / And profyte in vertuous dyscyplyne" ("Giles," lines 47–48). "Dysposed in vertu to profyte, / Lyk thy mastres wich tauht þe spelle and reede" (49–50), Giles becomes a compassionate youth, and Lydgate uses the legend's "ffirste myracle" to illustrate that compassion:

> As seith thy lyff, in almesse-deede
> Of compassioun castyst of thy weede,
> Gaff it freely to oon that quook for cold,
> Wich was maad hool reffreshed in his neede.
> (52–55)

As we can see, the miracle itself is less important for Lydgate than its motivation. It is also more briefly told and less sensational: instead of curing a sick man, Giles's coat warms a cold one. Lydgate continues to subordinate miracles to character throughout the narrative. Wonders are the by-products of Giles's kindness and generosity towards everybody he meets, whatever their station and whatever their affliction—the poor, the sick, the possessed, the anxious, the fearful. His compassion is an extension of his Christocentric piety. Where Jacobus's Giles had prayed for his wound never to heal because he sees perpetual pain as a way of increasing his *virtus*, Lydgate's Giles wants to remain wounded so that he will be continually reminded of that ultimate exemplar of compassion, Christ (Lydgate, "Giles," lines 158–68).

Lydgate wholly eliminates the saint's high-handed treatment of the unnamed king, whom he represents as eminently worthy of respect: "Curteys, gentyl, in al his gouernaunce" ("Giles," line 118). His Giles does not spurn the king's offer of "recompence" (133); he asks the king to build a monastery. The king does not cry and beg Giles to become abbot; he negotiates, agreeing to build the monastery on the condition that Giles takes charge of it. Though Giles is loath to leave his desert "mansyoun" (143), the king persuades him that doing so is in the interest of "comoun profyght" (144). It is often the case, Giles realizes, that "all a regioun myhte been amendyd / By o good man socoured and releued" (151–52).

Lydgate describes both king and hermit as "condescending" to each other (138, 146), thus reinforcing the mutuality of their relationship.

Lydgate also departs from the *Legenda aurea* in describing Giles's later dealings with another king, Charles. In the *Legenda aurea*, Jacobus uses the relationship between the two men to show the saint's reputation and authority. In the course of a conversation about salvation, the king requests Giles to pray for him "because he had committed an enormous crime, which he dared not confess even to the saint himself" (*Golden Legend*, 2:148). In answer to Giles's prayers on the king's behalf, a dove from heaven deposits a scroll on the altar while the saint is saying Mass. The scroll in essence gives the king nothing—it is only a spectacular iteration of the Church's teaching on penance: "The king's sin was forgiven due to Giles's prayer, provided that the king was truly repentant, confessed his sin, and abstained from committing it thereafter" (148). King or no, Charles must obey the Church's precepts, and so he does: "Charles acknowledged his sin and humbly prayed for pardon." In the scroll God also promises, rather more generously, to forgive the sins of anyone who prays to Giles. Jacobus concludes the episode with his characteristic emphasis on the saint's stature: Giles became "more honored than ever" thanks to his visit to the king.

Lydgate embroiders Jacobus's account into a story of compassion and friendship. King Charles is moved to confide his fears to Giles because he has just witnessed how the saint, "of compassion," "maad hool" a man possessed by demons (Lydgate, "Giles," lines 209–14). Lydgate conveys the king's anguish and heartfelt regret:

> He hadde offendyd of froward mocyouns,
> In a synne terryble to descryve,
> Weuer of purpos in his oppynyouns
> Therof to been confessed in his lyve.
> (221–24)

Giles's fervent prayers on the king's behalf result in a genuine concession, not just a heavenly admonition that the king confess. An actual confession of the sin is written on the scroll, just as if Charles had confessed it: "Alle circumstaunces pleynly out declaryd, / Atween you two, as thou lyst hym confesse, / Treuly in ordre there was no poynt I-sparyd" (238–40). God forgives the sin King Charles "confessed," and only Giles knows his secret: "What was wretyn no man knew riht nouht, / Woord nor sillable but thy-silffe alloon" (243–44). Lydgate emphasizes not the honor Giles gains from Charles but rather what Giles *gives* the king. Thanks to the saint's "notable Informacyoun," the king is not only "restoryd on-to goostly helthe," but he enjoys "gret encres of hys worldly welthe, / And gret prosperyte of all his regioun" (257–60). Instead of granting forgiveness to those who pray to Giles, the scroll in Lydgate's version more modestly grants them the will to change their lives (256).

Lydgate concludes by underscoring the friendship that grew between the two men. Their "ffervent love and trewe affeccyoun" is such that both men weep when Giles's visit ends—"To dysceuere ye tweyne were so loth" ("Giles," lines 262–64).

Lydgate's Giles is a "pastor . . . nat a mercenarye" ("Giles," line 183). Though he spends much time in his "lybrarye, / Euer in study or Contemplacyoun" (181–82), he uses the profits of study and contemplation to benefit others, teaching those in his charge "erly and eek late, / To profyte in ther Relygyoun" (175–76). What's more, he teaches by *example*:

> Fastyng, wakyng, and liggyng harde a-nyht,
> To thy discyples patroun and examplarie,
> Fyrst at matynes settyst vp the lyght,
> In ech party of the seyntewarye.
> (177–80)

Lydgate uses Giles to model qualities appropriate not only to an abbot but to any leader, religious or secular: "discressioun," "prudence," "consayl," "equyte," "resoun" ("Giles," lines 187–89). Balance is the mainstay of "prudent gouernaunce" (195): Giles was "loved and drad" (173); he "kept egal the ballaunce / A-tween cherisshyng and just correccyouns" (193–94); he "peised rigour and clemence, / Twen thextremytees hate or affeccyoun" (190–91). Respected by those around him, he rules "with soffte speche and with woordes ffayre" (198). His governance of others parallels his self-governance: he elicits "obedience" (192) and "set a-syde alle rebelliouns" among his "soggettis" (199, 175) just as he made his own "flessh meekly to obeye / To the spirit, voyde of rebellyoun" (185–86).

George was a soldier-martyr, Giles a hermit-abbot. Lydgate narrated George's life in the expected third person, Giles's in the surprising second person. Yet in both of his accounts, Lydgate emphasizes teaching, community, compassion, and pastoral care. As we shall see, the same themes inform his "Austin," another formal experiment, one in which the saint transforms a request for help into a "teaching moment," an opportunity to impress upon a fellow cleric the importance of compassion and tactful teaching.

Saint Austin at Compton: "Lyk as the Bible makith mencioun"

Lydgate's 408-line "Saint Austin at Compton" is another of Lydgate's innovative short hagiographies. The piece is, like "Giles," a hagiographical hybrid—part *vita*, part *miraculum*, part *exemplum*. It is less biographical than most *vitae*, but more biographical than most *miracula*. Though MacCracken's edition presents it as an *exemplum* on tithes ("Offre vp yowre dymes"[27]), Lydgate dexterously complicates that simple moral.

Lydgate's subject is the Augustine whom Pope Gregory the Great sent to England to convert the Anglo-Saxons. Bede had told the story of Austin's mission in his eighth-century *Ecclesiastical History*, and Bede's account was embroidered into a lengthy freestanding *vita* in the late eleventh century.[28] The miracle at Compton was a thirteenth-century accretion to the Austin tradition, and evidently a popular one. Lydgate calls it a "myracle remembryd many fold, / In many shire and many cité toold" ("Austin," lines 404–5), and indeed, it can be found in collections of miracles and of exempla and is incorporated into lives of the saint.

Lydgate's probable source is a late thirteenth-century miracle story in Latin that is found in multiple anthologies of edifying moral stories for preachers to incorporate in their sermons.[29] The exemplum presents itself as "the story of an excommunication and how Saint Augustine, apostle of the Angles, resurrected two dead people" (*Narratio mirabilis de sententia excommunicationis et beati Augustini Anglorum Apostoli qualiter resuscitauit duos mortuos*).[30] In that story, as Austin passes through the village of Compton, its parish priest asks him to remonstrate with the local lord, whom he has excommunicated for refusing to pay tithes. Austin obliges, but the lord remains obdurate. Later, though, Austin says the Mass in the parish church, and when he reaches the part where excommunicates are admonished to leave the church, a cadaver rises from its grave and exits. Under Austin's questioning, the deceased explains that he was once a lord, cursed for refusing to pay tithes, and he has been suffering the pains of damnation for the past one hundred fifty years. Austin thereupon resurrects (in God's name) the priest who had excommunicated the lord, hands him a whip, and tells him to punish the lord's sin and release him from damnation. That done, and the chastised lord returned to his grave, Austin invites the resurrected priest to remain among the living and help with his missionary work. The priest, however, demurs, for he prefers heaven's joys to earth's tribulations. The living lord, of course, can hardly fail to take the hint: trembling and crying, he repents and becomes Austin's follower. As we see, the Latin *narratio* keeps its focus on the unpleasant consequences of not paying tithes. The renegade lord learns that at *best* noncompliance will result in temporary pain (i.e., the flogging), at worst in eternal damnation.

At first glance, Lydgate seems to have the same straightforward agenda as the author of the *narratio*, namely, to warn people to pay their tithes. His "Austin" begins by invoking scripture—"Lyk as the Bible makith mencioun"—as the source of the Church's tithing requirements. Abel "gaff God his part, tenthe of his substaunce," and subsequent biblical patriarchs followed Abel's lead, proving that tithing was an ancient and venerable practice. This discussion of the Old Testament foundation for tithing takes up 64 of the poem's 408 lines. Lydgate thereupon asserts, but curiously offers no scriptural basis for, the claim that those who don't tithe won't thrive:

> And who fro God withhalte his dewté
> Lat hym knowe for pleyn conclusyoun
> Of warantise he shal nevire the,
> Lakke grace and vertuous foysoun,
> Of ther tresoure discrece in ech sesoun.
> ("Austin," lines 65–72)

To illustrate that claim, he turns to what "befyl in Awstynes tyme" (72).

Lydgate precedes the miracle story with a vivid portrait of Austin. That portrait is cast in the apostolic mold of the "good priest" known from Chaucer's portrait of the Parson, whom Lydgate, I suspect, was deliberately copying. Chaucer presents the Parson as "a lerned man, a clerk / That Cristes gospel trewely wolde preche" (General Prologue, lines 470–80).³¹ He taught by "noble example": "That first he wroghte, and afterward he taughte" (496–97). Though holy, he does not disdain sinners: "He was to sinful men nat despitous, / Ne of his speche daungerous ne digne, / But in his techyng discreet and benygne" (516–18). "Ful looth" to "cursen for his tithes" (486), his "bisynesse" was to "drawen folk to hevene by fairnesse" (520, 519). At the same time, he did not hesitate to "snybben sharply" "any persone obstinate" (521, 523).

Lydgate endows Austin with these same qualities, emphasizing the day-to-day "labour" ("Austin," line 131) he performs as a teacher and preacher. As he does with all of his saints, Lydgate celebrates imitable virtues—his "moost hooly conversacioun" (79), his "goostly elloquence" (103), and his zeal to "preche and teche devoutly the maneere / Of Cristes lawe abroad in every shire" (139–40). Picking up the scriptural theme of his introduction, he presents Austin as a scripturally oriented teacher: "Thoruh al the parties and provinces of the lond / Of Cristis gospel he gan the seed to sowe" (81–82). A "gracious" (75) man, "withouten pompe" (85), he teaches not only by word but by example: "His liff was lyk his predicacioun: As he tauht, sothely so he wrouhte" (77–78). Like Chaucer's Parson, he is "looth" to excommunicate—a quality not stated but rather demonstrated in (of all places!) the pro-tithing miracle story.

Though he freely embellishes the Latin *narratio*, Lydgate declines to associate the renegade lord with fifteenth-century grumblings and grievances against tithing.³² The lord doesn't dispute which of his earnings should be tithed; he doesn't claim a poor yield; he doesn't protest that tithes would be an economic burden; he doesn't argue that he ought to be able to give directly to the poor; he doesn't aver that the priest is unworthy. He simply doesn't want to pay: he "wyl" have the tenth part, and the other nine, for his own.

In contrast to the inflexible lord, the priest is a good and reasonable man. Respectful of rank and eager to avoid confrontation, he "entretid hym lik to his estat," "secrely" at first, and only later "afforn the toun" ("Austin," lines 153–54). He explains to the lord that "custom grounded on resound" dictates that "he was bounde by lawe of oold writyng / To pay his dymes" (157–59). Excommunication is a last resort. In setting the case before Austin "meekly" and "in pleyn language" (147, 149), the priest expresses his willingness to be corrected: "We shall obeye to youre ordynaunce" (168). Lydgate, indeed, has created a priest whose claims might seem reasonable even to many critics of tithes.[33]

The dead lord and priest are much like their living counterparts. The late priest had advised his lord "daily moore and moore, / To paye his tithes" ("Austin," lines 283–84); he "warnyd hym many divers tymes" (286); he explained the "pereil" he was putting himself in (284). He had resorted to excommunication only when all else failed. The defunct lord, for his part, admits that he was "ay contrayre, froward, and obstinat" (248). He laments his present condition, yet he shows no remorse. Indeed, rather than acknowledge that his misery results from his own choices, he styles himself a victim, with "greet cause" to "moorne and to compleyne" (251), and he blames the priest for his woes: "Loo! heer he lith, cheef cause of my grevaunce, / So fel a curs he did on me conclude" (271–72).

Lydgate has embellished his source to make the lord more arrogant and the priest more reasonable: the lord in the *narratio* neither pities himself nor blames the priest, while the priest does not claim to have pled repeatedly with the lord. If ever there were a case for excommunication, Lydgate has surely made it.[34] Who could possibly sympathize with this whiny lord? Who, indeed, but "Hooly Austyn," who "wepte of compassioun" ("Austin," lines 255–56)! Apparently forgetting all about the "froward" (177) living lord with whom he has just been arguing, he seeks only some means of retrieving the dead lord's salvation: "Austyn gan muse in his oppynyoun / To fynde a mene the sowle for to save" (257–58). Lydgate's Austin berates the priest for ignoring scriptural precedent: "Thynk He that bouht us is evir merciable; / By whoos exaumple we must be tretable / As the Gospel pleynly doth recoorde" (292–94); "Thynk how Jhesus bouht us with His blood, / Oonly of mercy suffryd Passioun" (297–98); "Many exaumple to purpoos thu mayst fynde / Of trespasours relesyd of there peyne" (309–10. He goes on to cite (mostly biblical) examples of forgiven "trespasours"—Peter, Paul, Thomas, Mary Magdalene, and Mary of Egypt. If scripture teaches laypeople to pay tithes, it also teaches the clergy not to curse those who don't. This focus on scriptural teachings and precedent is wholly absent from the Latin *narratio*, though it is wholly consistent with the biblical orientation evinced in Lydgate's introduction.

As in all his legends, Lydgate prefers diplomacy and tact to confrontation. The incumbent Compton priest remonstrates with the wayward lord privately and respectfully. Austin does likewise: he "took hym apart" ("Austin," line 176). Austin never publicly rebukes the lord; at the end of the story, he asks, nonjudgmentally, "Wilt thu ... paye thy dewté?" (396). The lord capitulates, giving Austin more than he asked for by vowing to give up the world and follow Austin. But he capitulates graciously, without weeping and trembling:

> He grauntith his axing and fyl doun on his kne,
> Moost repentaunt forsook al the world as blyve,
> With devout hert and al hymylité
> Folwith Seyn Austyn duryng al his live.
> (397–400)

Though he gives up the world, he retains his dignity.

Lydgate's Austin, of course, also has a message for the Compton parish priest, but he delivers it indirectly by rebuking the dead priest, a saved soul with no earthly status to lose. The living priest is left to infer what Austin thinks of his excommunication from the scolding Austin gives his predecessor. Thus, with the diplomacy and tact that he imputes to Austin, Lydgate urges restraint upon his clerical readers: he argues against the use of excommunication to enforce tithing even while unequivocally asserting the laity's duty to tithe and the clergy's *right* to curse those who don't.

Lydgate is by no means saying that diplomacy and tact are guaranteed to work. Austin's taking the lord aside and reasoning with him privately does no good; only a pair of apropos resurrections brings him around—and resurrections are not in the repertoire of most parish priests. More to Lydgate's point, though, neither do threats nor even excommunication succeed. As Austin points out, cursing the lord does not enrich the Church; it is mere vengeance ("Austin," line 295).

For Lydgate, then, getting one's way is less important than doing right, and doing right is not at all the same as doing what one has a right to do. The priests ought not curse the lords, though they have a right to do so, because they should value mercy over retribution; conversely, the lords ought to pay their tithes, not because they have a duty to do so, but for the reason Abel first tithed: "Oonly to God for to do plesaunce" ("Austin," line 6).

In a further twist, Lydgate departs from his Latin source in expressing a certain disdain for the deceased priest's preference to rest in peace rather than labor in the vineyard. It is clear from the way Austin phrases the choice where Lydgate believes the priest's duty lies. Which, Austin asks, does he prefer?

> To goon with hym thoruh this regioun,
> The feith of Crist by predicacioun,
> For his part groundid on scripture,
> To doon his deveere of hool affeccioun;
> Or to resoorte ageyn to his sepulture.
> ("Austin," lines 356–60)

In declining Austin's invitation, the priest describes his own happiness at length:

> I rest in pees and take of nothyng keep,
> Rejoisshe in quiete and contemplacioun,
> Voyd of al trouble. Celestial is my sleep
> And, by the meene of Cristes Passioun,
> Feith, hoope, and charité, with hool affeccioun
> Been pilwes foure to reste upon by grace
> Day of the general resurreccioun.
> (369–75)

In preferring this contemplative life—or, rather, death—he may be choosing the better part, but he is also taking the selfish road: "This choys is for *thy* beste!" Lydgate's Austin exclaims, addressing the priest (line 377; my emphasis). He then iterates the easiness of the priest's choice of a life "Contemplatiff, fulfilled of al pleasaunce" (378). Little surprise, though, that the priest who did not truly understand the lesson of Christ's sacrifice while alive isn't willing to interrupt a pleasant afterlife for the good of Christ's earthly Church.

And the Church is in dire need of help. Again embellishing his Latin source, Lydgate draws attention to the perils besetting it as he asks the priest to pray:

> That Petris ship be with no tempest drownyd.
> I meene as thus: that noon heresye

Ryse in thes dayes, nor noon that was beforn,
Nor no darnel growe nor multeplye,
Nor no fals cokkyl be medlyd with good corn.
Cheese we the roosys, cast away the thorn.
Crist boute us alle with His precious bloode:
To that He bouht us lat no thyng be lorn,
For our redempcioun He starf upon the Rood.
                          ("Austin," lines 384–92)

Indeed, Lydgate seems to be trying to provoke discussion among his readers of the priest's choice and to generate debate about whether prayer or preaching is more likely to save "Petris ship" from heresy. As for Lydgate's opinion, we need only think of his representations of Giles, Fremund, and Guy of Warwick, all celebrated as contemplatives who laid aside their chosen life when recalled to active duty on behalf of the Church precisely because prayer is not enough.

Alban and Amphibalus: Epic Hagiography

Lydgate's first epic saint's life was the *Life of Saints Edmund and Fremund*, composed in 1433–34 for the young King Henry VI at the request of his abbot, William Curteys. With this dual *vita*, Lydgate brought to the genre of the saint's legend the sweep and grandeur of *Troy Book* and its concern with secular governance. The saints' lives and deaths are woven into an intricate history of the struggle of Britain against the treacherous and violent Danes. Edmund and Fremund are models not only of holiness but also of governance—both good and bad.[35] As he uses the kingships of Edmund and Fremund to dilate upon secular rule, he also, as Catherine Sanok and John Ganim have argued, uses Edmund's postmortem miracles to assert "the exemption of Benedictine monasteries from ecclesiastical and secular jurisdictions."[36] The moral, rhetorical, and political complexity of Lydgate's *Edmund and Fremund* makes it one of the most extraordinary achievements of Middle English hagiography.

In 1439, Lydgate undertook his second epic saint's legend: a life of Saint Alban and Saint Amphibalus in three books and 4,620 lines "at request and prayer of Masteir Iohn Whethamsted."[37] Whethamstede, a fellow Benedictine, had been abbot of St. Albans in Suffolk for about nineteen years, according to the colophon. He had a reputation in his own day "as an eminent churchman, diplomat, preacher, letter writer, and encyclopaedist, a munificent builder at St. Albans and Oxford, a magnate, a patron and benefactor of scribes, scholars, composers, poets, goldsmiths, painters, and glaziers."[38] "One of the greatest patrons of learning in fifteenth-century England," D.R. Howlett called him, Whethamstede commissioned and encouraged the production of books on a wide range of subjects—"astronomical, devotional, documentary, historical, homiletic, legal, liturgical, philosophic, and poetic."[39] He was open to innovation, if it served the cause of Christian education, and he encouraged the production of "orthodox standard works useful for the cure of souls."[40] "Clearly a benefactor, not a bibliophile," he gave more than one hundred books to individuals and institutions.[41]

Lydgate's completion of *Edmund and Fremund* just a few years earlier may have prompted Whethamstede to request a life of his own abbey's patron saint. Whethamstede was as concerned as Curteys with the preservation of monastic privilege, and he probably expected that Lydgate would represent Alban as a champion of that privilege.[42] He may have known Lydgate from their student days at Gloucester College, Oxford, during the early 1400s. Certainly, the two men had much in common as scholars, and Lydgate praises his intellectualism, evinced not only in his library but in his writings about "poetes and prudent philosophris" (*Edmund and Fremund*, bk. 1, lines 890–96). With such a patron, Lydgate probably felt encouraged to continue his experimentation with historically oriented and morally complex hagiography. Lydgate used his dual life to develop two themes that were dear to his heart: good governance and Christian education. He also used it to demonstrate the intrinsic harmony of religious and secular ideals and the tragedy that ensues when those ideals are forced into conflict.

Lydgate began *Alban and Amphibalus* shortly after completing his mammoth *Fall of Princes*, a work commissioned by Duke Humphrey that had occupied much of his attention during the 1430s. This long immersion in the question of why princes fail informed his *Edmund and Fremund* and obviously remained on his mind as he was composing *Alban and Amphibalus*.

Hagiographical convention represented the Roman persecutors of martyrs as sadists under the leadership of a malign emperor, and Lydgate had hitherto adhered to that convention. Dacian is "furious and cruwel" and Olibrius a "cruel wolfe."⁴³ The Danish adversaries of Edmund and Fremund are cut from the same pattern, "wonder despitous and of gret cruelte," with no redeeming qualities.⁴⁴ In *Alban and Amphibalus*, however, Lydgate did something completely different, embellishing more historically oriented French and Latin sources to construct a more nuanced portrait of imperial Rome, its politics, its ideals, and its theory of government.

Lydgate begins his narrative by harking back to when Britain was "ouer-maystred . . . Bi Iulius swerd," thanks to the "fals divisioun" among Britain's leaders. In the tradition of the "advice to princes" genre, Lydgate moralizes:

> Record the gospel: wher is divisioun,
> Frowarde discencioun, of cas or aventur,
> Thilk region may no while endur
> In prosperite, for bi discord of tweyn
> To subieccioun was brouht all Briteyn.
>   (*Alban and Amphibalus*, 1.136–40)

Caesar's victory had nothing to do with whether his "titil" were "wrong or riht" (1.123); he prevailed "rather bi fors than any title of riht" (1.142).

It might seem that Lydgate is laying the groundwork to expatiate on the iniquities of an illegitimate regime, but he is not. In fact, he goes on to represent the Romans as paragons of good governance, who implemented prudent policies that served the "comoun profite" (*Alban and Amphibalus*, 1.164). Those policies, though born of their self-interested determination to maintain their tenuous hold over a conquered people, were broadly beneficial. To ward off "newe rebellioun" and secure allegiance, the Romans decreed that no one can receive knighthood except at the emperor's hands and by swearing allegiance to Rome. They appoint stewards to govern each region through laws ordained "in rihtwysnesse" (1.188), in order to "restreyn" the "comouns" "fro willfull surfeits" (1.189) and to "set a-syde" "stormy troublis . . . a-mong the comountees" (1.205–6). The Romans work by "reforme" (1.208) rather than repression, amending outrages rather than perpetrating them (1.196). Rebels are promptly punished, but, perhaps more important, with less incentive to rebel, there are fewer of them.

The emperor nourishes principles of knighthood that would have been broadly endorsed (if not practiced) in fifteenth-century England. Those knighted were

> . . . iust and stable,
> Manly of hert and of condicioun,
> Sobre, nat hasty, feythful, honorable,
> For comoun profit previd profitable,
> Benyngne of port, nat proud, but debonaire.
> That woord and werk for nothyng be contraire.
> (*Alban and Amphibalus*, 1.409–13)

Roman knights "wrouht no thyng but bi wise counsaile" (1.403). They served widows, virgins, and poor people, and they used their "marcial violence" to chastise "fraud and extorcioun" (1.424–26). They were willing to shed their blood in the service of "comoun profit" (1.529). If only Roman ideals of chivalry prevailed today! Lydgate laments. Such knights would not stoop "t'apper at cessiouns or at shyres / Bi meyntenaunce of fals extorciouns," they would not "supporte bi ther proteccciouns / Causis vnleefull," nor would they "bi procurage maad to-forn / . . . make iuroures fully to be forsworn" (1.542–46). The Romans, he avers, were more concerned with "riht" than "ther clyent" (1.549–50).

Lydgate appears to be asserting that an illegitimate regime can nonetheless govern justly and in so doing earn its legitimacy. To reinforce that point, he recounts the iniquities of Carausius, a Roman naval commander who slays a British king who rules "bi iust successioun" (*Alban and Amphibalus*, 1.715) and with Roman approval. Deeds and disposition are what distinguish Carausius, who has "no titill to the regalie" (1.728), from Caesar, who likewise conquers "bi fors" rather than "title of riht." "Greetly disposid to slen and blood to sheede," Carausius has a "fals claym of mordre and tyranny" (1.711, 728). His revolt, thus construed as usurpation and falsehood (1.734), also shows that even the "prudent Romaynes" (1.163) make mistakes: after all, they appointed Carausius to the position of power that he eventually abused and betrayed.

Lydgate further complicates his representation of the Roman Empire by situating his account of its persecution of Christians amid his effusive praise of Roman rule. After enthusing about Roman justice,

Lydgate reports that the emperor, when informed that Christianity was spreading, immediately commands Christians to be brought into "his presence bi force" (*Alban and Amphibalus*, 1.342). The emperor's men, however, are unable to catch any Christians, and the subject of forcibly detaining them is dropped as Lydgate proceeds to even greater tributes to Roman chivalry. Lydgate thus ostentatiously discards the stereotypes of good or evil in favor of a more nuanced political vision. Impulses towards wrong might lurk within the hearts of wise princes; the question is whether they will act upon those impulses. Diocletian, of course, ultimately does. News of mass conversions stirs "gret envie" and "confusioun" within him, moving him to "malice" and "disdeyn" (1.826–27). In keeping with his penchant for nuance, Lydgate first shows the emperor behaving reasonably: he assembles his lords and senators to consult them about what he apparently believes to be a genuine threat to the empire. But the emperor and his advisors are too quick to condemn: in "hasti iugement," they order Christians killed, their books burned, and their churches razed. In so doing, they violate their own ideals of knighthood.

As Lydgate presents it, the Romans missed a great opportunity. In book 1, Lydgate shows emperor and pope engaging in parallel and complementary civilizing endeavors, fostering many of the same values. The emperor encourages the very qualities in his knights that Lydgate, both in *Alban and Amphibalus* and elsewhere, praises in saints and martyrs—"mekenesse," "gentilnesse," "humylite," "pacience," "sobirnesse," "clennesse" (*Alban and Amphibalus*, 1.450, 362). Roman knights were "sobre, nat hasty, feythful, honorable," "benyngne of port, nat proud, but debonaire" (1.411, 413)—just like the heroes of hagiography. Lydgate specifically points to the compatibility of Roman chivalry with Judeo-Christian principles when he praises the Romans for not shedding innocent blood: "Blood crieth vengeaunce to God of rihtwissnesse / Fals homycidis, contrarie to natur, / God soffreth hem no while to endur" (1.417–20). The Romans understood that "this noble vertu of humylite / Was in som cas nedefull to knyhthood" and that "verray meekenesse vsed in prudent wise / Is nat attwytid with no cowardice" (1.505–11). Their knights were to "avoide al dowbilnesse" and to "live chast" (1.361, 455). They were to protect the helpless. They were to honor and defend their religion (1.370–71)—and although the religion is wrong, the principle is right. The pope's goal is to match these admirable knights with the right faith. It seems only natural to him that men who are "so fresh, so seemely, and so honorable" should also be Christian. But where emperor and pope might easily have been allies, the emperor chooses to see the pontiff as his rival, a fellow expansionist whose conversions threaten his hegemony. In creating an enemy where there was none, he brings chaos and division to his empire.

Lydgate further indicates the compatibility of Christian values with Roman principles of governance in his development of the story of Alban and Amphibalus, who are among 1,500 British youths sent to Rome by King Severus, who was doing his "busi peyn" to please the emperor (*Alban and Amphibalus*, 1.234) and hoped to impress Diocletian with a spectacular demonstration of British respect and loyalty. Once in Rome, Alban is recruited by the emperor, Amphibalus by the pope. The two later meet up again in Britain, in the city of Verulamium (present-day St. Albans): Alban is residing in the city as the emperor's steward, appointed to keep order in the wake of the Carausius rebellion, while Amphibalus has fled persecution in Rome and is on his way back to his native Wales.

Lydgate takes pains to establish Alban as an ideal governor, loved and feared by all, who rules through "prudent pollicie" for the "comoun profit." As steward, he settles disputes, punishes slander, and disregards flattery and gossip; he punishes crime and redresses wrongs. "Nat slaw nor rekeles" (*Alban and Amphibalus*, 2.70), he "gaff nevir doom til trewthe wer out founde" (2.96). What's more, Lydgate shows that the very qualities that secure the emperor's favor and make Alban a just and trustworthy governor also make him receptive to Amphibalus's Christian teachings. Alban behaves "lik a prynce benygne and vertuous" when he recognizes his old companion, destitute and friendless, and welcomes him into his home (2.168). Though Alban's initial reaction to Amphibalus's Christian message is disbelief (2.433–35), he weighs Amphibalus's teachings, raises questions and objections, and accepts Christianity when his doubts are satisfied. In short, unlike the emperor, he acts with the prudence and even-handedness that were integral to the Roman ideal of governance.

As much as Alban is a paragon of just governance, Amphibalus is a model of effective religious instruction. As he did in his "Austin," Lydgate emphasizes the scriptural orientation of Amphibalus's teaching: a "clerk groundid in scriptur," he prechid Goddis worde" (*Alban and Amphibalus*, 3.194, 196); "he did teche / The worde of God" (3.97–98). His arguments are founded in scripture:

> Amphibalus is entrid of resoun
> On the Gospel to groundyn his processe
> And to conferme his disputacioun.
> Off Hooly Writ he took iustly witnesse
> How our bileve recordith in sothnesse
> Of God the Fadre and God the Soone also.
> (2.198–203)

Like Austin and Giles, Amphibalus practices what he preaches through "his lyvyng and parfit holynesse" (3.93). He is thus another ideal pastor, cut from the same pattern as Chaucer's Parson.

Amphibalus, Lydgate shows, is a patient teacher, undeterred by skepticism and hostility. He perseveres when Alban scolds him: "Ye be nat wys, your doctryne is in veyn" (*Alban and Amphibalus*, 2.413). And he woos the pagan crowds with the same gentle determination he uses with Alban:

> Tho folk that wer come to hym of newe
> Fro Verolamye his prechyng for to her,
> Lik a doctour in Cristis faith most trewe,
> Receivid them with al his hert enteer,
> Enformed hem, and tauth hem the maneer
> Of Cristis lawe with besi dilligence,
> And thei wer glad t'abide in his presence.
> Litill and litill in he gan hem drawe
> To catche savour and feith in his doctryne.
> (3.169–77)

Amphibalus, moreover, is flexible, sensitive to the needs of his converts. When the newly converted Alban protests his decision to leave Verulamium for other parts of Britain, declaring that he needs further instruction, Amphibalus immediately yields. He thus recognizes that the establishment of Christianity is not simply a matter of baptizing converts and moving on but rather of providing them with a thorough understanding of "doctrine" (2.794).

Though Amphibalus usually plays a bit role in lives of Alban (in the earliest accounts and in many later renderings, he is not even named), Lydgate's Amphibalus is at least as important as Alban, if not more so. Indeed, one might argue that, as much as Alban is praised for his courage and suffering, his "maistir" Amphibalus is the real hero of Lydgate's legend. Repeatedly, Lydgate emphasizes that Alban is Amphibalus's convert, Alban's passion a tribute to Amphibalus's good teaching. When Alban professes his faith before the pagan judges, he declares, "*Of my maistir* I confesse the doctryne" (*Alban and Amphibalus*, 2.1103; my emphasis). Those who witness Alban's death declare that, since God has shown such "vertu" through Alban, his "maistir" should have "grete auctorite" to address their doubts (3.79–84).

Lydgate clearly demonstrates the superiority of teaching to alternative methods of instilling faith, such as revelation, miracles, and the testimony of a martyr's death. True, when the initially skeptical Alban receives a moving vision of the Passion, Amphibalus tells him that he is privileged to learn through revelation rather than merely "of a man" (*Alban and Amphibalus*, 2.764), but Lydgate shows that such learning through revelation is limited. Alban's vision fails to convert him, because he does not understand it; its real value is to make him more receptive to Amphibalus's teaching (2.668–70). It is not until Amphibalus "expounned" the vision "with ful instructioun" and "supportacioun" that Alban embraces Christianity (2.474–76). Similarly, although the miracles attending Alban's martyrdom astound the pagan bystanders, they are open, as Lydgate shows, to interpretation: one is attributed to the gods generally, another to sorcery (2.1665–67, 1789–90, 1953–59). Signs alone do not thoroughly signify; they do not effect the instant conversions we find in many thirteenth- and fourteenth-century lives. Instead, signs inspire beholders to seek the *instruction* that can effect conversion. After witnessing Alban's heroic death, one bystander declares:

> Go seeke menys for our salvacioun,
> In dyvers contes to fynde vp the man
> Which bi his labour and predicacioun
> Convuertid Albon.
>   (3.58–61)

The miracles that attend Alban's death inspire the bewildered bystanders to urge that Alban's "maistir in al hast may be souht" (3.73), for they suggest that "his maistres techyng feithful was and trewe" (3.79–84).

Set against the Christians' effective teaching is the violence with which the Romans attempt to repress it. The pagans are also anti-intellectuals, who try in vain to stamp out Christianity by ordering that its teachers "be slayn and ther bookis brent" (*Alban and Amphibalus*, 1.854). When the Romans come to "debate" the Christians, soldiers brandishing swords are met by confident Christians armed with "connyng and eloquence" (3.187, 241). But violent repression brings death not only to the Christians but to peace and stability, as family members are set against each other and the Roman regime is devoured by Lydgate's dreaded serpent of division (3.282–301). Though swords trump eloquence in the short run, Albion is converted in the long run, proving words mightier than weapons.

Lydgate's hagiography varies tremendously in form; his lives range in scope from epitome to epic. He appropriates the conventions of paean, chronicle, romance, and exemplum. But in all of his saints' lives, we find a humane and humanizing Christianity, founded on compassion and understanding, propagated through the preaching of scripture, and reinforced through the example of its teachers.

Andrew Cole and Shannon Gayk have found in Lydgate's devotional verse a flexibility, a willingness to experiment, and an impulse towards reform that is odds with the agenda of "aggressive orthodoxy" associated with the Lancastrians and embodied in the "Constitutions."[45] The same independent, reformist thinking is very much evident in Lydgate's hagiography. His monastic credentials, combined with his position as a poet trusted and sought after by the Lancastrians, gave him great authority and credibility, which he used to promote a return to a more capacious orthodoxy, asserting as orthodox an emphasis on biblical precedent and preaching and reclaiming for orthodoxy the figure of the priest as good shepherd. Read, admired, and imitated into the sixteenth century, Lydgate's hagiography continued, as we shall see, to shape ideals of holiness on the eve of the Reformation and beyond.

CHAPTER TWO

Osbern Bokenham's Holy Women

In 1443, the Cambridge friar Thomas Burgh persuaded his friend Osbern Bokenham of the Austin priory at Clare to compose a verse life of Saint Margaret of Antioch. Bokenham was none too pleased with the assignment, at least so he says in the life he grudgingly provided.[1] After all, he was fifty years old; writing for long stretches strained his eyes, cramped his hands, and taxed his wits ("Margaret," lines 869–920). What's more, people's "hate" and "despyht" for him would make them likely to "blame" anything he wrote (36–37). Bokenham therefore exhorted Burgh to keep his authorship a secret, especially from his fellows at Cambridge, whose "wyttys . . . manye ryht capcyows / And subtyl," would soon "aspye" the "lewydnesse" of a "symple wreche" (208–10, 70). Let him tell his savvy confreres that "Margaret" was sent to him by a friend who used to sell horses at fairs and lives in the city of Burgh, near Castle Bolingbroke (200–225).

Who would have guessed that this crotchety friar would go on to become medieval England's most prolific vernacular hagiographer? "Margaret" was the first of an astonishing series of female saints' lives that occupied Bokenham into the 1450s, perhaps beyond. At least thirteen of those lives were written during the 1440s and appear to have circulated individually among East Anglian readers in booklet form.[2] In 1447, Burgh paid thirty shillings to have them copied into an anthology for a "holy place of nunnys."[3] That anthology survives as British Library, MS Arundel 327, and scholars have long known it as the *Legendys of Hooly Wummen*, the title of its modern edition. Many more saints' lives, probably later compositions, are found in a larger and more diverse legendary: Bokenham's adaptation of Jacobus's *Legenda aurea*, preserved in the Abbotsford Special Collection of the Faculty of Advocates Library in Edinburgh, Scotland.[4] This second collection, which I will be examining more broadly as an anthology in chapter 5, attests that Bokenham was by no means exclusively interested in women. Here, however, my focus is his women, for the number and diversity of Bokenham's lives of female saints establish him as the most prominent representative of the fifteenth century's preoccupation with female sanctity. I will first look at Bokenham's presentation of himself and his heroines in the lives he is known to have composed during the 1440s (i.e., those anthologized by Burgh) before considering the more diverse and ambitious representations of the experiences of holy women in lives found in the Abbotsford manuscript. We shall see that in the Arundel lives Bokenham shows a pronounced tendency to create saints whose behavior, insofar as possible, conforms to contemporary norms for women. In his Abbotsford lives, by contrast, he imagines a broader range of action for his heroines as scholars, teachers, even preachers. He does this while maintaining, indeed amplifying, the careful attention to the feelings and emotions that would surely have facilitated the identification of lay readers with the saints. In his Abbotsford lives, moreover, he shows himself more willing to probe the darker recesses of family life and the values that inform the relationships between parents and children, husbands and wives.

"A symple wreche"?

Bokenham comes across as quite a character. A man of moods, he could be diffident and boastful, servile and bossy, affable and grumpy. His eccentricity is abundantly evident in "Margaret." Even as he insists that Burgh conceal his name, he reveals more personality than any other Middle English hagiographer had done in a saint's life. "Margaret" is full of offbeat digressions. He assures readers that his devotion to the saint should not surprise them, for he experienced firsthand the power of her foot, which was kept in a splendid reliquary near the town of his birth ("Margaret," lines 132–70). He lets everyone know how frustrated he was when his pen started blotting midway through the project and no amount of rubbing its "sowt" against his "thombys ende" helped! His pen's malfunction forced him to take a break from writing for a few days, but he needed a break anyhow because of all his aches and pains (896–920).

Though Bokenham protests his unworthiness as an author, he vigorously defends the quality and the authority of his work: "Margaret," he brags, is like the rose that grows from a thorny branch, the pearl that emerges from a worthless shell, and so forth (lines 43–58).[5] In fact, "Margaret" the narrative is much like Margaret the saint, whom he also likens to a pearl and to a rose (250–56, 348–50). After Bokenham has told us we shouldn't judge a book by its author because scripture says one shouldn't judge the son by his father (60–72), how can we fail to compare the saint, who "sprong ... of the hethene blood" (348–50), to her "life," which sprang from the pen of "a symple wreche"? As for the details of that life, Bokenham obtained them on his latest trip to Italy, where Margaret's story was well known among the residents of Montefiascone (108–12). Let skeptics travel there and see for themselves! His own journey was far from pleasant, he adds; heavy rains stranded him at Montefiascone, where the locals "begyle" "wery pylgrymys" with trebbiano instead of muscatel (114–18).

Was Bokenham really such a garrulous eccentric? Or was the "personality" of this "symple wreche" a construct, an attempt to create a distinct narrative voice in the tradition of the three "fresh rethoryens" he so admired: Chaucer, Gower, and Lydgate ("Margaret," lines 416–17). Certainly, we must question his professed zeal for anonymity. His ramblings about the horse-seller read more like a joke at the expense of know-it-all Cambridge friars (whom he assumes—or pretends to assume—would be gullible enough to believe such a tale) than a sincere attempt to divert suspicion from his authorship. In any case, Burgh didn't seem to worry about betraying his friend's confidence when, in 1447, he identified Bokenham as the author of the thirteen female saints' lives ("Margaret" among them) contained in Arundel 327.[6]

Arundel 327: "Hooly Wummen" for Special Friends

If in 1443 Bokenham really *was* worried about being disdained as an author, his attitude had evidently changed by 1447. He certainly did not betray any such anxieties in 1445, when, in the prologue to his "Mary Magdalene," he recalled chatting about his writings with Isabel Bourchier at a Twelfth Night party she was hosting at her castle. As the young people reeled about the dance floor, Bokenham rattled off a list of seven "legendys . . . of hooly wummen" that he had written to date ("Mary Magdalene," lines 5038–40). When Bokenham mentioned his life-in-progress of Elizabeth of Hungary—undertaken at the behest of Elizabeth Vere, Countess of Oxford—Isabel cajoled him into adding a life of her own favorite saint, Mary Magdalene, to his to-do list.

Bokenham wrote most of the other lives found in Arundel 327 for his East Anglian friends and acquaintances.[7] Besides "Margaret," "Mary Magdalene," and "Elizabeth," he penned a "Dorothy" for the Hunts, an "Anne" for the Denstons, a "Katherine" for Katherine Howard and Katherine Denston, and an "Agatha" for Agatha Flegge. Clearly, he had a receptive and supportive audience. That he wrote an additional six lives—"Christina," "Ursula," "Agnes," "Lucy," "Faith," and "Cecilia"— for nobody in particular indicates that, for all his talk of "rudnesse" and "lytyl experyence" (lines 5038, 5078), he was not all that reluctant to take pen in hand.

Indeed, Bokenham's writing exudes a confidence that belies his ostentatious self-deprecation. He asserts that it is important "to eschewyn prolyxite" ("Mary Magdalene," line 1612), but he doesn't curtail his digressions and grumblings. "A-statys preyer" is his command, he avers (5083), and he declares himself wholly committed to the "consolacyoun" and "conforte" of his friends (6365–66). Yet he is no slave to their wants and whims. Isabel Bourchier asks specifically for a legend of Mary Magdalene the "apostyllesse" (5068); as Bokenham presents Mary's story, however, the action is driven precisely by her *failure* to convert the king and queen of Marseilles through her preaching: "Maryis wurdys auaylyd no thyng" (5808–9). In "Elizabeth" he inveighs against the "men & wummen . . . þese dayis" who are "froward" enough to "compleyn" when clergymen chastise them—though he expects that "sum folk wolde haue greth indygnacyoun" at his "dylatacyoun" ("Elizabeth," 9841–55). For John and Katherine Denston, so eager for a son, he writes a life of Saint Anne, who was blessed immeasurably by a daughter.[8]

Literary Competitors and "Ianuence"

Bokenham shows an independent spirit, not only in dealing with friends and patrons, but also in following literary authorities. Even as he praises the loftier accomplishments of others, he promotes his own efforts. Bokenham pays tribute to "maystyr" Capgrave's recently compiled *Life of Saint Katherine*, with its "balaadys rymyd ful craftyly" ("Katherine," lines 6354, 6359). Yet he discreetly plants doubts about the credibility of Capgrave's account of Katherine's conversion, claiming to know nothing of "alle þat" (6360). Bokenham admits that he lacks the "crafty eloquens" ("Agnes," line 4048) of a Cicero. In fact, Pallas Athena *drove* him from her meadows, saying that Chaucer, Gower, and Lydgate had already gathered the "most fresh flourys" of rhetoric (4059–62). Yet he evinces an unmistakable pride as he touts himself as a homespun author, whose offerings are rude but honest, inexperienced but earnest, and delivered "pleynly / Aftyr þe language of Suthfolk speche" for the comfort and consolation of his friends (4063–64).[9]

Though Bokenham emphasizes how different he is from contemporary hagiographers Lydgate and Capgrave in the style and scope of his work, his vision of holiness is much like theirs. He follows Lydgate's lead in promoting the saints as exemplars for ordinary men and women. In so doing, he, like Lydgate, departs from the paradigms popularized by Jacobus de Voragine, systematically muting the conflicts that dominated Jacobus's legends and bringing out his heroines' more "feminine" qualities. Though he purports to convey "Ianuencys [Jacobus de Voragine's] purpose" and "entent" ("Lucy," lines 8948, 8962), his professed deference to the popular Latin author masks his pursuit of an altogether different agenda.

I have discussed elsewhere Bokenham's transformation of virgin martyrs in Arundel 327 from the obstreperous viragoes who populated the *Legenda aurea* into models of gentility and decorum that would suit a conservative lay readership.[10] In retelling virgin martyr legends, Bokenham typically uses Jacobus's prologues, which dwell on the saints' virtues, but he either replaces Jacobus's narratives altogether or supplements them with material from monastic sources that dwell on the saints' devotional lives. Here, I will examine his approach to telling the stories of holy wives Elizabeth of Hungary and the Virgin Mary's mother, Anne, whose stories are found in Burgh's collection. "Elizabeth" represents Bokenham's characteristic modus operandi as he translated lives from the *Legenda aurea.* "Anne" shows most clearly the interest in psychology and in complex family relationships that, as I will show later, also characterizes many of the lives of his Abbotsford collection.

Elizabeth of Hungary: Beyond "Ianuence"

We clearly see the strategies Bokenham employs in his pursuit of exemplarity in his life of Elizabeth of Hungary (d. 1231), the only late medieval laywoman whose life Jacobus de Voragine included in his *Legenda aurea*.[11] Bokenham immediately identifies "Ianuence" as "myne auctor" ("Elizabeth," lines 9456, 9467), when, in his usual fashion, he begins with an etymological meditation of Elizabeth's virtues, "as seyth Ianuence in hys golden legende" (9456). But his life of Elizabeth, though based on Jacobus's, is more a free adaptation than a translation.

Jacobus's life is marked by the extreme antiworldliness and the emphasis on saintly power and perfection that characterizes the *Legenda aurea* as a whole.[12] Jacobus details heroic feats of asceticism that waste Elizabeth's body, and he describes in lurid detail her contact with the filth, disease, stench, and squalor of poverty. Yet even as he praises Elizabeth's willingness to humble herself in God's service, he never allows his readers to forget that she is "unsurpassed . . . in freedom of high station" (*Golden Legend*, 2:305) and that her "position was of the highest dignity" (306). Elizabeth humbles herself on her own terms, calculated to enhance her status in the kingdom of heaven. She says, "I *choose* to give my obedience to Master Conrad, a poor, undistinguished man, rather than to some bishop" in order "to gain merit" (309; my emphasis). She *orders* her servants to address her as a social inferior (309–10). Moreover, she does not hesitate to invoke her social or heavenly privilege to compel others to serve God. When a girl with beautiful hair visits the hospital Elizabeth founded, Elizabeth has her seized and her hair shorn, "despite her sobs and her struggles" (312), to deprive the girl of a source of vanity; when a sick old woman refuses to confess and take Communion, Elizabeth "has her whipped to change her mind" (311). Jacobus demonstrates Elizabeth's continued power after her death through his accounts of numerous posthumous miracles.

Jacobus's Elizabeth is a reluctant wife, "compelled to enter the state of marriage in obedience to her father's order" (*Golden Legend*, 2:304). She had sex only "out of respect for her father's command, and in order to procreate and raise children for the service of God" (304). Jacobus observes that although Elizabeth "was bound by the law of the conjugal bed, she was not bound to enjoyment," adding that it was "obvious" that she did not enjoy sex because she vowed to her confessor "that if she survived her husband she would practice continence for the rest of her life" (304). Elizabeth did not allow marriage to "change... the way she intended to live" (304). When her husband died in the Holy Land, in a crusade he undertook at her behest, she "embraced" widowhood, rejoicing that "her long-standing desire for poverty was fulfilled" (308). Though Jacobus praises Elizabeth's husband for his supportiveness, Elizabeth expresses no affection for him while he is alive, nor does she grieve his passing. She only once admits to having loved her husband: that admission occurs in a prayer after his death, when she is trying to impress the Deity with her far greater love for Him (308). Of her children, she boasts, "I care for my children no more than for others around me" (309).

Bokenham liberally rephrases and embellishes his source. He goes well beyond Jacobus in praising Elizabeth's virtues—humility, hospitality, patience, charity, diligence, temperance, restraint, and prudence. Moreover, he discusses those virtues as they might be practiced by anybody, for example, "pacyence / In suffraunce of trouble & of aduersyte" ("Elizabeth," line 9495), "loue & eke pyte, / Of god & our neybours both hy & lo" (9503–4), "largenesse / And pyte to the pore" (9708–9). Even when he describes actions his readers could not be expected to imitate, he draws attention to their eminently imitable motives. For example, "tendyrnesse" and "mekenesse" lead her to personally wash and anoint a sick servant whose sores repulse everybody else (9769–84). In recounting Elizabeth's obedience, he explicitly distinguishes between the laudable virtue and Elizabeth's extreme interpretation of it: obedience to one's confessor is "blyssyd," Bokenham says, but submitting to a confessor's floggings could not be expected of anyone these days— "neythyr prest ner munk, chanoun ner frere" (9840).

Bokenham's Elizabeth is a "merour" to "alle wyuys" ("Mary Magdalene," line 5047). Though he retains Jacobus's claim that she would have preferred not to marry ("Elizabeth," 9673–80), he precludes the inference that Elizabeth's vow against remarriage indicates her distaste for sex by having her make that vow *before* her marriage (9681–88). At every opportunity, he emphasizes her love for her "dere spouse, whom next god most tendyrly / I loue & euere haue done treuly" (10076–77). She admits to missing him when he was away from home: "Sumtyme I sorwyd whan thow wentyst fro me" (10125). She heeds him when he begs her "to sparyn hyr body & hyt yeuyn sum rest" (9728), undertaking her most rigorous feats of asceticism only "in hyr lordys absence" (9874).

Though Elizabeth sacrifices the husband she loves to the God she adores by convincing Louis to take the cross, Bokenham stresses the magnitude of that sacrifice. He adds a poignant scene in which Elizabeth professes her love to Louis as he departs for the Holy Land: "Wyth what affeccyon & how enterely / I þe loue, dere spouse, & euyr haue do, / No man knowyth but god & þou & I" ("Elizabeth," lines 10113–15). It is "impossible" to undo the "knot of spousayle" than has joined them, she swears (10117–20). And she acts on her words, for in Bokenham's account, Elizabeth's refusal to remarry signals her devotion not only to God but also to Louis. When her husband's remains are brought home from the Holy Land, she tells the uncle who has been advocating her remarriage, "Syr, syth my lord ys now comyn home to me, / Othyr husbonde wyl I neuere haue noon, certeyn" (10255–56).

Bokenham omits many of the miracles that set Elizabeth apart from ordinary women. He also omits at least some of the incidents in which she asserts her authority over others, for example, her flogging of the old woman who refuses to confess. By not stressing her singularity and her superiority to those around her, Bokenham creates a more fully human Elizabeth. He thus makes it easier to see the many compromises she makes as she negotiates her competing obligations to husband, father, relatives, children, subjects, confessor, and God. She bows to her father's will as a young girl but not as a widow. She curbs her asceticism to please her husband. She reveres her confessor but skips his sermon to entertain a marchioness ("Elizabeth," lines 9825–28). She indulges her dream of living in poverty only after she has provided for her children (10175–76).

Anne: Marriage

Although "Elizabeth" illustrates Bokenham's usual modus operandi in the Arundel lives—keeping the details of his source(s) but developing the saints' imitable virtues and emphasizing their emotions, in Elizabeth's case, her love for her husband—the most innovative of the Arundel lives is "Anne."

Bokenham may have felt freer to adapt Anne's life because his "auctour" ("Anne," line 1611), Jacobus de Voragine, had so very little to say about her in his account of the Virgin Mary's birth. As Anne's husband,

Joachim, is making his offering at the temple in Jerusalem, he is reproached by the officiating priest for having no children after twenty years of marriage: "It was not proper . . . for a sterile man . . . to stand among men who begot sons" (Jacobus, *Golden Legend*, 2:151). Ashamed to face his neighbors, Joachim goes off to live with his shepherds. An angel appears to him, explaining at length how his childlessness was part of God's plan and ordering him to go home. The angel then "reveals the same things he had told Joachim" to Joachim's distraught wife (2:152). As instructed by the angel, Anne meets Joachim at the Golden Gate of Jerusalem. They are "happy to see each other" and Anne conceives a child, just as the angel promised. As this summary indicates, Jacobus's account is not exactly a *vita*, and to the extent it *is* a *vita*, it is Joachim's.

By Bokenham's time, Anne was the object of a burgeoning cult, which thrived in England well before its official recognition in 1382.[13] Anne's following was especially strong in East Anglia, where Abbot Anselm of Bury and Osbert of Clare were already in the twelfth century promoting her veneration. Numerous chapels, guilds, and altars were dedicated to her. The earliest literary accounts of her life date from the fifteenth century, when her story was dramatized in the N-Town Cycle, and it was relayed in at least three distinct Middle English verse lives, not counting Bokenham's.[14]

All five of these fifteenth-century renditions of Anne's life participate in the vigorous trend towards more accessible saints. Gail Gibson observes that the author of the life written for a guild and preserved in the commonplace book of Robert Reynes of Acle, Norfolk, "transforms ascetic and gospel paradigms by his enthusiastic bourgeois piety," rendering Anne and Joachim "a merchant's saints par excellence":

> The Acle poem closely follows the canonical history of the life of Saint Anne in the *Golden Legend* but adds elaboration and emphases that make of Saint Anne a model East Anglian matron, tending to her tithes, her alms basket, and her prayer book. This is sanctity envisioned as a busy, comfortable, and pious life in which only the temporary martyrdom of childlessness must be suffered—to be overcome in the fruitful triumph of becoming the grandmother of God.[15]

The other two anonymous verse lives likewise represent the couple's childlessness as a "temporary martyrdom," eclipsed by "triumph."

Only Bokenham and the N-Town playwright dwell on that "martyrdom," but they develop it in completely different ways.

In the N-Town play, the "martyrdom of childlessness" demonstrates the strength of the couple's commitment to each other. As he sets out for the Temple, Joseph anticipates the humiliation that awaits him there and confides his fears to his "blyssyd" wife, who feels his pain and tries to comfort him ("Joachim and Anna," lines 42–81). When his offering is spurned, Joachim immediately thinks of his wife:

> For hevynes I dare not go hom to my wyff,
> And amonge my neyborys I dare not abyde for shame
> A, Anne, Anne, Anne, al oure joye is turnyd to grame!
> From ȝoure blyssyd felachepp I am now exilyd
> And ȝe here onys of þis fowle fame,
> Sorwe wyl sle ȝow to se me thus revylyd.
>
> (123–28)

When he doesn't return home, Anne understands his anguish and reproaches God: "Why do ȝe thus to myn husbond, Lord? Why? Why? Why?" (167). Heartbroken, she resolves to "seke hym whatsoevyr befalle" even though she has no idea where he went (214–15). Joachim and Anne each claim full responsibility for their childlessness: Anne speaks of "*my* barynes" (168); Joachim calls himself a "wrecche, werse þan an hownde," whose "synful steppys an vemynyd þe grounde" (152, 150). Joachim will gladly accept his punishment for his "offens" (158); he asks only that God spare his wife: "Punchyth me, Lorde, and spare my blyssyd wyff Anne / Þat syttyth and sorwyth ful sore of myn absens"; "my lovyngest wyff Anne, Lord for þi mercy, kepe" (159–61, 164). Each rejoices at the angel's good news, not only because they will finally have a child, but also because they will be reunited. Anne exclaims:

> Þer can no tounge telle what joye in me is!
> I to bere a childe þat xal bere all mannys blys,
> And haue myn hosbonde geyn! Ho myth haue joys more?
>
> (232–34)

The play ends with the couple embracing at the Golden Gate and returning home together, grateful for God's blessing and secure in their happiness. The N-Town playwright thus models a marriage based on compassion, affection, and mutual respect. He celebrates a love uneroded by twenty years of disappointment that emerges from a crisis stronger than ever.

Bokenham tells a more complex and disturbing story of pain and isolation.[16] He begins with the "solenne" wedding of the wealthy and well-bred Anne "to a man acordyng to hyr degre" ("Anne," line 1628). Joachim is

> A ryche man & of gret dignyte
> Whos lyf of youthe was euer vertuous,
> Symple, ryhtfulle & eke petous,
> Aforne god & man ryht comendable
> To whom Anne was wyf ful conuenable.
> (1632–36)

Bokenham iterates that the two were well matched, not only in goods but in goodness: "vertu to vertu is agreable; / Werfore anne to ioachym was wyf ful able" (1642–43). They live as they were brought up to live, that is, giving generously to paupers and pilgrims, supporting their church, and maintaining their household (1654–57). The disappointment of childlessness they meet "wyth offrynge & wyth deuouht prayer" (1664), and despite that blemish on their "chast maryage" they live harmoniously together, "ryhtful to god & to man petous" (1660, 1658)—until the incident at the Temple.

Unlike his counterpart in the N-Town play, Bokenham's Joachim has no inkling that he will be singled out for censure:

> Iochym in his best aray
> To ierusalem went wyth deuocyoun
> To make his ofrynge as he was woun,
> Wyth other burgeys of hys cyte,
> Eche man as longyd to hys degre.
> ("Anne," lines 1674–78)

"Stondyinge ful sturdyly" among his fellows on a routine visit to the Temple, he is stunned when the bishop turns on him and denounces him for being "bareyn and frutles," "cursed" and "condemptable" in the eyes of God (1681–99). The humiliation of being "rebukyde . . . / Of þe byschop in þe temple opynly" (1700–1701)—not childlessness or fear of God's curse—effects a profound transformation. "Aschamyd of þat caas" and fearful that "his neybures . . . Hym wolde repreue," he withdraws from society and joins his shepherds in the "wyldernesse" (1702–9). Bokenham gives no indication that Joachim thinks of his wife until an angel appears to him, asking why he doesn't return home to her (1825–26).

Bokenham's Anne evinces a love for her husband every bit as profound as that of her counterpart in the N-Town play:

> . . . lorde, þu knowyst how affecteuously
> I hym now loue and euere haue do,
> Syth we fyrst knyt were lawfully,
> Past alle creatures.
> ("Anne," lines 1742–45)

Expressing the anguish and isolation of a woman without children and now without a spouse, she asks God: "What haue I trespascyd geyn thy mercy / That þus my spouse þu takyst me fro?" (1730–31). Though she may not be able to have a child, she longs to be a wife to Joachim. But how can she do so, when she has no idea where her husband is, or even whether he's still alive?

> . . . yf I knew where [to find Joachim], wyth-owt letynge
> I wolde hym seke, yf he were lyuynge,
> And yf he ded were, his sepulture
> I wolde enbelshyn wyth besy cure.
> (1738–41)

Even the angel's "glad tydynges" that she will soon conceive a child do not dispel her gloom: "astoyned" and "dysconsolat," she retreats to her chambers to pray, rejoicing only when the angel returns to announce her husband's homecoming (1787, 1793–97).

Joachim displays no such fervor. "I loue my wyf as affectually, / I dar wel seyn, as any man doþe his" ("Anne," lines 1828–29), he tells the angel, his "affectually" a cold echo of her "affecteuously" (1742). For Joachim, Anne is now just one of his financial responsibilities, which he can discharge as effectively from the fields as he can at home:

Hom ageyn I wyl neuer more go,
But here wyth myn herdys I wyl abyde,
& wyth good avyhs I wyl prouyde
To sende þe part whiche longeþe hem to
Both temple & wyf & pore men also.
          (1856–60)

The rejoicing at the Golden Gate is conspicuously one-sided. As soon as Anne spots "hyr dere spouse," she runs towards him "as fast as she myhte":

She toke heed of non oþer thynge
But of hym alone, for in veraay blysse
Here þowte she was for his comynge.
& a-non she gan hym halsen & kysse,
No ioye wenynge þat she myht mysse
Syth she hym hadde.
          (1966–71)

Compare Bokenham's rendering with the mutual happiness described by Jacobus de Voragine and the N-Town playwright, and with the Acle poem's "eyther kyssyd other and were ful blythe."[17]

Bokenham makes it abundantly clear that in fleeing to the pastures Joachim has taken the easy way out. He moves from a scene of Anne weeping "wythowten consolacyon" ("Anne," line 1818) at a servant's insolence to one of Joachim walking with his sheep in "mountes grene" (1821). His life is not so bad: his shepherds are affable companions and respectful subordinates; he's even equipped to entertain a guest at his "tabernacle" (1900). Whereas Anne struggles vainly to understand, or at least accept, God's will, Joachim appears content in his new life. He asks for no answers and prays for no heavenly intervention. Perhaps Joachim accepts his new life with equanimity because it's the life he chose. Or perhaps he's complacent because, as Bokenham presents him, he doesn't think deeply about much of anything. A decent man, he doesn't need to live extravagantly or to shine among his peers. All he wants is to be respected by those around him, and he can achieve that among the shepherds.

Joachim's simplicity and desire for respectability is abundantly illustrated when the angel visits him in his pasture. Obviously still smarting from the bishop's imputation that he was to blame for his lack of issue, Joachim defends his manhood, regaling his heavenly visitor with assurances that he sowed his seed diligently but that he labored in vain. It was "vylany" for the bishop to despise his offerings and bar him from the Temple. When the angel urges him to return home to his wife, giving multiple examples to show that "bareynesse" has often been visited on good people as part of God's plan, Joachim seems not to have heard. His response: "Com & suppe wyth me, I þe pray, / In my tabernacle her be-syde þe wey" ("Anne," lines 1899–1900). Though impressed and honored by the angel's visit, and eager to please through his hospitality, he falls asleep wondering "what best was to do" (1932) and he takes no action until the angel haunts his dreams with a directive unencumbered with exegesis:

> ... of my comynge, lo, þis is þe entent,
> In hasty wyse þat þu home hye the.
> ȝoure prayeris ben harde, & ther-fore ye
> Swich a chylde shul haue as neuer to-fore,
> Ne neuer schal aftur, of woman be bore.
> (1940–44)

This terse message—much like the one delivered earlier to Anne (which sent Anne weeping and confused to her room)—is all that's needed to make Joachim a happy man: he "made hym redy wythowt lettyng" and headed home with his animals and herdsmen, praising God along the way: "Of goddes goodnesse þey dede speke & talke" (1951).

Curiously, "Of goddes goodnesse þey dede speke & talke" is the last we hear of Joachim's feelings or opinions. I have already noted that Bokenham conveys none of Joachim's emotions when he meets his wife at the Golden Gate. Bokenham does not even speak of his joy at Mary's birth. What's more, Catherine Sanok points out, Anne's prayer at the Temple "leaves Joachim out altogether"; she speaks only of God's singular grace to her and of the comfort he gives to all those who are in distress.[18] Though Bokenham describes the reunion of Joachim and Anne, he stops short of assuring his readers that they lived happily ever after. Even back home with his family, Joachim remains marginalized.[19]

In his prologue, Bokenham claims that he is writing "Anne" for the sake of his friend, Katherine Denston ("Anne," line 1466). In his conclusion, he prays that John and Katherine might have a son (2090–92). Yet, as I suggested earlier, there is also a hint of reproach. Bokenham's Anne prays that God might grant her "sone *or dowgter*," and even the surly Joachim complains that he has "neythyr son *ne dowghter*" (1775, 1836; my emphasis). The Denstons, by contrast, will only be happy with a son: they already have a "yung & fayre" daughter, Bokenham explains, as he enlists the intervention of Anne, a mother of three children, all daughters (2077, 2092–95). Did the Denstons catch the irony?

A more intriguing question: Did this fifteenth-century couple have more in common with Anne and Joachim than childlessness? In other words, was Bokenham's probing portrait of a troubled marriage based on his perception of how matters stood within the Denston household? That question, too, is unanswerable. All we can say is that something inspired Bokenham to transform Anne's life into the story of a husband and wife who have drifted apart, and to tell that story with extraordinary sensitivity and compassion.

Bokenham's "englische boke"

Though Bokenham appears to have begun his career as a hagiographer by writing freestanding saints' lives in verse, at some point, probably during the 1450s, his "specialle frendis" persuaded him to undertake a more ambitious project, which he describes in his *Mappula angliae* as "the englische boke the whiche y haue compiled of legenda aurea and of oþer famous legendes."[20] That "englische boke," preserved at the Library of the Faculty of Advocates, in Edinburgh, Scotland, consists of 175 chapters on the saints and on major Church festivals, all arranged according to the liturgical calendar.[21] Bokenham's principle source is the *Legenda aurea*, but he freely adds lives not found in Jacobus's collection, or substitutes other versions of saints' lives for Jacobus's. Unfortunately, the manuscript is incomplete, missing its beginning and ending and some parts in the middle. We can thus only speculate about the identity of Bokenham's special friends and how they persuaded him to take on such a massive project. The manuscript breaks off towards the end of the Winifred legend, so lives of saints whose feast days fall after November 3 are missing.

Though mostly written in prose, the Abbotsford legendary contains fifteen verse lives, including eight found in Arundel 327: the lives of Agnes, Agatha, Dorothy, Margaret, Mary Magdalene, Christine, Faith, and Ursula. (Since the feasts of the other saints celebrated in the Arundel collection fall after November 3, their lives probably were originally part of the collection.) These eight lives are unchanged from their incarnation in the Arundel manuscript, except that Bokenham excised all references to his original addressees and to the circumstances of their commission (for example, the colorful account of Isabel Bourchier's Twelfth Night party is completely gone). The other seven verse lives—Barbara, Vincent, Apollonia, Mary of Egypt, Ambrose, Audrey, and Winifred—were probably also originally freestanding compositions, but if they were directed to particular readers, Bokenham erased the evidence. That Bokenham was working on the collection after 1449 is clear from his reference to Lydgate's death. Individual lives might have been composed earlier, but the lives of female saints not found in Arundel 327 were almost certainly written after 1445, for Bokenham does not mention them in the conversation he reports with Isabel Bourchier as being among the lives of holy women that he has written so far. "Winifred" was written after 1448 because Bokenham mentions a visit to her shrine in that year ("Winifred," Abbotsford 217r).

The contents of the Abbotsford legendary attest to Bokenham's continued interest in "hooly wummen." Virgins, especially virgin martyrs, figure prominently among its female saints. Four of the five women celebrated in the additional verse legends are virgins, and three of these were virgin martyrs if we count Winifred, who was resurrected after her beheading. In addition, Bokenham provides the first Middle English translations of the lives of the virgin martyrs Martina and Priscilla, whose lives were not told in Jacobus's *Legenda aurea*. But the Abbotsford collection also attests to Bokenham's interest in female saints who were not legendary virgins. The lives he adds to the *Legenda aurea* include the first Middle English life of Augustine's mother, Monica, and an extended life of Clare of Assisi, the only Middle English life of Clare and one of the few lives of "modern" female saints that were written in England.

Not only are the women whose lives are told in the Abbotsford legendary a diverse lot, but Bokenham shows a greater tendency towards experimentation in narrating their lives. He draws from a more diverse body of sources—not just Jacobus's *Legenda aurea* and classic monastic *passiones*, but "modern" Continental renderings—and he also shows a greater inclination to alter and amplify his sources. As he did in "Anne," he uses saints' lives to convey emotions and moral dilemmas and to explore tensions and conflicts within families, even Christian families. As he does with his Arundel saints, he endows his heroines with qualities that would be deemed praiseworthy in contemporary laywomen, but he also shows them engaging in controversial behaviors, including studying scripture and even preaching. Indeed, a strain of radicalism permeates the Abbotsford collection that is wholly absent from Arundel 327.[22]

Matrons: Monica and Paula

Bokenham's late antique matrons, Monica and Paula, are prime examples of women who reconcile family responsibility with their pursuit of holiness. Both women are deeply attached to their husbands and children, and they only indulge their extreme ascetic inclinations after their husbands are dead and their children grown. Though rigorously ascetic as a widow, Paula enjoys the comforts of her class during her marriage: "delicacy and affluence," "longe laughyng," "softe shetis," and "plesaunt silken clothis" ("Paula," 98r).[23] "Busy with al [her] wittes to plese" her husband, she is so upset at his passing that "she lamentid and byweiled liche as she shulde han diyed hir self." As he did in "Elizabeth," Bokenham omits comments found in the *Legenda aurea*, his immediate source, which might suggest that marriage was a burden to Paula. He doesn't speculate that Paula was so ardent in God's service, according to Jacobus, "that she might seem to have desired her spouse's death," nor does he suggest that his readers "understand" from the fact that she bore no more children after the birth of her son Toxocius "that she did not wish to engage in conjugal union any longer" (Jacobus, *Golden Legend*, 1:122). Following Augustine's reminiscences in the *Confessions*, Bokenham presents Monica as an ideal wife and mother, who "governed hir hous to goddys worship." "Paciently marveilous and marveilously amyable," she "servid with al humbilnesse" an irascible spouse, bringing out his best qualities and converting both him and their son to Christianity by her "maners and condicions" ("Monica," 101v).

In addition to describing their harmonious marriages, Bokenham attests to the saints' good relationships with other women. He praises Monica for having "the grete singuler yifte . . . to setten rest and pees bitwix womman and womman" by not spreading gossip:

> So pesibly she had hir and so prudently bitwix hem that what so evir either partie seid to hir of othir in hir absence were it nevir so cruelly uttird and seid as commonily rancour and discorde usith she nevir wolde tellen the absent partie more therof than ony thyng myght availen to her reconciliacion and to setten pees and rest bitwix hem. ("Monica," 101v)

Through her example and her sage advice, Monica helps her fellow wives achieve better relationships with their husbands. Bokenham similarly describes Paula as "an example to al the matrones of the cite" of Rome "in al hir porte and governaunce." When she becomes head of a community of virgins, she is a natural peacemaker: "yf ony strife grew amonge hem with a light word she coude maken hem at oon" ("Paula," 50v).

Monica and Paula model religious practices that were popular among Bokenham's contemporaries, including devotion to the Eucharist, pilgrimage, and contemplation. Paula practices the meditative strategy that Nicholas Love described in his widely circulated *Mirror of the Blessed Life of Jesus Christ*, when he instructed the reader to "ymagine" and "þenk in þi herte as þou were present" scenes from the life of Christ.[24] Paula, Bokenham relates,

> sawe with the inward eyen of hir soule clerely the byrth of criste and hym lyeng swathed in the assis cribbe his bissid modir and maiden Marie and Joseph hir keper the sheperdis commyng by nyght to see the eternall worde of the hevenly fadir made man temporal of his erthely modir. She seid also that she sawe the bright new sterre stondyng ovir the shedde by conduct wherof the thre kyngis commen with mysty yiftes to worshippen cristis new birthe. She sawe ferthermore the Holy Innocentis slayne thurgh Herodis cruelnesse for Cristis sake and Marie and Joseph fleyng with childe Jhesu into Egypt. ("Paula," 50r)

Paula also exhibits the more extreme manifestations of affective piety. When, on pilgrimage to the Holy Land, she visits Calvary and the Holy Sepulcher, her devotions result in uncontrollable tears:

> And whan she came before the holy crosse she fel downe prostrate and worshippid it as fervently and as devoutely as though she had seyn criste hangyng theron bodily ffro thens forth whan she entrid the sepulcre and sawe the stoon which the aungel remevid from the grave dore and the place where cristis body was biried in she kissed hem with grete fervour of devocion. And how moche habundaunce of teeris of sobbyng sighyng and sorowes she pored oute there al the citee of Jerusalem berith wittenesse in erthe and god for whos loue she did it testifieth it. (50r)

Paula's experiences are reminiscent of those described by Margery Kempe, Bokenham's East Anglian contemporary, who also recalls that she "myght not stondyn ne knelyn" at Calvary and that she burst into uncontrollable fits of loud crying "as thow sche had seyn owyr Lord wyth hir bodyly ey sufferyng hys Passyon."[25]

Monica, too, is visited by "teerys brongyn oute thurgh the presse of the crosse" ("Monica," 101v). Her tears, like Kempe's, are uncontrollable; the more she tries to stop them, the harder they flow. Bokenham writes, "So parfitely the loue of god had woundid hir hert" that "she bare contynuelly the passion of criste in hir mynde." Monica's meditations result in the kind of ecstasies that were often described in Continental mystical tracts and saints' lives of the late Middle Ages. Her soul was "ravasshhid with so grete a drunkeship of the holy goste" that she lost all feelings in her body, much to the consternation of her friends and neighbors: "Unnethe the matrones and hir next neighbours pluckyng and prickyng hir myght exciten hir and awaken hir from that pricke of devocion" ("Paula,"101v–102r). In the presence of the Eucharist, she was "so rapt with the spirite of compunccion and devocion that she was seen lyfted up a cubite from the erthe" (102r).

Along with this profoundly affective spirituality is an equally profound intellectualism. Paula is well versed in Hebrew; indeed, Bokenham quotes the Church Father Jerome wondering at how easily she mastered a tongue that had always frustrated him. An avid reader of scripture, she cherishes not only the Bible's literal sense but its loftier and more abstruse spiritual sense: "Though she loued wele the story aftir the lettir as the grounde and the fundament of truthe yit she folowed alwey more the gostely undirstondyng as for most singuler edificacion of the soule" ("Paula," 50v). Jerome encourages her studies, telling her that she should "sparen hir eyen from wepyng and kepen hem to redyn with holy scripture"—advice, by the way, that she politely declines to take, thus asserting her independence from her spiritual advisor. Though Monica lacks the erudition of Paula, her "natural witte enflamed with natural wisdam" so impresses Augustine that he consults her on matters of theology: "I provided and ordeyned that whan leyser and oportuniyte haboundid that ony thyng of divinite shuld be communed and disputid that she shuld nat ben absent so grete excellence of witte and reson I fonde in hir communing" ("Monica," 102r).

Daughters: Audrey, Winifred, Barbara

As he did in the virgin martyr legends found in the Arundel collection, Bokenham endows the virginal heroines of his Abbotsford lives with qualities that would make them suitable models for laywomen. Of Audrey (also known as Etheldreda), he writes:

> In hir demeanyng she was amyable
> In contenaunce and port sad and demure
> In communycacion benygne and affable
> In hir aray honest and in hir vesture
> Noyeng ner hurtyng noon erthely creature
> But glad she was evir to helpen eche wight
> As far as hir kunnyng strecchid and hir myght.
> ("Audrey," 117v)

Though exceptional in being "twyes wife and evir maide" (117v), Audrey is in other respects an exemplary wife, who manages to retain her husband's "hole affeccion" along with her chastity: "as gode loue was bitwix hem thoo / In speche and in talkyng and eche othir wise / As it is ony man possible to devise" (118r). Bokenham's Winifred similarly possesses the qualities befitting a good wife: "wummanly honeste," "eloquence in speche and affabylnesse" ("Winifred," 215r).

In both "Winifred" and "Audrey," Bokenham cultivates his interest in family dynamics, exploring the ways in which the saints' spiritual longings conflict with the legitimate expectations of their parents (and, in Audrey's case, her spouse). Audrey is the daughter of a "noble" East Anglian king, famous not only for his "temporal and worldely habundaunce" but also for his "cristen and religions governaunce," and "joyned togider" with his "worthy" queen, "in parfite charite / As the lawe of mariage wolde it shuld bene" ("Audrey," 117r).[26] Though marriage is "ageyns hir plesaunce," Audrey "assentid therto / For hir fadir and hir modir wolde han it so" (117v). When her husband dies (before consummating their marriage), she hopes to dedicate herself to God, but, Bokenham explains, she doesn't confide her desire to anyone, not even her mother. When the unwanted suitors present themselves ("Desired she was in mariage of many oon / But in truthe she hir self desired noon"), Audrey's parents see no reason not to give their blessing to King Egfrid of Northumbria, "a right manly man":

> Thei bothe gladly assentid therto
> Thynkyng wisely that it was to doo
> With so worthy a kyng to han alyaunce
> And that hir kynrede it moch myght avaunce.
> (117v)

Audrey, who had hoped and expected to "reioyssen hir libertee" as a widow, is "astoyned" (117v). "In hir privey thought she gan to silogise": refusing to marry without disclosing "privey counseil" and "inward entent" would offend her parents; assenting, however, would jeopardize her virginity (118r). Confiding in them was out of the question. After much thought, she "comitted al thyng to goddis wille / And hir frendis counseil she assentid tille" (118r).

With his characteristic coyness, Bokenham does not say how Audrey avoided consummating her second marriage: "But what maner meanys she usid certeyn / To preserve with maidenly integrite / Withoute the kyngis maugre I ne can seyn" ("Audrey," 118r). He intimates, however, that her exemplary behavior has much to do with it. In an extraordinary passage, he describes Audrey through her husband's eyes:

> For wele he perceived and did aspye
> That she womman was of gode livyng
> And he eche day sawe with his eye
> By vigiles preyers and by fastyng
> And of almesse by hir large yivyng
> And with hem familiarly for to talke
> Pittous she was and ful of mercifulnesse
> To them geyns hir which did trespace
> Was noon so redy to aske foryivenesse
> As she was redy to offren hem grace
> In etyng and drynkyng was hir solace
> Yf she ony fey which she thought had nede
> More busily them than hir self to fede.
>
> (118r)

For these "causis" and "many othir moo," Egfrid would "for no thyng . . . represe" his wife or "doon ner seyn" anything that "hir myght greve" (118r).

With the same sympathy and sensitivity as he portrayed Audrey, he portrays Egfrid as desiring nothing of his wife except "safe oonly / Aftir mariages licence knoulech flesshly" ("Audrey," 118r). Whatever his "entitlements," he is a decent man and not about to force himself on her "withouten hir propre assent":

> Hir he therto wolde nevir constreyn
> Al be it he nevir so sore brent
> And in his sensal felyng suffrid grete peyn
> Yet lever he had his passions to refreyn
> Than ought of hir his flessh with to pese
> Desire or aske that hir shuld displese.
>
> (118r)

The most he will do when "titillacion / Of flesshly lust hym ought did greve" is to entreat Audrey's confessor to remonstrate with her (118r). After twelve years of chastity, he realizes that "he ne myght hir doon more solas" than to allow her to enter a convent (118v). Though Audrey "wins," Bokenham inspires tremendous sympathy for the good man who could only please her by wholly subordinating his desires to hers.

Though Winifred manages to avoid marriage, Bokenham explores the *potential* for the kind of conflict that played out in "Audrey." Winifred's parents have much in common with Audrey's. Her father, Tenythe, is of royal blood, "a man of gret rychesse and of gret myht" ("Winifred," 214v), who not only has "habundaunce of temperal possessyoun / But also dayly in hys thouth inward / He hym commyttyd to goddys proteccyoun" (214v). Tenythe's spiritual advisor is a monk, Beuno, whose "lyvyng was so hooly and good / And so edificatyf his communycacyoun" that Tenythe puts him in charge of the education of his only child, Winifred, "Wich al his ioye was and al his delyth" (214v).

Beuno's instruction, however, threatens to disrupt the harmony of this Christian family. Because Winifred is Tenythe's only child, "thelyneal descens of hys kynrede" ("Winifred," 214v) depends on her marriage. He and his wife fully expect that Beuno's instruction will prepare her to be a good Christian wife. They thus encourage her "famylyaryte" with him, urging her to attend his sermons, "Hyre chargyng ententysly for to lere / What he seyde and yt awey to bere," with the "entent"

> That she shuld kun lyuyn verteuously
> Whan she to maryage aftyr were sent
> And advouterye fleen and al lecherye
> As goddys lawe byddyth certeynly
> And in trewe weedlok hyre so to reule and gye
> That . . . in honeste she myht multyplye.
> (215r)

Beuno's instruction in fact instills desires that are "contrarye to that hyre fadyr ment": "he hyre purposyd to ben a wyf / And god hyre disposyd to a contynent lyf" (215r). Having promised her virginity to God, Winifred, Bokenham tells us, would rather die than yield it to any living creature.

We never find out how this potential family conflict would have played out. As the story develops, Winifred's religious vow is challenged not by her parents but by the lecherous Prince Caradoc, who proposes to make her his mistress. When she tries to flee, he strikes off her head. Following her "cruel hefdyng" at the hands of the spurned prince, Beuno obtains her resurrection on the condition that she will enter God's service, and her parents fully endorse her religious vocation.

The human drama of this episode clearly appealed to Bokenham.[27] He expresses young Winifred's "prevy drede," home alone and facing a man who threatens to rape her if she doesn't submit to his embraces: "Sche vex in hyre herte inwardly" ("Winifred," 215r). At the same time, he captures her resourcefulness as she "owtwardly / Dissymulyd," and, "Feynyng glad chere," flatters her "suitor":

> Syre for sothe y am ryht sory
> That thus unwarly ye come up on me
> Ffor of youre comyng yf y had wytst treuly
> Myche bettyr arayid y shuld haue be
> And more plesauntly to youre dygnyte
> Ffor on to plesaunce of a kyngys sonys lust
> On the fresshest wyse a wumman aray hyre must
> Therfore syre syth of youre ientylnesse
> Ye lyst youre affeccyoun to settyn on me
> Ffor the embesshyng of my sympylnesse
> Wiche as ye seen stonde dyschevele
> That y more plesauntly arayid may be
> Suffryth me a while to myn chaumbyr goon
> And fresshlyere arayid y shal returne anoon.
>   (215r)

Articulating at such length Winifred's answer to Caradoc underscores her underhandedness. The rogue, "wenyng that she / Wold haue doon lych as she promysyd," allows her to retreat to her bedroom. He is less enraged by her escape than by her deceit: "Bethyngkyng how she hym deceyuyd had / For very malyncolye he wex ner maad" (215r). Whereas in the Latin *passio* Caradoc gives her an ultimatum to submit or die, Bokenham's villain, no longer caring for the prize of her body, avenges his humiliation:

> Why woldyst thou thus han maad my berd
> Thou shalt dye therfore, and owt hys swerd
> Anoon he drow and with owte more lette
> Hyre heed of at a oo strook he smette.
>   ("Winifred," 215r)

Caradoc's ultimatum in the *passio* provides an occasion for Winifred to reject his love and profess her commitment to Christ before she dies in the conventional manner of a virgin martyr. In keeping with his interest in his characters' inner life and his tendency to de-emphasize confrontation, Bokenham has Winifred express her sentiments to herself, as she stands alone in her bedroom, in "perplexyte" about "what she myht doon" (215r). Keeping her promise was out of the question—"What so euere wyth hyr god wold do":

> Ffor weel she wyst yf she ageyn went
> To hym the flour ofhyre virgynyte
> Sche shuld haue lost geyns hyre entent
> And levere she had onborn to haue be
> For that to god beheest had she
> To noon erdly creature wiche dede lyue
> To be deed therfore she nevere wolde yive.
> (215r)

This realization prompts her to seek safety through flight. Bokenham conveys the implicit message of the Winifred legend, namely, that deceit is justifiable in a good cause, even as he shows that it may have the effect of escalating violence.

In "Barbara," Bokenham conjoins the themes of parent–child relationships and justifiable deception that he examines separately in "Winifred." Barbara, whom Bokenham once described as one of his "valentyns," is by far his most complex character.[28] Here Bokenham demonstrates his willingness to abandon hagiographical "classics" that had long been his staple and adapt more unusual, Continental sources. His source for Barbara is an extended life by Augustinian John of Wackerzele, composed in the Low Countries at the end of the fourteenth century, steeped in the tradition of *devotio moderna*.[29] We meet Barbara as a young girl yearning to understand God, whom she reasons must be a single entity and cannot possibly abide in the statues of sundry scurrilous "deities" that she has been taught to revere. She worries about what she'll do if she's called upon to kneel before the "stokkis and stoones" that are being worshipped in the temple ("Barbara," 6r). She doesn't want to have any part of what "in hir hert she dempt . . .

supersticion," but she also doesn't want to cause trouble. What will she say if people ask her why she isn't kneeling? She doesn't know enough about the true God to state her beliefs. Her solution: to feign compliance with prevailing religious customs until she acquires an informed faith. She comforts herself with the thought that

> ... though I knele doun
> With my knees bodily, my spirit affeccioun
> To that lorde which moste is of myght
> Without any variance shal stonde upright
> And nevir doun enclyne ydoles to honoure.
>   (6r)

As it turns out, by pursuing a strategy of subterfuge, Barbara both acquires the knowledge she yearns for and defers the inevitable conflict with her virulently anti-Christian father, Dioscorus. When she learns of a teacher in Alexandria, Origen, who might be able to teach her the truth about the one true God, she sends him a letter "ful pryvely / By oon whom she trustid right singulerly" ("Barbara," 7r). Anxious for her messenger, she prays, but she does not trust the success of her endeavor wholly to God. She deceives her father "by pretence of sikenesse" (7r), not exactly a lie, for in her anxiety and eagerness, Barbara does make herself sick; her malady was just not *bodily* "sikenesse" (8r). Bokenham explains: "Enflaumed inward with the gostely fire / Of the loue of goddis knowlecchyng / In hir hert she was languryng" (8r). The priest sent by Origen then exploits Barbara's "pretence" with his own equivocation, which allows him to "atteyn" her presence "withoute hir fadris offense." He identifies himself as an expert from Alexandria who "coude heel / Eche sikenesse that ony body coude feel" (8r). Though the sight of the priest immediately cures Barbara's complaint, news of her father's approach immediately sends her scurrying back to bed: "But anon enfourmed that hir fadir cam nere / To hir bedde ageyn she start without taryenge / Hir fadir to illuden so desiryng (8r). The old man who is attending her, she tells her father, is a physician ("leche") whose ministrations, including a bath (baptism), will have her well again within a matter of days. Barbara does not exactly lie:

> ... this man certeyn
> Is of Alisaundre a leche ful crafty
> Which seith that he wol right hastily
> Make me ful hole of al my sikenesse
> For he affermyth in verey sikeronesse
> That at Alysaundir a maister hath he
> The which of kunnyng hath such sotilte
> That ageynis the common use of looris awe
> Not oonly bodies but he soulis doth cure.
>
> (8r)

The priest *is* a healer, and the "bath" he recommends does indeed bring Barbara "releef and cure of hir langoure" and make her "heil and sounde in eche degre," just as she assures her father it will.

When Dioscorus later raises the subject of marriage, Barbara again resorts to equivocation. Her father is in no hurry to lose Barbara to a husband, but when suitors call, he consults her wishes in the matter. Barbara, for reasons she does not share with her father, does not desire her marriage any more than he does. Her response is calculated to please:

> In this mater myn hert is accordaunt
> To your and in no wise variant
> Ffor neither youthe beaute ner hye noblesse
> Myght ner strength ner grete richesse
> Shal me nevir mevyn to ben a wife
> As long as endurith my present life.
>
> ("Barbara," 9r)

Dioscorus is naturally delighted "that she so applied was to his entent." Bokenham immediately points to his misunderstanding: "he no thyng wist what she ment."

Barbara's stratagems work precisely because her father loves her so dearly and never imagines that she will betray his trust. Distraught at his daughter's illness, he is all too willing to encourage anyone who might heal her. She later manages to receive the sacrament of baptism by telling her father that her "doctor" advises that a "bath" will restore her health ("Barbara," 8r). His joy at her recovery is genuinely moving:

> Which tidyng to hym was the moste solas
> That he myght han for in erthe here
> Was no thyng to hym so leef and dere
> As was his doughtir and hir prosperite.
>
> (8v)

He expresses his concern for "his doughtir dere" in the specifications of the tower he has constructed for her to live in. The tower, he orders, should have only two windows, one on the north side and the other on the south. A window facing east might disturb her sleep by waking her too early; a window facing west might also hinder her rest if "the sunne bememys bright" should cause her room to become too hot or too light (9r).

Yet even as Bokenham reveals the intensity of Dioscorus's love, he shows that it is based on an unhealthy obsession. When he rebuffs her suitors, he does so because he cannot bear the thought of parting with one whom he thinks of in terms more befitting a lover than a daughter: "His oonly hope, the ioye of his household, / The fulcyuient and the strength of his life oonly, / And the light of his eyen which he saugh by" ("Barbara," 8v). He later consults her desires to "assay" her (8v). What, one wonders, would he have done had Barbara told him to by all means negotiate a suitable alliance? What ultimately throws Dioscorus into a frenzy is not simply the fact of Barbara's Christianity but that she claimed Christ as "hir husbonde" (10r).

The tower Dioscorus constructs is a concrete realization of his sick love, "a token of covenant" between them when she "promised hym had of hertely entent / That she nevir in hir life wolde to mariage assent" ("Barbara," 9r). Though he claims to consider only Barbara's comfort when he designs the tower, Bokenham says that he in fact constructed the tower "as he loued *his* and his doughtris welefare" (9r; my emphasis). Dioscorus's fury at the addition of a third window exposes his self-interest. Barbara had persuaded the builders to add the window by using indisputable logic. Knowing "that for my loue my fadir this toure doth edifye, / For my plesaunce than and at my request" (9r), the builders should be confident undertaking a modification that she herself proposed. That he objects so strenuously only shows that the tower was ultimately more for his welfare than for hers.

Bokenham does not resort to stereotypes in depicting Dioscorus as a parental pervert; his villain is a tortured soul whose excessive "love," once frustrated, drives him to monstrous acts of violence. Bokenham conveys Dioscorus's mental instability as he wavers between love and hate. Though angered at the intrusion of a third window into his original design for the tower, he is soothed at the sight of his daughter:

> Anon Barbara came forth to his presence
> And welcomed hym home with grete reverence
> And he hir anoon gan halse and kisse
> Thynkyng noo ioye that he myght misse
> Sith he this wise hir had founde
> In his returnyng both heil and sounde.
> ("Barbara," 9v)

Her explanation—that she ordered the third window in honor of the Trinity—sends him into a murderous frenzy. She flees; he pursues her. But when she gives herself up, he "he gan to han compassion" on her—to a point. After sheathing his falchion, he "pullid hir in boistously by the here" and "shett" her "in a derk hous"; "Evir hym bithynkyng how he myght be wreke / His angir on hir whom he had lovyd so wele" (10r). He retaliates against her by denouncing her to the authorities, urging them to use violence to expunge her "fonned bileve," and offering his services as an executioner (10 r-v). Her subsequent tortures are his design: "At hyr fadris suggestion and connseil," she was "made nakid" and "beetyn" "with yerdis" (11v.)

Though I have emphasized Barbara's repeated deception of her father, she does not show the contemptuous antagonism characteristic of virgin martyr legends. She deceives him in part because she fears him, in part because she doesn't wish to defy him. Indeed, she tries to convert him, using the tower to explain the mystery of the Trinity. Bokenham's Barbara, much like his Winifred and his Audrey (and, as we have seen, much like Lydgate's protagonists), prefers conciliation to confrontation.

Preachers: Martha and Apollonia

In the majority of his female saints' lives, Bokenham goes out of his way to reconcile his heroines' pursuit of holiness with contemporary norms of femininity. He extols dutiful wives and daughters, showing that spiritual ambitions do not trump familial responsibilities. As we have seen, even his virgin martyr Barbara tries to be a good daughter, insofar as she can do so without offending God. Yet Bokenham also endorses a broader range of actions for women than one would find in the typical conduct manual. Some of his women, as we have seen in the case of Paula and Barbara, are not merely well-read but scholars. Martha and Apollonia are formidable preachers.

Though Bokenham's usual practice was to tone down the social radicalism of many of Jacobus de Voragine's lives of holy women, in his life of Martha he if anything embellishes Jacobus's emphasis on Martha as a preacher, producing a legend that portrays Martha's preaching as fully compatible with her socially normative role as Jesus's hostess.

As we might expect in a life of Martha, Bokenham, following Jacobus, takes care to present his heroine as being on a par with her more famous sister, Mary Magdalene. He praises Martha as "cristis ostesse," and, departing from the scriptural source of the story, allows Martha's opinion of Mary's behavior during Christ's visits to stand unchallenged:

> This Martha had never noon as ferforth as we kan redyn but beynge stylle a maydyn was oftyn cristis ostesse and herbeiour and diligently and deuouhtly mynistrid on to hym and servyd hym and wolde that hyre sustir Marie shulde have doon the same. For as hyre servyd to semyn so wurthy a gest al the word suffesyd not. ("Martha," 146r)[30]

Going beyond Jacobus, Bokenham emphasizes the contrast between Martha and Mary as exemplars, respectively, of the active and contemplative lives. Following the Resurrection, Martha, Mary, Lazarus, Maximian, and others, having been cast adrift in a rudderless boat, arrive at Marseilles. Bokenham *implies* that as soon as the party landed, Mary retreated to the wilderness, contrasting her retreat with Martha's active engagement with the populace:

> Aftyr that hyre sustyr Marye was goon to wyldyrnesse, she abood stylle and convertyd to the feyth myche peple by hyre doctrine and techynge, for she was ful facunde and ful eloquent in spekyng and

prechynge and ful exempler in al hyre conversacion and lyuyng and ful myghty in wundris and miraclis werkyng. (146r)

In Jacobus's account, by contrast, Martha's efforts were subsumed within the missionary activities of the entire company of Christians (including Mary): "They went to the region around Aix and converted the local populace to the faith." Her efforts, moreover, were not specifically characterized as preaching: "Martha spoke eloquently and was gracious to all" (*Golden Legend*, 2:23).

Martha's career merges activities found in the lives of male saints with traditionally female qualities and pursuits. A sort of female Saint George, but now armed with prayers rather than a sword, she rescues a region from a man-eating dragon. She founds a community of religious women, where she practices the customary asceticism while remaining active as a preacher. Bokenham emphasizes that her doings are authorized by the Church hierarchy of her day, namely, "by licence of hyre maistir Maximilian" ("Martha," 146r). Following her death, her disciple Marcella follows in her footsteps: she "went in to a cuntre or a cyte clepyd Salanoma and prechyd there cristys gospell and ten yer afftyr hyre maistiresse she deyid" (146v). Marcella traverses traditional gender boundaries not only by preaching but by authorship: she "wroot the lyf of hyre maisteresse" (146v).[31]

Bokenham's "Apollonia" offers a more radical portrait of a female preacher in a life that further belies the impression obtained of him from many of his lives—including all those in the Arundel manuscript—as a social conservative. Showing no interest in exemplary feminine conduct, as it was traditionally construed, Bokenham jettisons Jacobus's conservative life, replacing it with a ripping tale of rebellion and filial defiance. Jacobus, following an account in Eusebius's *Ecclesiastical History*, represented Apollonia as an elderly deaconess whose teeth were bashed in by anti-Christian rioters and who willingly sacrificed herself for Christ by leaping onto a pyre her tormenters were preparing for her.[32] Following a Continental tradition abundantly represented in the miniatures found in Books of Hours, Bokenham represents Apollonia as a beautiful princess whose conversion to Christianity infuriates her pagan father and leads to her martyrdom.[33] What distinguishes Bokenham's narrative from any other version of the Apollonia legend that I know of is his emphasis on preaching, the activity that defines

Apollonia's character and brings her into conflict with her father, Corsus, king of Alexandria.

Educated by a local hermit, Bokenham's Apollonia is determined to share her faith with others:

> Criste god allone to ben prechid she
> Even openly and in wordis pleyn
> And al othir goddis to be voide and veyn
> And moche people with hir doctryne
> From ydols worship she did inclyne.
> ("Apollonia," 64r)

When Corsus finds her preaching to his citizens, he summons forty scholars to convince her of her error. She converts them all. Corsus has her teeth broken and yanked out by the roots "principally for . . . that entent" that she should not be "so eloquent . . . in prechyng . . . as she was whan she first bigan" (64v). But she continues to preach. He starves her for forty days, then drags her to the temple, but instead of kneeling to the gods, she preaches against idolatry. When he casts her from a tower, she picks herself up and resumes her preaching. "Moche peple thurgh help of grace divine / She convertid there by hir doctrine" (64r), we are told.

Though Bokenham's Apollonia traverses gender boundaries through her preaching, Bokenham mitigates the radicalism of her actions in two ways. First, he takes care to emphasize that the knowledge she conveys is imparted by a bona fide representative of Holy Church, namely, the hermit to whom she was sent by "speciall grace." Second, he portrays Corsus's concern with family and appearance as obsessive and destructive.

Corsus, indeed, possesses the status-consciousness of Joachim taken to its logical extreme, a man less concerned with religion than with how his daughter's ostentatious Christianity might interfere with his plans and damage his reputation. When he first hears that she "prechid criste openly," he immediately regrets that his daughter "wil al hir kynrede shame and reproue" ("Apollonia," 64r). He beseeches her to "restreyn" her "tung" from "such langage" because her actions will "blemshyn and hurten al thi kinrede" (64r). When she says that she has vowed her virginity to Christ, he remonstrates: "For I wil thou know that I the / Promysed haue in mariage / To oon born of ful high lynage" (64v). His plans dashed, he resorts to violence; his zeal to uphold the honor of his family leads him to abandon not only truth and integrity but "fadirly pitee" (64v). Bokenham thus invites readers to see the obsessive father, not his Christian daughter, as the greatest threat to family values.

Bokenham's Holy Women Revisited

In the twenty years or so after undertaking "Margaret" for Thomas Burgh, Bokenham grew to be one of England's most prolific and versatile hagiographers. His lives of female saints demonstrate his willingness to draw on different types of hagiographical sources, to adapt those sources to his own ends, and to explore different models of sainthood. He consistently portrayed his heroines as women whose desires and experiences a fifteenth-century audience could understand, and even identify with, but he also challenged his readers to imagine "ordinary" women passionately and successfully serving the Church in extraordinary ways—as scholars, teachers, and preachers. His gallery of women illustrates the fifteenth century's interest in female sanctity, which we will continue to trace throughout this book.

Bokenham's hagiography has significant affinities with Lydgate's, which doubtless inspired him. Lydgate's hagiography is more rhetorically and formally adventurous than Bokenham's; however, Bokenham, as I will discuss in subsequent chapters, produced in "Barbara" a hagiographical "epic" along with a legendary whose commingling of verse and prose narrative was unprecedented in Middle English hagiography. Both men focused more on the emotional and spiritual lives of the saints than on their extraordinary achievements, whether surviving extreme torment or performing miracles. Both celebrated saints as scholars and teachers; moreover, both construed the saints as exemplary figures whose experiences could speak to the lives of lay readers. Lydgate placed a premium on diplomacy and tact in the lives of both his male and female saints. Indeed, he emphasized most of the same virtues in his lives of holy men as he did in his lives of holy women, including modesty, humility, discretion, and kindness. In Bokenham, too, we see a convergence not only of the qualities of holy men and women but of their roles. Bokenham presents his women as scholars, teachers, and preachers—roles Lydgate reserved for men. In that respect, Bokenham's lives exhibit a radicalism that Lydgate's mostly lack. Both hagiographers were deeply invested in Christian communities, nurtured by holy scholars and teachers. But Bokenham was far more interested in families than Lydgate, whose protagonists are specifically virgins, professional celibates, or singles. Lydgate's Alban and George are laymen but not family men; many, if not most, readers probably presumed their virginity. Only Petronilla is shown interacting with a parent, Saint Peter, but her relationship with him is untroubled by any of the friction found in Bokenham's legends. Bokenham, as we have seen, shows family relations in their complexity and diversity as his heroines juggle their responsibilities to husbands, parents, children, and God. His characters undergo more inner conflict than Lydgate's, perhaps because Bokenham himself experienced more. His oeuvre, as I have argued in this chapter and will elaborate in the next, shows a shift towards a more radical vision of sainthood as more women in his later hagiography take on traditionally male roles. Bokenham's radicalism is also evinced in his promotion of Christian intellectualism through theologically sophisticated "teaching hagiography." Chapter 3 explores his and other teaching hagiographies as constituting an important new current in fifteenth-century hagiography.

CHAPTER THREE

Holy Educators and "Teaching Hagiographies"

Sometime during the 1420s, Symon Wynter, a Bridgettine brother at Syon Abbey, delivered to his spiritual daughter, Margaret, Duchess of Clarence, a *Life of Saint Jerome* that he had been promising for some time.[1] In his prologue, he likened the life to a "scoole" wherein "scolers" may learn how to live and die.[2] They could learn penance by studying the example of a master penitent and "hear" one of Christianity's most illustrious Church Fathers dilate on purgatory and eschatology. The "holsom lesson" conveyed in Jerome's life was "needful" to "man or womman," and Wynter urged Margaret to "latte other rede hit and copye hit, whoso wyl" (Wynter, *Jerome*, 180). In thus disseminating Jerome's life, Margaret, along with Jerome and Wynter, would participate in the crucial process of Christian education.

Education is a ubiquitous theme in fifteenth-century hagiography. We have seen its centrality in the lives by both Bokenham and Lydgate. Here I will look more broadly at the proliferation of lives of holy educators and also discuss the emergence of what I will call "teaching hagiographies," lives so saturated with expositions on doctrine and morality that they are as much vehicles of religious instruction as biographies of the saints. After surveying fifteenth-century lives of Christian teachers and scholars, I will focus on the treatment in fifteenth-century hagiography of what many medieval theologians considered the loftiest mystery of the Christian faith: the Trinity. I will show that the same, thoroughly orthodox Trinitarian doctrine recurs in lives of this period, but hagiographers differ in how they present that doctrine, in how much of it they present, and in how accessible to human understanding they consider the Trinity to be. Their diverse treatments confirm that a culture of inquiry and exploration was finding expression in the vernacular only a generation after the promulgation of Arundel's "Constitutions." Indeed, I strongly suspect that the burning of heretics in the present kindled a heightened appreciation for holy teachers of the past and that the specter of censorship inspired the production of theologically adventurous hagiography. By using their saints' lives both to celebrate educators and to educate, hagiographers were asserting an informed, intellectualized faith as orthodoxy's best weapon in the war against error.

Holy Educators

The interest in holy educators is variously manifested in Middle English hagiography: in the composition of new lives of missionaries, apostles, and Church Fathers; in the representation of saints as educators who had not hitherto been thus represented; and in the greater attention to saints' educational backgrounds and intellectual pursuits. It is further evinced in the strong presence of teachers and scholars within fifteenth-century legendaries as well as in the production of the first anthology dedicated to holy educators. It is also seen in the only surviving Middle English saint's play, the so-called *Digby Mary Magdalene* composed at the turn of the century.

Wynter's *Life of Saint Jerome*, the first freestanding life of the Church Father in Middle English, was one of several such freestanding lives of Christian scholars and educators written during the fifteenth century. The Augustinian friar John Capgrave produced the first freestanding life of Augustine circa 1451 for a local noblewoman eager for a life of the "grete doctoure of þe church."[3] Osbern Bokenham's verse "Ambrose," though it survives only as part of his Abbotsford legendary, was probably originally also a freestanding narrative—and the first in Middle English. At the same time, the first freestanding life of John the Evangelist was published, along with a life of John the Evangelist conjoined with a life of John the Baptist, Christianity's first preacher.[4]

The appearance of these lives is consistent with Eamon Duffy's observation that Church Fathers and apostles were, along with the perennially popular virgin martyrs, the most frequently represented subjects on fifteenth-century rood screens.[5] Freestanding lives of British teachers were also being produced, as we saw with Lydgate's life of Austin of Canterbury and of Alban and Amphibalus. As chapter 4 will show, lives of late medieval women engaged in public speaking and teaching, such as Catherine of Siena and Bridget of Sweden, were also being translated into English for the first time.

Certain saints not traditionally represented as teachers, scholars, or even readers became such in the hands of fifteenth-century hagiographers. We have already seen how Lydgate transformed the ultimatum-issuing George, who will slay the dragon if those it's been terrorizing will accept baptism, into a knight who converts the people he has rescued by the force of his teaching; and how Bokenham renders as an eloquent young preacher pious old Apollonia, who in earlier versions of her legend says nothing as she flings herself into the flames. Capgrave devotes most of his short account of Saint Cecilia to establishing that she was a devout reader of scripture, who carried the Gospels around with her so that she could peruse them when she could. Capgrave reports that Cecilia converted her husband, her brother-in-law, and many others; however, he says nothing of how she avoided consummating her marriage, the key episode in most renderings of her life.[6] Later in this chapter, we will see how both Bokenham and an anonymous contemporary embellish the legend of Barbara to include an extensive account of her clandestine education.

Lives of renowned scholars and teachers were also being rewritten to place even greater emphasis on scholarship and education. This practice is well illustrated in the prose life of John the Evangelist, which takes pains to establish the evangelist, the son of a poor fisherman with no "connynge of clerge," as a sage whose accomplishments surpass those of any Church Father (see Waters, *Virgins and Scholars*, 128).[7] The hagiographer shows John refuting heretics and instructing the faithful so effectively that his enemies sought to kill him (144, 148, 154, 156). He avers that John was the only evangelist to address "the Godhed of oure Lorde" in a Gospel that is "most excellent aboue alle scriptures and wrytynges that euere [were] write from the begynnynge of the worlde, or euer shall"; his writing was "a ryuer. . . . to slekken te thirst of alle that desire to knowe the right faith of the euerlastynge Godheed of the blessed Trinite" (148). John, he concludes, is "a doctor, and amongst alle doctors moost marvelous and wurshepful" because "his doctrine passeth alle othirs," because he converted "a greet parte of the worlde," and because he saved those who "were infecte by heresye" (174). Everything that Peter, Paul, and the other apostles accomplished through their preaching would have been destroyed by heretics "had not this holy doctor Saynt Iohn haue put theragenst the defense of his holy doctrine and wrytynge" (176). Saint Matthew wrote a Gospel and Paul and Peter wrote epistles, but John wrote a Gospel *and* epistles. Moreover, his writings surpass his colleagues': "His Gospel is moost hyge in diuinyte, his pistles are moost ful of charite, and his prophecye ys hylled wyth moost mysteries and meruelous priuyte" (176).

Two fifteenth-century lives of Katherine of Alexandria play up the saint's identity as a scholar and a teacher: a prose life composed circa 1420, and Capgrave's verse *Life of Saint Katherine* (ca. 1445). Katherine is one of the few female saints who was from the outset represented as a scholar.[8] The earliest extended account of her passion, composed during the eleventh century, presents her as the only daughter of a Greek king who gave her a superb liberal arts education.[9] Following his death, she inherited his kingdom and lived frugally and piously until the Emperor Maxentius arrived in her capital city of Alexandria and required everybody to sacrifice to the pagan gods. Katherine confronted the emperor, and her wisdom so stymied him that he summoned the wisest philosophers in his realm to discredit her faith in a public debate. She converted them, along with myriad spectators, then went on to convert the emperor's wife and his best friend. Unable to intimidate or convince her, the emperor had her beheaded.

The anomaly of being a sovereign and scholar probably helped Katherine become one of Western Europe's best-loved saints. Yet she was not uncontroversial. A Middle English version of her life composed during the fourteenth century represents her not as a queen but as a young princess whose "debate" with the philosophers consists of little beyond her declaration of faith.[10] Capgrave and the anonymous author of the prose life, by contrast, celebrate Katherine as a scholar par excellence. Both authors preface the traditional story of Katherine's passion with an elaborate "prequel" that recounts her upbringing, her conversion to Christianity, and her mystical marriage to Christ. Capgrave describes at great length the rigorous liberal arts curriculum she masters and the magnificent palace her father constructs for her education, whose floor plan is specifically tailored to the needs of different academic disciplines. Both describe the steady progress Katherine makes towards an erudition so profound that the scholars hired to train her are now eager to learn from her. Her early mastery of her teachers anticipates her later triumph over the fifty pagan philosophers.

The two lives offer rather different portraits of Katherine as a scholar. In the prose life, her thirst for knowledge informs all she does. Education makes her a judicious ruler and an effective proselyte. Indeed, the life concludes by reflecting that Katherine's wisdom was evinced not only in her "knowing of the mysteryes of the faith" but in her "wisdom of gouernance of meyne and of puples and of remes whiche [sche] had vnder cure" (see Waters, *Virgins and Scholars*, 416). By contrast, studiousness leads Capgrave's Katherine to neglect her worldly responsibilities, eliciting complaints of financial ruin and rampant crime from her unhappy subjects and leaving her realm vulnerable to invasion. She rises to heroism only when she abandons her isolated life of study and uses her learning to teach and inspire others and to defy tyranny. Though in both lives Katherine repudiates her pagan learning following her conversion, both show how her pagan knowledge helps her pursue her Christian agenda. She can convince the pagan philosophers because she speaks their language: she can spot rhetorical swindles; she can argue by reason and also explain the limits of reason; she can quote the philosophers' own authorities against them. Knowledge of all kinds is valuable, both texts show: what matters is how it's used.

Both of these intricate and learned lives of Katherine were successful, to judge by surviving manuscripts. Four copies of Capgrave's *Katherine* are extant, and their transmission suggests that it was in demand shortly after its production.[11] Versions of the prose life were anthologized in the 1438 *Gilte Legende*, in Caxton's *Legenda aurea sanctorum*, and in the anthology of scholar/saints I will discuss shortly. Though Caxton jettisoned Jacobus de Voragine's narrative of Katherine's life in favor of the more capacious prose life, he translated Jacobus's conclusion to his chapter on Katherine: a point-by-point enumeration of Katherine's academic accomplishments, which praises her mastery of all three branches of philosophy (theoretical, practical, and logical), describes exactly what knowledge pertains to each of these branches ("theoretical" philosophy covers mathematics, and so forth), and explains how Katherine demonstrated her command of each. His life thus joins the humanizing portrait of a young scholar with a scholastic disquisition on her credentials.[12]

EDUCATORS IN ANTHOLOGIES

The penchant for teaching saints is evident in hagiographical collections. Jocelyn Wogan-Browne has pointed out that one fifteenth-century manuscript of the *South English Legendary* (Oxford, Bodleian MS Bodley 779) supplements the standard contents of the popular thirteenth-century legendary with "thirteen unique biographies of saintly popes," each of whom "is celebrated for a particular reform or innovation"; "together they build a corporate history of doctrine and practice."[13] The manuscript variants of the *South English Legendary* are only beginning to be studied, and similar doctrinally oriented clusters of additional lives may well occur within the twelve full copies produced during the fifteenth century. Lives of missionaries, scholars, teachers, and devout readers were added to all three "translations" of Jacobus de Voragine's *Legenda aurea*: the 1438 *Gilte Legende* and the legendaries of Bokenham and of William Caxton. Woodcuts in the 1487 edition of Caxton's *Legenda aurea sanctorum* draw readers' attention to the lives of these apostles, teachers, and missionaries. Katherine, one of only three female saints illustrated in Caxton's edition, is shown holding an open book, reminding readers of her identity as a scholar.

Bokenham's Abbotsford legendary places the greatest emphasis on scholars and teachers, both women (as we saw in chapter 2) and men. Bokenham mined Bede's *Ecclesiastical History* and other sources for stories about illustrious British educators. In his legendary, we learn about Bishop David of Wales, who would "incomperably superexcellen and excedyn al the doctouris of Britaigne," converting Pelagian heretics through his eloquence. Trained in "the undirstondyng of holy scripture," John of Beverley travels "in divers cuntrees" to "sew abrode the sede of goddis word" (Abbotsford, 102r) before commencing a thirty-three-year episcopal career. Patrick, Dunstan, Botholf, Aldhelm, and Austin of England are similarly praised as teachers, as are several lesser known figures, including the East Saxon bishop Cedd and the East

Anglian bishop Felix. Through these lives, Bokenham reminds readers of the crucial role that education played in their own past. His focus on educators distinguishes his collection from the late thirteenth-century *South English Legendary*, whose compilers shared his interest in British saints but included more royals than teachers. Bokenham's concern with education is also evident in his portrayal of saints dear to the Augustinian order. Cynthia Turner Camp has identified eight such "fraternal" hagiographies, each of which celebrates a saint who had a rich contemplative life but also sustained fellow Christians through edifying "conversation."[14]

Sometime during the mid-fifteenth century, Wynter's *Life of Saint Jerome* and the prose *Life of Saint Katherine* were collected, along with the conjoined life of John the Baptist and John the Evangelist, to form a collection unlike any other—at least any other in Middle English.[15] Whereas "specialist" anthologies were most often devoted to the lives of virgins or the passions of martyrs, this one featured Christian teachers. The four saints could not be more different. Jerome is the quintessential educator—fluent in multiple modern and ancient tongues, translator of scripture, author of learned tracts. He teaches not only during his life but after his death, appearing to friends and colleagues to expatiate on eschatology, purgatory, and other topics. The Baptist and the Evangelist had no formal training; they obtained their "learning" through revelation and through direct contact with Jesus. Being a woman, Katherine is as unlikely a teacher as the son of a poor fisherman; nonetheless, she is, like Jerome, a member of the intellectual elite, beneficiary of the best education money can buy, and superior to every male scholar she encounters. Together the lives of Jerome, of Katherine, and of the two Johns celebrate Christian learning in all its diversity. Knowledge, the collection demonstrates, can be variously obtained by research, revelation, and reason. It is available to rich and poor, to women and men. It can be variously imparted, through preaching, debating, conversing, and writing. What matters is that it be sought, devoured passionately, and passed on to others.

The rise in Middle English lives of holy educators, along with the increased attention to reading and teaching within the lives of all kinds of saints, shifts the traditional association of holiness with virginity and martyrdom. Dying is not the only way to witness. One can show one's love of Christ by living for him, and, more specifically, by teaching for him. Readers are being challenged to read, to think, to learn, and to share their knowledge with others. They are being shown that people of all backgrounds and of both genders, married or single, can join forces with the saints in helping to create an informed Christian community.

Teaching Hagiographies

Some lives not only promoted learning and teaching by celebrating holy educators but provided religious instruction, embedding in their narratives sometimes substantial passages of doctrine and other edifying material. Hagiographers tackled diverse matters. Capgrave's Katherine of Alexandria dilates on the arcane doctrine of adoption, while Wynter's Jerome covers purgatory and eschatology. The sacraments and the Incarnation were popular topics. Wogan-Browne finds in the thirteen lives of popes in Bodley 779 reinforcement of the Church's "doctrine on the nature of God and humanity" and reflections on "the rich and strange orthodoxies of body and blood."[16] Juliana Dresvina notes that the fifteenth-century life of Margaret (preserved in Bodlian Library MS Eng. Th. E. 18) includes carefully identified scriptural references, "perhaps with an intention to educate their audience"; one-third of Margaret's life, she further notes, consists of Margaret's "soliloquies."[17] The first edition of Caxton's *Legenda aurea sanctorum* is a conduit for scripture, with close translations from the Old Testament packaged as the lives of "saints" Noah, Isaac, Joseph, Moses, David, Job, and others. As Helen White observes, when Caxton published his collection, "the prohibition of 1408 against circulating the Bible in English was still in force."[18] Caxton's inclusion of these biblical translations is evidence indeed that "lay people were not going to tolerate any attempt on the church's part to 'letten christen peple to knowe, here, rede, write and speke holy writ in Englisch.'"[19]

The most flamboyant of the fifteenth-century's "teaching hagiographies" is the first surviving saint's play in English: the play of Mary Magdalene, composed in East Anglia at the turn of the century (preserved in Oxford University Bodleian Library MS Digby 133).[20] A remarkable extravaganza with more than fifty speaking parts and nineteen settings, the play combines scholarship with spectacle to "illumyn ower ygnorans" (*Mary Magdalene*, line 712). It opens with Mary

Magdalene's dying father bequeathing his property to his three children: Mary, Martha, and Lazarus. Enticed by Lechery, Mary soon trades her affluent respectability for a scintillating life of sin. In its scope and its attention to so much that happened before Mary's encounter with Jesus, it is the dramatic equivalent of such "epic" hagiographies as Capgrave's *Life of Saint Katherine* and Lydgate's *Lives of Saints Edmund and Fremund.* In its concern with family life, it resembles the hagiographies of Bokenham and Capgrave.[21] Also in the tradition of Lydgate, Bokenham, and Capgrave is its rendering of the psychological complexity of Mary's fall—she succumbs to Lechery's sweet-talking in part because bereavement has made her vulnerable: "For my father, I haue had grett heuynesse—/ Whan I remembyr, my mynd waxit mort" (454–55). The playwright follows his extrabiblical prequel with episodes drawn from the Gospels, including Mary's interaction with Jesus at the house of Simon the Pharisee; Jesus's raising of Lazarus; and the encounter of Mary and the apostles with the risen savior. The second half of the play mostly recounts Mary's mission to Marseilles and conversion of the king and queen. It concludes, briefly, with her retirement to the desert and encounter in her old age with a hermit, who serves her the Eucharist before she dies.

With the exception of the extended prequel, the plot follows Jacobus de Voragine's *Legenda aurea* and many other lives of Mary Magdalene.[22] What sets the Digby play apart from its predecessors is the amount of direct exposition it relays. The play not only tells us *that* Mary preaches; it tells us *what* she preaches. Moreover, Mary's encounters with Jesus are not only based on passages from scripture; they are translations from scripture. Jacobus summarizes scripture as he describes the meeting with Jesus at the house of Simon the Pharisee recounted in Luke 7: "Now Simon the Pharisee thought to himself that if this man were a prophet, he would never allow a sinful woman to touch him; but the Lord rebuked him for his proud righteousness and told the woman that all her sins were forgiven."[23] The Digby playwright, by contrast, dramatizes scripture, translating almost verbatim Jesus's rebuke to Simon along with his minatory parable of the two debtors (compare lines 649–77 of *Mary Magdalene* with Luke 7:39–48). His rendering of other biblical scenes, including the raising of Lazarus and Mary's meeting with the Risen Christ at the tomb, also is largely scriptural. For example, John 11:21–27 reads:

Martha therefore said to Jesus: Lord, if thou hadst been here, my brother had not died. / But now also I know that whatsoever thou wilt ask of God, God will give it thee. / Jesus saith to her: Thy brother shall rise again. / Martha saith to him: I know that he shall rise again, in the resurrection at the last day. / Jesus said to her: I am the resurrection and the life: he that believeth in me, although he be dead, shall live: / And every one that liveth and believeth in me shall not die for ever. Believest thou this? / She saith to him: Yea, Lord, I have believed that thou art Christ, the Son of the living God, who art come into this world.[24]

The Digby play renders this exchange almost verbatim:

Martha
Lord, and þou haddyst byn her, werely
My brother had natt a byn ded—I know well thysse.
Jhesus dicit
Martha, doctor, onto þe I sey,
Thy brother xall reyse agayn!
Martha
Yee, Lord, ar þe last day;
That I beleve ful pleyn.
Jhesus
I am þe resurreccyon of lyfe, þat euer xall reynne,
And whoso belevyt verely in me
Xall have lyfe euyrlastyng, þe soth to seyn.
Martha, belevyst thow þis?
Martha
3e, forsoth, þe Prynsse of blysch!
I beleve in Cryst, þe Son of Sapyens,
Whyche wythowt eynd rygne xall he,
To redemyn vs freell from ower iniquite!
     (*Mary Magdalene*, lines 875–88)

Mary's encounter with the risen Jesus is similarly close to its scriptural source (1061–77; John 20:15–18). Lines and also full scenes in the play are also drawn right from the Bible; for example, "Blyssyd be þey . . . / That sen me nat, and have me in credens" (699–70; John 20:29). In conveying Mary's teachings, the playwright emphasizes that Mary's preaching is scriptural: "As holy wrytt berytt wettnesse" (1501); "as skryptur declarytt pleyn" (1522). That Mary was learned in "holy wrytt" was suggested from her first encounter with Jesus, when she said that Jesus's mercy has restored her faith in the "techeyng of Isaye in scryptur" (697).

The playwright elaborates the scriptural underpinning for Mary's status as "apostle," namely, that Jesus told her at the tomb, "go sey to my bortheryn I wyll pretende / To stey to my Father In heu[n]ly towyrs" (*Mary Magdalene*, line 1076–77; John 20:17). After the apostles have departed to spread the gospel far and wide, Jesus sends the Archangel Raphael to give Mary her own apostolic mission, namely, that "she xall converte þe land of Marcyll" (1371). In Jacobus de Voragine's *Legenda aurea*, she is, under Maximin's care, one of many missionaries to Marseilles, but in the Digby play she *is* the mission, undertaking a role that clearly demonstrates that she is "amyttyd as an holy apostylesse" (1381). "Alle þe lond xall be techyd alonly be the" (1382), Raphael tells her.

The somewhat later play *The Conversion of Paul*, also preserved in Digby 133, likewise celebrates a penitent turned preacher. Though it praises Paul as "so nobyll a doctor" and encourages viewers to consult scripture for more information about his teaching career, it conveys little of Paul's teaching itself.[25] That preaching figures more prominently in the play about Mary Magdalene than it does in the play about the Apostle Paul continues the broad trend in fifteenth-century hagiography whereby the most doctrinally charged teaching hagiographies are lives of female saints. For the remainder of this chapter, I will look closely at hagiographies that address one of the most fundamental and challenging doctrines of the faith: the Trinity. This doctrine was explored most fully in the lives of two women: Katherine of Alexandria and Barbara.

The Trinity: "ouer hiʒe, ouer reverend and hard"?

The Trinity was a cornerstone of medieval Christianity, and its greatest mystery. In late medieval England, churches and guilds were named for the three-personed God. Images sought to convey the unity of Father,

Son, and Holy Ghost. Sermons and meditations stirred the faithful to devotion. Yet few pedagogical tracts undertook to explain the Trinity in any detail beyond its simple articulation in Archbishop Thoresby's catechism, which, to quote its English translation, states that "Iesu crist goddes son of heuen is sothefastly god euen til his fadir," that "the hali gast that samenly comes of bothe the fadir and the son, is sothefastly god, and euen til tham bothe," that Father, Son, and Holy Ghost are "bot thre se[r]e persons and noght bot a god,'" and finally that "the trinite Fadir and sone and haligast, thre persons and a god, is maker of heuen and of erthe and of all thinges."[26]

Pastoral literature of the fourteenth and early fifteenth centuries generally diverts attention from Trinitarian doctrine to devotion. The anonymous author of *Speculum Sacerdotale* refers only in passing to the nature of the Trinity in his sermon on its feast: "Sires, in syche a day ȝe schul haue the solempnite of the Holy Trinity, scilicet, fader and sone and Holy Gost, þe whiche Holy Trinite is oo God," he says, before passing on to the wonders wrought by that "oo God, almyȝtty and euerlastynge" and wrapping up with an explanation of why it is important to honor the Trinity.[27] John Mirk's much longer sermon on the feast day has more to say about the nature of the Trinity, but not much more. Mirk, too, devotes more attention to *why* the Trinity should be honored than to *what* is being honored. Following the common practice of explaining the Trinity by analogy, he compares Father, Son, and Holy Spirit, all manifestations of one God, to water, ice, and snow, all manifestations of water. But even as he enjoins his audience to believe in "þre persons in on godhed" he warns that to "study how þis may be, hit is but a foly; for monnys wyt may neuer comprehend hit."[28] He concludes with an exemplum of how a "gret maystyr of diuinyte" learns the futility of attempting to understand "why God wold be leuot on God in þre persons."

The reticence of vernacular authors is hardly surprising, for the Trinity was high-stakes theology, even for "gret maystyrs of diuinyte." Augustine warns that "in no other subject is error more dangerous, or inquiry more laborious," but he also avers that in no other subject is "the discovery of truth more profitable."[29] Quoting Augustine, Peter Lombard writes that "this highest and most excellent of topics is to be approached with modesty and fear."[30] Even more cautious, Jacobus de Voragine, archbishop of Genoa, asserts in his Latin sermons on the saints, "No subject is more elevated, or more fraught with danger than to speak of the most profound mystery of the Trinity."[31] He concludes, "Let us, therefore, speak of open and lowly subjects, and leave lofty concerns to wise men." The author of the prose life of John the Baptist I mentioned earlier averred that the Trinity is not easily known through words, however erudite.

William Langland's Anima would have agreed. In passus XV of *The Vision of Piers Plowman*, she inveighs against the "freres and fele other maistres that to the lewed men prechen" who, more eager to dazzle the faithful with their erudition than to actually teach anything, "moeven materes unmesurables to tellen of the Trinité."[32] Their efforts are worse than useless, in that they risk raising more doubts than they settle. Instead of preaching matters best left to theologians, these friars and masters ought to teach the Ten Commandments or the seven deadly sins. As if to confirm this stance, passus XVII finds Will baffled after Faith's confusing disquisition on the Trinity, unable to reconcile the apparent contradiction between Faith's admonition to believe in a triune God and Hope's exhortation "to byleve and lovye in o Lorde almyghty," which makes no mention of the Trinity. Yet Langland goes on to demonstrate that the Trinity, properly expounded, *can* be accessible to "lewed peple." Through extended analogies comparing the Trinity first to a fist and then to a candle flame, the Samaritan of passus XVII demonstrates the unity of the three persons and further shows that believing in the Trinity has everything to do with Hope's message of loving God and one's neighbor.[33]

Langland's object of providing an explanation of the Trinity that was comprehensible to the faithful was taken up by Reginald Pecock over a generation later, in what, to my knowledge, is the most extended treatment of the doctrine in Middle English. In his *Reule of Crysten Religioun*, composed circa 1443, Pecock took issue with those who claimed that the Trinity was too lofty a topic for the laity: "þese trouþis and her profis ben esily aweeldeable of ech competently wittid lay man if he wolde take bisynes þerto."[34] In fact, they are no more complicated than so many of the business matters that laypeople deal with routinely "in plees of dette and of trespace, in rekenyngis to be maad of receivers and rente gaderers in þe account of an audit," and so forth (*Reule of Crysten Religioun*, 94). The risk of falling into error, he argues, is minimal for those who are willing to be guided and corrected by the bona fide representatives of Holy

Church (96). The error is in preventing "a man fro profitable labouris in redyng, in heryng, in studiyng, resonyng, enquering, encerching, wherbi he may be edified and edifie oþere and preise god, þe deuoutlier drede god and wondre of god, þe more loue god and serue" (97). Religious understanding makes for better Christians.

Pecock's exposition on the Trinity is consistent with his career-long promotion of a reasoned Christianity.[35] He avers that although the existence of God *as a Trinity* is something that can only be known through revelation, once revealed there is much about the nature of the Trinity that can be deduced "bi discurse and liȝt of natural resound" (*Reule of Crysten Religioun*, 76). In his ensuing discussion he first documents the revelation of the Trinity in scripture, then expounds the essentials of the doctrine as "schewid bi resoun and bi feiþ" (85). He is careful to differentiate between the Son's being "gendrid" by the Father and the Holy Ghost's being "spirid" from the Father and Son (81), while emphasizing that the same substance is communicated by the Father to both Son and Holy Spirit (76–80): one substance, one God. The begetting and proceeding that produced the Trinity occur out of time, he emphasizes: it had no beginning and will persist throughout eternity (82–84). Pecock's approach to the Trinity differs most markedly from that of most other Middle English authors, including Langland, in his reliance on reason rather than analogy to convey his points. Indeed, his entire exposition contains not a single analogy.

Though bold in its extended and intricate coverage of the doctrine, Pecock's discussion is nonetheless laced with anxiety about those who "juge þat þis doctryne is ouer hiȝe, ouer reverend and hard forto be lerned and kunnen of þe comoun peple in her moderis langage" (*Reule of Crysten Religioun*, 85), those who believe that there "is no nede þat þe lay peple haue so myche and so hi ȝe and sutil knowing of god in trynyte of persoonys" (88). Demonstrating that he has been selective in which points of doctrine to treat, he alludes to "more and hardir doctrynes and oþere consideraciouns vpon þe godhead" that are expounded in Peter Lombard's *Sentences*; then, in an odd move, he summarizes some of those "consideraciouns" in Latin (86, 88–89).[36] He allows that his entire discussion of the Trinity could be cut, but he hopes that will not be deemed necessary (85). After all, he protests, the Trinity, unlike, say, the Eucharist, is not a topic that lay people are prone to speculate about (94).

Pecock's anxieties may help explain why some of the most detailed explanations of the Trinity occur in hagiography, a genre that stresses its ancient (and irreproachably orthodox) sources and in which excursions into theology are to some degree camouflaged by narrative. I will now turn to the three most complex treatments of the Trinity in Middle English hagiography, which occur in texts roughly contemporaneous with Pecock's *Reule*: Capgrave's *Life of Saint Katherine of Alexandria*, and two lives of Saint Barbara, one in verse by Bokenham and the other in prose by an anonymous hagiographer.

Capgrave's Katherine: "The Holy Trinité she provyde ... be kynde"

The Trinity figures prominently in Capgrave's *Life of Saint Katherine*. A Cambridge-educated doctor of divinity, Capgrave authored numerous Latin commentaries, and his theological training informs his vernacular saints' lives.[37] A theological orientation is particularly evident in his life of Katherine, who, as we have seen, manifests her renowned learning in debate against fifty pagan philosophers. Capgrave enhanced the theological content of Katherine's life well beyond that of the prose life, even though he, like his anonymous contemporary, humanized his heroine by delineating her emotions and developing her relationships with family members, thus making it far easier for his targeted audience "of man, mayde, and of wyffe" to identify with her—to feel with her, and, most audaciously, to think and to learn with her.[38]

Theological discussion had formed part of Katherine's debate with the philosophers since the eleventh-century "Vulgate" passion; however, that discussion had revolved around Christ's dual nature rather than the Trinity per se. Even while retaining—indeed amplifying—the discussion of the dual nature, Capgrave made the Trinity the theological center of his life. When, after Katherine's mystical marriage to Christ, the Savior gives the hermit Adrian the task of instructing her in the essentials of faith, he first mentions the Incarnation, but he emphasizes the Trinity:

> ... thu schall hir teche
> Of Myn incarnacyon the manere speche;

Teche hir the feyth eke of the Trinité,
The Fadyr, the Sone, and the Holy Gost;
Teche hir of the Godhede the unyté.
    (Capgrave, *Life of Saint Katherine*, 3.1322–26)

When, later in the narrative, the fifty philosophers declare themselves ready to learn about Christianity, Katherine begins by telling them about the Trinity (4.1667–80).

Adrian's instruction to Katherine is vigorously conveyed in the simple and direct language that readers might encounter in pastoral writings of the day. However, he relies on iteration rather than analogy to make his point. Each time he elaborates on God's "kynde" he repeats, in different terms, the key point that God is "on in substauns and in nature" though he is "thre eke in persones" (*Life of Saint Katherine*, 3.1390–93): "pluralyté of persones is no prejudyse / Onto the unyté of Godhed" (3.1399–1400); "dystynctyoun in persones, in nature unite" (3.1408). What's more, Capgrave tackles intricacies and nuances that prior Middle English writers (Pecock excepted) tended to gloss over, for example, the distinction between the *begetting* of the Son and the *procession* of the Holy Spirit. Though power "longyth" to the Father, wisdom to the Son, and goodness to the Ghost, Capgrave emphasizes that the Holy Ghost and the Son have no less might than the Father, the Father and Son no less goodness than the Ghost, and so forth.

In her debate with the philosophers, Katherine must defend the doctrines she learned from Adrian—Christ's dual nature, unity in plurality, "filiacion" versus "procession," and so on—against learned and skeptical critics. The experience of her mystical marriage had left Katherine herself more than willing to accept the tenets of Christianity on faith alone, but the philosophers pose tough questions: How can Christ have created the universe if he was born in Bethlehem no more than three centuries ago? If Father, Son, and Ghost are one, how can the Son alone become flesh? What's more, the philosophers demand logical proof. They exhort her to eschew "crafty circumlocucion" (*Life of Saint Katherine*, 4.1887) and to "teche" her "thingis" by "naturall resones," explaining that it is "harde" to "constreyn a mannes wil / To trow a thing whech he cannot prove" (4.1779–80). Though Katherine initially responds by protesting that some things cannot be proved but must simply be believed, by the end of the debate she has "provide" the

Trinity "be kynde" (4.2302) and forced the chief philosopher to admit that "he coud fro the resones no wey fynde" (4.2303).

Capgrave's treatment of the Trinity is the most unusual I have encountered in vernacular hagiography because he explains not merely the *doctrine* of the Trinity but its *motivation*. Katherine tells the philosophers:

> Oure auctoures sey that if Godd had be
> Oonly o persone than schuld not His holy blys
> Be comounde to other so parfytly as it is,
> For creature non myght receyve no swech:
> Therfore He ordeyned be His eterne counsayle
> That thre persones in myght and nature lych
> In oo Godhed, to us ful gret mervayle,
> Schuld be consederyd to mannys grete avayle;
> And ech of other His substauns schuld thus take,
> Non lesse, non more; thus oure feyth we make.
>   (*Life of Saint Katherine*, 4.1671–80)

Capgrave's object seems clear enough. He is extending to dogma the goal he pursued in his deeply affective account of Katherine's conversion and mystical marriage to Christ, that of making God accessible to ordinary people. The Trinity exists because the Godhead—just like the debonair Son, who marries Katherine—is reaching out to those he created in his desire to be known by them.[39] Yet presenting the Trinity in this fashion to a general audience "of man, mayde, and of wyffe" was risky. Capgrave's source for this passage appears to be the unimpeachably orthodox *De fide et symbolo* of Augustine: "God the Father, on the other hand, who possessed both the will and the power to declare Himself with the utmost truth to minds designed to obtain knowledge of Him, with the purpose of thus declaring Himself begat this [Word] which He Himself is who did beget."[40]

Nonetheless, Capgrave's discussion risks raising thorny questions. It is worth noting that Peter Lombard found this passage from Augustine potentially problematic; in his *Sentences*, he takes pains to show that Augustine is *not* intimating that God begat himself.[41] Though the issue of begetting does not arise in Capgrave's discussion, his audience might well wonder, for example, how the Father, Son, and Holy Spirit could be both absolute and eternal essences and a form of self-presentation ordained for man's benefit. I have found no analogue to this discussion anywhere in Middle English, not even in Pecock's oeuvre. Here and elsewhere, Capgrave was willing to risk misunderstanding in order to convey a fuller, more substantial understanding of faith, counting on his ample discussions of the singularity and coeternity of the three-personed God to keep his readers from falling into error.

Osbern Bokenham: "Resoun here faylyth"

Not all hagiographers were willing to take such risks. Capgrave's fellow Augustinian Bokenham is an intriguing example of a hagiographer who evidently overcame his reluctance to tackle matters of doctrine.[42]

About a year after Capgrave had completed *Katherine*, Bokenham undertook his own version of Katherine's passion. He had read Capgrave's *Katherine*. But his own account, he declares in his prologue, will be nothing like Capgrave's—and indeed it is not. Not only does he omit Katherine's conversion and mystical marriage, claiming to know nothing of "alle þat," but he also strips her debate with the philosophers of its theological meat.[43] As Paul Price observes, Bokenham's Katherine converts the philosophers with a simple statement of faith, a paraphrase of the Apostle's Creed or the Nicene Creed (but without the latter's lines on the Trinity).[44]

Shortly after he completed "Katherine," Bokenham composed a life of Saint Cecilia. As he did with his "Katherine," Bokenham used the *vita* found in Jacobus de Voragine's widely circulated *Legenda aurea* as his source, but here he *amplifies* rather diminishes his source's theological content. Jacobus has Cecilia startle a prospective convert, Tiburtius, by declaring, "All things that were made, the Son begotten of the Father has established in being, and all the things that are established, the Spirit who proceeds from the Father has enlivened" (Jacobus, *Golden Legend*, 2:320–21). Tiburtius protests: "Surely you assert that there is only one God! How then can you testify that there are three?" Cecilia answers, following Augustine (*De trinitate* 10.12): "Just as in human knowledge there are three powers, namely, thought, memory, and understanding, so in the one divine being there can be three persons" (Jacobus, *Golden Legend*, 2:321). But she then moves on to the Incarnation and Passion, graphically describing Christ's sufferings, and it is her affective presentation of the human Christ, not her theology lesson, that moves Tiburtius to conversion. There is no further discussion of the Trinity, or of any other doctrinal matter, in Jacobus's *vita*.

In Bokenham's retelling, Cecilia's passing allusion to the Trinity is elaborated into a concise summary of the doctrine, replete with jargon. Christ, she says, was born both "temporally / Of a mayde" and "eternally" "of hys fadyr"

> ... to-forn al tyme, to whom egal
> He is & was & euere be shal;
> In whom, by whom, al thyng was wrouht,
> And wyth-oute whom was neuere maad noht;
> To whom wyth þe fadyr consubstancyal
> The holy gost ys & coeternal;
> And þow þei personelly dystynct be,
> Yet in substaunce but oon þei arn al thre,
> Vndeuydyd outward in her werkyng.
> ("Cecilia," lines 7801–11)[45]

Tiburtius objects that "þis manere talking" is "ageyn al resoun," a "thing" to which his "wyt can not incline" (7812–15). Undeterred, Cecilia promises to "preue" "naturally" and "by resound" that it is indeed possible for a single substance to have "powers condystynct thre" (7822, 7824, 7827). Yet after rehearsing a couple of common analogies that "coniecturally / may be conseyuyd of the trynyte" she retreats to the same line Jacobus's Cecilia followed, admitting that such analogies fail to fully convey "þe treuth" (7836–37, 7840). "Resoun here faylyth, & oonly feyth / Preuaylyth," she declares, urging Tiburtius to "forsake euydence" and trust "doctryne of scryptur" (7841, 7845–46). As in Jacobus's telling, discussion of theology ceases; Cecilia launches into a vivid and moving account of Christ's suffering, concluding with the promise that if Tiburtius converts to Christianity he will be able to see angels. Tiburtius capitulates.

In light of Bokenham's refusal in "Katherine" to treat matters of doctrine in any depth, it is easy to see in his "Cecilia" a conservative message aimed at the likes of Capgrave, namely, that it is pointless to convey theological intricacies to the hoi polloi. Yet Bokenham's view is not so simple. Cecilia's lesson, after all, is being relayed not only to the clueless Tiburtius but to Bokenham's own readers.[46] The gist of what Cecilia says is not much more elaborate than what Bokenham's lay readers might have read in manuals such as Thorlesby's *Catechism* or heard from pastors like Mirk. What differs is the Scholastic language she uses to convey her message. Terms such as "consubstantial," "condistinction," and even "coeternal" are not found in any other version of the Cecilia legend I know of, in Latin or the vernacular; nor do they commonly occur in the Latin reference works that pastors were likely to consult. Was Bokenham merely showing off, indulging in the very sort of tour de force that Langland's Anima denounced, by bandying about terms that were more likely to baffle than to enlighten? Or was he seeking to create lay readers who would *not* be mystified by Anima's supercilious "masters" by introducing technical terminology in a context that makes its meaning obvious? His subsequent life of Barbara, most probably written in the next decade, suggests the latter, namely, that in "Cecilia" Bokenham was moving away from the conservatism of "Katherine" and demonstrating an interest in Christian education. As we will see, "Barbara" is one of the most theologically sophisticated saints' lives in Middle English, a work that is very much in the spirit of Capgrave's *Katherine* but marked by the propensity for Scholastic terminology that characterized "Cecilia."

Two Approaches to Teaching the Trinity through Saint Barbara

Barbara is the saint most closely associated with the Trinity. Indeed, her emblem, the tower, represents the Trinity. Her martyrdom came about when she incurred her father's anger by changing the two-window design of the tower he was constructing for her to a three-window design in honor of the three-personed God. Though Barbara's legend had always celebrated the Trinity, it did not necessarily expound it. An English account written in the early fifteenth century, based on a popular Latin *vita*, has only this to say, as Barbara is explaining to her father why she changed his plans:

> For thre wyndowes I have ordeynid so
> That the byssidful Trenite it schuld represent,

In that on God schal ben worschepyd and no mo,
Aboven alle creatures with hol entent,
That also lythnyth alle erthly creature,
That is comyn in this wordis here for to dwelle.
                               ("Barbara," lines 105–10)⁴⁷

During the mid-fifteenth century, Bokenham and an anonymous prose hagiographer each adapted the lengthy account of Barbara's life composed in the Low Countries at the end of the fourteenth century and attributed to the Austin friar John of Wackerzele.⁴⁸ In the tradition of *devotio moderna*, the *vita* is marked by its attention to the saint's spiritual, emotional, and intellectual experiences.⁴⁹ Its accounts of Barbara's conversion and of her failed attempt to convert her father include lengthy disquisitions on the Trinity. It celebrates Barbara for attaining the four crowns—of virgins, martyrs, doctors, and preachers. Mathilde van Dijk, who has studied the Latin and vernacular incarnations of Barbara's legend in the Low Countries, observes some ambivalence on the part of translators about the theological and intellectual orientation of the Latin *vita*. Some vernacular versions, especially those intended for women and lay brothers, omitted much of the theologizing and also dropped the reference to Barbara's having obtained the crowns of preachers and doctors.⁵⁰

Bokenham (as we saw in chapter 2) and the prose author retained the Trinitarian orientation of the *vita*, and they likewise retained its detailed description of Barbara's thoughts and of her complex relationship with her father. In so doing they, like Capgrave, allowed readers not only to sympathize with but to identify with a scholarly laywoman and her ways of thinking. Nonetheless, the two Middle English versions express somewhat differing theologies, which affect their presentations of the Trinity. The anonymous prose life, following the emphasis of the Latin original, presents Barbara as a conduit of God's grace who is stirred by the Holy Spirit to reject the pagan pantheon and to reason that there is a single God.⁵¹ Her inquiries into the nature of the divine, the author emphasizes, are divinely inspired: "by the special light of grace geven to her of God sche founde by her owen wytte and natural reason howe yt was oone to be veray God in hymselfe."⁵² Bokenham, on the other hand, presents Barbara as an intellectually enterprising pagan who, evidently prompted by natural reason alone, becomes convinced of the existence of a single god through a vigorous process of syllogizing. Indeed, Bokenham devotes hundreds of lines to her "musings," "reasonings," and "syllogizings," and he consistently omits references to the Holy Ghost or God's grace as the source of her inquiries.

Both Barbaras learn about the Trinity through the teachings of the Church Father Origen. However, the prose account condenses and simplifies Origen's presentation of the doctrine in the *vita*, while Bokenham elaborates and complicates it. For example, where the prose author writes, "These .iij. lyke as they be oo God in substaunce, right so in persones they be verely .iij." (Anonymous, "Barbara," 398), Bokenham writes:

> But yit although these persones thre
> Ben condistincte asundir in the trinyte
> Eche from othir by personal nocion
> Yet eche is that othir by substanciall unyon.
>   ("Barbara," 7v)

Similarly, the Middle English prose life renders *pater igitur in filio et filius in patre, spiritus vero sanctus a patre et filio* as "alwey hole togedyr the son in the fader, the fader in the son, the holy goste in bothe two, whose charite and communyon knytteth alle .iij. in oon and togedyr dothe theym combyne" (Anonymous, "Barbara," 398); the hagiographer's elaboration works to demystify the terse original by linking its abstruse theology to concepts of charity and community that would have resonated with ordinary readers. Bokenham, by contrast, takes the opportunity to teach his audience some clerical jargon:

> The fadir is in the sonne and in the fadir is he
> The holy goost in her either by a propirte
> Clepid of clerkis circumincessioun.
>   ("Barbara," 7v)

Again, where the English prose life asserts the coeternity of the Trinity in simple terms ("noon before another by any processe of tyme" [Anonymous, "Barbara," 398]), Bokenham dresses the point in theological terminology:

> And yit noon dooth othir in tyme precede
> For eche of hem to othir is coetern
> So that two hem can no man discern
> First ner last so that coequal
> Is eche to othir consubstancial
> Of tyme withoute ony prioryte
> > ("Barbara," 7v)

This terminology, with the exception of "coeternal," was Bokenham's addition to his Latin source.

Bokenham and the author of the prose life also differ in their presentation of Barbara's attempt to explain the Trinity to her father. In both versions, Barbara uses the three-windowed tower as an analogy for the three-personed God. The substance of the saint's teachings is the same; what differs is the packaging. The anonymous prose writer again conveys theological points concisely, using simple syntax and mostly familiar language. His Barbara starts with a simple definition of the Godhead as "that thynge whiche hathe made alle that ever ys of nought, both visible and vnvisible" (Anonymous, "Barbara," 413). The Godhead, she goes on to say, consists of three persons: Father, Son, and Holy Ghost. She then explains how the Deity can be both "departable in persones" and yet "oone in godhede, vndevided, vnseparable and vndepartable": "Thof the fader be fader by hymselfe in that he is fader, yit he may never be withowt the son nor withowte the holi goost in that he is God"; the same holds for the Son and Holy Ghost.

In contrast to the prose version's simple declarative sentences, the disquisition of Bokenham's Barbara is a syntactical jungle in which key points are packed into subordinate clauses, fitting the synopsis of the doctrine into one convoluted sentence:

> Thou shalt leere that thou nevir knew yit
> That is to seyn how marveilously is puyt
> The sovereyn godhede in the nombre of thre
> Which al thyng hath wrought the holy trinite
> Distincte in thre persones and of myghtis moste
> The fadir and the sone and the holigoste
> In whom althogh ther be personal variaunce

> Yet al thre essentially arn but oon substaunce
> Individibly divisible
> And divisibly indivisible
> For though the fadir as fadir divisible be
> From the sone and the spirite yit as god is he
> Indivisible from hem and in liche wise
> Of the sone and the holigoste men must devise
> For notwithstandyng personal distinction
> Bilevid must nedis substancial unyon
> Which by the toure and the wyndowes thre
> By a maner of liknesse may seyen be.
>
> (Bokenham, "Barbara," 9v)

Bokenham's Barbara uses the tower as an analogy for the Trinity, but she also points to the analogy's limitations:

> The similitude egally doth not procede
> For in the high and souereyn trinite
> Personal distinction excludith not ydentite
> Of substaunce ner substantial ydentificacion
> Forbarrith in no wise personal seperacion
> So that the fadir the sone and the holi goste in fer
> Thre ben in oon and in ineffable manere.
>
> (10r)

The writer of the prose life, by contrast, only explains in simple and direct language how the three-windowed tower is like the Trinity, "oo veray God aloone, fader, son and holi goste, distincte in persones and not in godhead" (Anonymous, "Barbara," 414).

Bokenham differs from his English contemporary not only in how he relays the doctrine of the Trinity but in what he relays. In transmitting Origen's teachings, the prose author skips the Latin *vita*'s discussion of begetting and proceeding. After explaining the unity of three distinct persons in one God, Origen warns Barbara that the Trinity is a mystery that must be accepted on faith because it cannot be fully understood: its "habitudis or relacion, natures, processe and generacion . . . passyth mannes wytte clerely to speke or ever so high to clymbe" (Anonymous, "Barbara," 399). Bokenham, by contrast, shows no such reticence. On the subject of generation, he follows the Latin *vita* in writing, "the fadir of hym self is oonly iwys / The sone of the fadir by generacion is / The holigoste of hem bothe doth procede" (Bokenham, "Barbara," 7v). He then moves on to "habitude," "relacion," and "nature." Knowledge appears to be a guiding principle for Bokenham, as it was for Capgrave. Where the Origen of the prose life says that anyone who fails to believe in the Trinity "schal never be saved nor never come to the presence of God" (Anonymous, "Barbara," 399), Bokenham's Origen says that those who do not believe "may nat to the *knoulech* of god atteyn" (Bokenham, "Barbara," 7v). Bokenham's "Barbara" uses narrative to convey much the same message that Reginald Pecock does in his *Reule of Crysten Religioun*, namely, that although the existence of the Trinity cannot be deduced through reason, once revealed it can be comprehended through reason.

The theologically oriented saints' lives of the mid-fifteenth century point to a contingent within the clergy eager to reverse the "pedagogy of infantilization" associated with Arundel.[53] These lives both teach basic theology and model approaches to teaching it. Through hagiography, writers were examining (and sometimes, as in the case of Bokenham, reexamining) complex issues, such as the capacity of reason to comprehend the divine. They were experimenting with ways to bring together affective and intellectual modes of piety. Though it might seem surprising that the Trinity—that loftiest and most "dangerous" of mysteries—should occur so frequently as a topic of discussion, it also makes perfect sense that writers should focus on a central tenet of Christianity, especially one that was not being disputed by the heterodox. Their strategy appears, indeed, to have been similar to Pecock's, who, as James Simpson has argued, deliberately chose to expatiate on "topics that were not sources of contention between the orthodox and Lollards."[54] In the spirit of Augustine, these hagiographers, like Pecock, realized that study of the Trinity has great rewards and also great risks, and they were willing to take risks in order to spread the rewards beyond an elite class of theologians.

Their work is further evidence that the fifteenth century was, as Kathryn Kerby-Fulton put it, "an age of *failed* censorship."[55] But I wonder to what extent the appreciation and promotion of Christian intellectualism was propelled by the very spirit of repression that we associate with the "Constitutions." Though they wrote in a more tolerant environment, hagiographers such as Bokenham and Capgrave grew to intellectual maturity in the shadow of the "Constitutions," educated in universities that were grappling with issues they raised about the dissemination of religious thought. These authors must also have realized that, though intellectual repression might be out of fashion, it was not out of the question—as Pecock found. It is no coincidence that the most extensive theological discussions occur in martyr legends that pit Christian intellectualism against the censorship and violence of a persecuting society. It is also, I suspect, no coincidence that the most deeply theological lives are lives of women rather than of Church Fathers. Intellectually ambitious women had long been the emblems of a rebellious laity prone to speculation and error, the products and purveyors of heresy. In constructing Barbaras, Katherines, and Cecilias who can purvey a cogent and orthodox theology, hagiographers of the generation after Arundel were saying, in the strongest terms, that it was time to move on.

CHAPTER FOUR

Holiness and the Modern Woman

In the entry for 1243 of his *Chronica Majora*, Matthew Paris reported the presence "chiefly in Germany" (which would, for him, have included the Low Countries) of laypeople, "mostly women," who donned a religious habit and "made profession of continence and simplicity of life by a private vow, without, however, being straitened by the rules of any saint, nor as yet shut up within the precincts of any cloisters."[1] Paris estimated two thousand such layfolk living in or around Cologne.

The women Paris described were beguines, members of a movement that began circa 1200 in the diocese of Liège and quickly spread to other parts of northwestern Europe and even into the eastern part of central Europe.[2] The earliest beguines lived with their families or with like-minded women. They often worked to support themselves and volunteered among the poor or in hospitals or leprosaria. Though many remained beguines for life, they were not bound to do so, and some married, joined convents, or entered anchorholds. Beginning in the 1230s, amid rising suspicion of unregulated religious women, walled "court beguinages" were established. These campuses, equipped with churches, hospitals, apartments, and refectories, might accommodate hundreds.[3] Walter Simon writes that they "attracted women from all walks of life" for "the opportunity they afforded to pursue economic independence in a safe environment"; they "sprang up in virtually every major town or city of the Low Countries, where they still form a typical feature of the urban landscape."[4] Another movement popular with women was the *devotio moderna*, which arose in the Netherlands during the late fourteenth century. Like the beguines, its adherents embraced poverty and service but did not follow a rule. Some formed communities, "brethren and sisters of the common life."[5] New forms of religious life also flourished in southern Europe, where women were becoming Dominican and Franciscan tertiaries or leading lives of poverty under the guidance of Augustinian canons.[6] The "Poor Clares," or "Second Order of St. Francis," established in 1212, offered a more traditional monastic experience for those wishing to embrace apostolic poverty. Beguine-like communities in southern Europe included the Pinzochere of Tuscany and the *beatas* of Spain.

Many holy women of continental Europe wrote.[7] Bridget of Sweden recorded more than seven hundred visions, while Catherine of Siena left a copious correspondence, along with her visionary writings. Hildegard of Bingen's enormous corpus ranged from liturgies to treatises on medicine and sexuality. Beatrijs of Nazareth kept a journal in Dutch.[8] Holy women also wrote saints' lives, allegories, poetry, dialogues, and moral tracts. Their lives and writings inspired a rich and diverse hagiography as confessors celebrated their friends and spiritual mothers.[9] In certain convents in Germany and the Netherlands, nuns wrote lives of each other.[10] Lives survive of nuns, canonesses, beguines, anchoresses, tertiaries, and *beatas*, and also of women who fit neatly into no category, such as Catherine of Genoa, Bridget of Sweden, and Isabelle of France. Seven manuscripts preserve the life of the French peasant woman Alpais of Cudot (ca. 1150–1211) and lives of battered wives form a subset of Scandinavian hagiography.[11] Most countries of Western Europe, indeed, left a rich hagiography about holy women along with a substantial corpus of writings by them.

But not England. English holy women are, to be sure, attested, though in fewer numbers.[12] In addition to cloistered women, there is some evidence of urban women pursuing beguinesque vocations in *maisons dieu* and hospitals, and there is more ample documentation of several hundred anchoresses.[13] Though English clerics wrote guides instructing anchoresses how to live, only one wrote an anchoress's life.[14] The incomplete *vita* of that anchoress, Christina of Markyate (1096–1155), commissioned by Abbot Geoffrey of St. Albans and discontinued following his death, is the only extant biography of a late medieval Englishwoman.[15] The piety of noblewomen—Elizabeth de Burgh (d. 1360), Elizabeth

Berkeley (d. 1478), Anne Neville (d. 1485), and others—is attested through their bequests and acts of patronage but not commemorated in *vitae*. English holy women also wrote far less than their counterparts in Italy, Germany, France, or the Lowlands. Only a few female-authored saints' lives in Anglo-French survive from the twelfth and thirteenth centuries, alongside Julian of Norwich's accounts of her visions, Eleanor Hull's commentaries on the psalms, undertaken shortly before her death in 1460, and the *Book of Margery Kempe* (1436–38). Though some lives of Continental holy women appear to have circulated in Latin, the only life of a "modern" (by which I mean late medieval) holy woman available in an English vernacular prior to the fifteenth century was Nicholas Bozon's life of Elizabeth of Hungary.

Lives Untold

Two intriguing bits of untold lives occur in John Capgrave's *Abbreviation of Chronicles* (1462–63). These bits were evidently of particular interest to Capgrave because he signals each with a marginal trefoil, his personal *nota bene* mark.[16] In his entry for 1337, Capgrave writes:

> At a little town cleped Berwik, v myle fro Walsyngham on þe west syde, [was] a woman þei cleped Jewet Metles, so cleped for sche ete no mete but receyued þe sacrament on þe Sunday, and þerby lyued al þe weke. Prestes assayed þat sche schuld receyue a hoost not consecrate, but sche knewe it. Sche was examined be þe officers of þe Cherch and no defaute fond þei in hir faith, ne no synne in hir conuersacion.[17]

This Jewet was obviously something of a local celebrity. But who was she? A nun? An anchoress? A widow? A spinster? Perhaps a pious wife, like Margery Kempe? On the Continent, the kind of extreme devotion to the Eucharist that Jewet displayed inspired hagiography, as Rudolph Bell and Caroline Walker Bynum have abundantly documented.[18] But not in England. The priests Jewet encountered evidently cared only about her orthodoxy. The details of "hir conuersacion" didn't matter.

Capgrave might have written more about Jewet had more information been available to him. But perhaps not. The other English holy woman whose commemoration he marks with a trefoil was rather better documented: Joan of Acre, daughter of King Edward I and mother of Elizabeth de Burgh. Capgrave writes of Joan in his entry for 1287, the year she was "weddid onto Gilbert, herl of Gloucetir."[19] He goes on to say that she was a "ful holy woman." Though he does not elaborate on the nature of her holiness, he writes that, three years following her burial at the Austin priory at Clare, her body was exhumed and discovered uncorrupt. Capgrave details its condition in such a way that readers would immediately recognize the conventional indicators of sanctity:

> Sche was found hol in all membris: hir tetis, whan þei were pressid with handis, þe flesch ros up ageyn; hir eyeledes, left up, fel down ageyn. The cloþis þat were aboute hir, whech were dipped in wax and rosyn, þoo were roten, but þe lynand cloth whech was next hir, þat was dite with no craft, þat was found clene and hool. (131)

By conjoining the record of Joan's marriage with the physical evidence of her sanctity, Capgrave conveys a forceful message that is also conveyed elsewhere in his own hagiography and in the hagiography of his contemporaries, namely, that Jesus loves wives just as he does virgins.[20] But his entry is hardly a *vita*, and if any English woman were to be the subject of a life, it surely would have been Joan, the daughter of a king and patron of the order of two of England's most prolific hagiographers, Capgrave and Bokenham. Patronage of the Austin friars at Bokenham's home institution of Clare, Cynthia Turner Camp writes, "was not only part of Joan's duties as countess, but also a function of her personal piety," and "the friars were thriving during her tenure."[21] Bokenham was certainly cognizant both of her generosity and of her saintly reputation. In his *Mappula Angliae*, he ranks her with such well-established saints of preconquest England as King Edward the Confessor, King Edmund the Martyr, Alphege, Cuthbert, and Etheldreda, and reports that "many gret miracles" were performed at her gravesite, particularly on behalf of those who suffered from toothaches, backaches, and ague.[22] A poetic dialogue inscribed on a scroll to decorate Joan's tomb is attributed to him.[23] The dialogue begins with a secular asking a friar who "lyeth here" in "this chapel." The friar identifies the deceased as Joan and goes on to praise her and the many other patrons of the priory who were of the

Honor of Clare. Though writing the life of a holy person interred on the premises was a time-honored means for religious houses to attract wealthy benefactors and pilgrims, Joan remained, as Camp puts it, a "potential saint," whose potential was never realized in hagiography.[24] That she did not inspire a life, even by Bokenham, a path-breaking hagiographer fascinated by female sanctity, suggests just how foreign writing the lives of contemporary compatriots was to hagiographical practice in postconquest England.

A somewhat ampler "life fragment" is an account of the daily routine that Cicely, Duchess of York, followed during her widowhood.[25] This account was entered into a household ordinance sometime between 1483 and 1495. Its anonymous author, C. A. J. Armstrong hypothesizes, was probably a member of Cicely's household, writing with the "consent and . . . approval" of the duchess.[26] It describes the many and various devotions that she accommodates amidst meals, public appearances, business meetings, and recreation. Reading is an important part of her routine: at meals she listens to extracts from the *Golden Legend*, *On Infancy of the Savior*, Walter Hilton's *Treatise on the Mixed Life*, and Nicholas Love's *Mirror*; she evinced an "obvious predilection" for the lives and writings of the female mystics, including Mechtilde of Hackeborn, Catherine of Siena, and Bridget of Sweden. Tapestries depicting the Passion, along with the lives of Saint George, John the Baptist, and Mary Magdalene, adorned her chambers. Had Cicely lived on the Continent, where the lives of at least some pious rich widows were memorialized in hagiography, the details embedded in this entry might well have been embroidered into a life. But in England, it seems, if a woman wanted her story told, she would have to tell it herself. Hence, as I will discuss later, *The Book of Margery Kempe*.

An Anthology of Modern Women

If English hagiographers of the fifteenth century did not write about their own holy women, even in Latin, a few of them did translate into English the *vitae* of modern Continental women, whose lives had hitherto been available to English readers only in Latin.[27] With the establishment in 1415 of Syon Abbey, the first Bridgettine monastery, it is hardly surprising that Bridget's life and writings should have been translated. Lives of beguines were likewise Englished. Bokenham, who, as we have seen, wrote a verse life of Elizabeth of Hungary for Elizabeth de Vere, included in his Abbotsford legendary a prose life of Clare of Assisi, whose story also appears in Caxton's *Legenda aurea sanctorum*.[28] Circa 1493 and again in 1500, Wynkyn de Worde printed an English translation of Raymond of Capua's monumental life Catherine of Siena, the longest life in English of any saint.[29] In addition to their *vitae*, the revelations of Bridget and Catherine were translated, along with the visions of other Continental mystics.[30]

The earliest translations into Middle English of lives of modern women were the lives of three thirteenth-century beguines: Christina Mirabilis (ca. 1150–1224), Marie d'Oignies (ca. 1170–1213), and Elizabeth of Spalbeek (ca. 1247–1304). Their lives, along with the translation of a letter supporting Catherine of Siena's canonization penned by her Carthusian follower Stephen Maconi, are found together in a manuscript dating from the second quarter of the fifteenth century (Bodleian Library MS Douce 114).[31] The Latin *vitae* on which these lives were based had different authors, each of whom had a different relationship with his subject and took a different approach to composing her life. Writing of Marie d'Oignies, his close friend and spiritual mother, Jacques de Vitry steeped his biography in personal information. Thomas of Cantimpré, biographer of Christina Mirabilis, did not know his subject personally and perforce relied on the testimony of others. Philip of Clairvaux's "life" of Elizabeth consists mostly of his observation of her devotions during a single visit, fleshed out with information supplied to him by friends, family, and spiritual advisors.

Jennifer N. Brown, who edited the Douce lives, considers it likely that a single author translated the three lives from a Latin collection. Brown observes that the lives—first Elizabeth's, then Christina's, and finally Marie's—progress strategically from the least to the best known of the three holy women: "A reader who may not understand the nature and depth of Elizabeth's devotion has it reinforced with a more familiar name in Christina, and finally it is exemplified in Marie d'Oignies."[32] Though Douce 114 was owned by the Carthusians of Beauvale in Nottingham, the translator addresses a broad audience of "deuoute soulless that are not leeryd in Latyn tunge," women and also men.[33]

The heroines of Douce 114 engage in devotional practices that had no known counterparts in late medieval England.[34] Elizabeth daily delivers a performance of Christ's passion that on Fridays culminates in her receipt of the stigmata. Her Middle English life vividly details the cruelties she inflicts on her own body as she plays out the roles of both Christ and his tormentors. Christina, following a near-death experience, becomes "the Astonishing," whirling like a top through the streets, dangling from gibbets, leaping into hot ovens, and drinking from her own breasts. After parting company with her husband, Marie d'Oignies, often considered the first beguine, pursues a life of asceticism and charity in the company of like-minded women.

It is consistent with the conservative reputation of English spirituality that no English translations of these women's lives were made while the beguine movement was sweeping the Continent during the thirteenth and fourteenth centuries. But their translation during the early fifteenth century is something of a puzzle. Though the early beguines attracted the support of powerful clergymen such as Jacques de Vitry, their enemies grew more vocal and influential in the later thirteenth and fourteenth centuries.[35] Beguines were accused of subscribing to the heresy of the Free Spirit, and in 1310 one of them, Marguerite Porete, was burned as a heretic. The Council of Vienne in 1312 denounced the beguines for their preaching and speculative theology. What could have possessed an English translator to make available the stories of women associated with a movement that had been denounced as heretical at a time when the English Church was preoccupied with stamping out its own heretics?

One explanation, as Jennifer Brown and Patricia Kurtz have proposed, is that whoever translated or commissioned the lives actually considered them an effective answer to heresy, much as their authors appear to have done.[36] Dyan Elliott observes, "The sponsorship [by thirteenth-century Continental clerics] of certain holy women associated with the Beguine movement was an extension of the antiheretical campaign associated with Lateran IV. In the writings of these men, female piety comes to exemplify devotion to the sacraments, particularly confession and the Eucharist."[37] The same two sacraments were, in fifteenth-century England, the targets of lollard criticism. Elizabeth, Marie, and Christine combine a deep reverence for the sacraments with a creative spirituality that might appeal to fifteenth-century readers. Elizabeth's "reuelacyouns and spiritual lyfe ... figurith ... the sacramente of the auter, and of confessyon"; she confesses her sins scrupulously and demands that her devotees do likewise (Brown, *Three Women*, 45–47). Christina is restored to life precisely so that she could "stire men to repentauns and penauns" (56). Her example is meant to shame those who "dreed to do penauns for oure selfe and for oure synnes" (83). Of Marie, we are told, "if happely hit semyd to hir that she hadde trespassed any litil venial synne, she shewyd hir to a preste with so grete sorow of herte, with so mykel schame, and with so longe contricyone that . . . she was constreyned to crye loude in maner of a woman trauelynge of childe" (95). Not only are her own penitential practices detailed, but her life also includes a lengthy account of how her prayers deliver a nun who will neither confess nor partake of the Eucharist (105–8). Receiving "Crystes body" was "euen lyfe" to Marie, and "that was deth to hir to abstene and be desseuered from this sacramente" (392). The recipient of Eucharistic visions, "she sawe bytwix the prestys handes the lyknes of a feyre childe and an ooste of heuenely spirites doune-commynge with mykel lighte" (368), and "she sawe the Maydens sone as a childe with fulle grete brightnesse aboute the box in whiche the sacrament of the auter was put" (390).

The translator is aware that he is writing in an environment hostile to vernacular theologizing. Claiming to be "but symple letterd," he promises to convey faithfully the "substaunce" of his "story," while "leuying legeauns and auctorites of holy writt that wolde be ful dymme to vndirstonde if they were turnyd into Englissh withoute more declarynge of glose" (Brown, *Three Women*, 27). He omits, for example, Jacques's prologue to Marie's life on the grounds that it contains "legeauns and figuratif spekynges that are not lighte to be turnyd into Englische langage withouten moor expounynge" (86).

Yet the lives—especially Christina's and Marie's—offer a capacious definition of holiness. Like the legends we have examined in the previous chapters, they celebrate an active and informed lay Christianity that was nonetheless respectful of clerical prerogative. Christina "vndirstood soothly alle Latyn and knewe plenirly alle the menynge in scripture, thof sche neuer knewe lettir sythen she was borne" (Brown, *Three Women*, 73). She was, however, reluctant to answer "dyuyne questyons of holy wrytte" and did so "ful gretely ageyns hir wille and ful selden," "seyyng that hit byfelle to clerkys to expoune holy writte and that siche mater felle not to hir" (74). Marie, likewise, "was suffyciently byshyned with holy writte" and "bare in herte wordes of holy writte" (146). But even though she was "enformed suffycyently with holy writte," her "houge plente of mekenesse" led her to "lowe hirselfe gladly and deuoutly to othere mennes councelle" "leste she shulde seme wyse in hir owne sighte" (153).

Both blend radicalism with restraint. For example, at moments Christina behaves rather shockingly like a priest. We are told that a certain count, "knelynge byfore Cristyns feet, rehercyd to hir with ful many terys alle his synnes that hee hadde doon fro the eleuenthe yeere of his age vnto that daye" (Brown, *Three Women*, 76). Lest readers be shocked, the hagiographer quickly adds that this "confession" was made "not for indulgence—the whiche sche hadde no powere to gyf—but atte she shulde be the more stired thereby to praye for hym." Elsewhere, Christina asserts "ageyne the opinyone of alle" that a recently deceased man "hadde forgifnesse of penauns and contricyone" (66). Marie's preternatural knowledge of sinners' hearts leads one confessor to demand of his confessee, "Whethere yee haue seyde youre synnes to dame Marie?" Marie, apparently, had on a recent visit enumerated this man's sins to the confessor "as if she had sene hem writen byfore hir in a boke" (180). The beguine, readers are to understand, was not trying to infringe on the confessor's prerogative; she was only trying to work *with* him to secure a sinner's salvation. This cooperation of laity and clergy, however, could not help but challenge a rigid hierarchy that subordinated laypeople—especially laywomen—to clerical authority.

Though both Marie and Christina revere the Church and show an appropriate respect for the clergy, they are not uncritical. When a priest does not satisfy Christina's demand for the Eucharist promptly enough, she finds one who will. She reproaches a powerful lay admirer for doing "anythinge agayne righte, or holy chirche, or ministres of holy chirche," but she also "monyshed esely and priuey . . . prestys and clerkys that synned" (Brown, *Three Women*, 283). After the breaking of the Eucharistic host, Marie would see "oure Lorde abidyng in the prestys soule," illuminating his soul "with a meruelous cleerte" (149). If a priest performed the sacrament "unworthily," she "sawe that oure Lorde wente aweye with grete indignacyone and the soule of the wrecchid preste was laft tome and voyde and ful of derknesse" (149). Though there's nothing unorthodox here, some readers might find something uncomfortably lollard in the notion of a lay woman like Marie critiquing the clergy and pronouncing this or that priest fit or unfit to administer sacraments.

Though the letter from Stephen Maconi that concludes the anthology of lives is not itself a life, Jennifer Brown has discerned in it some of the same features that we have traced in the beguine lives.[38] Maconi recalls Catherine "demonstrating her theological and intellectual superiority to the pope's advisers" while still "maintaining her humility."[39] Maconi, moreover, emphasizes Catherine's devotion to the sacraments, particularly her "reliance on confession."[40] Brown postulates that Maconi's letter serves at once to establish Catherine as an important saint and "to validate the other women in the collection," whose mysticism is more "exuberant" than her subdued piety.[41] His emphasis on her teaching and intellectualism reprises a theme that pervades fifteenth-century English hagiography generally.

Clare, Elizabeth, Bridget, and Catherine

The other modern women whose lives were told in English were, by the fifteenth century, international luminaries. All were canonized: Elizabeth of Hungary in 1234, Clare of Assisi in 1255, Bridget of Sweden in 1391, and Catherine of Siena in 1461. Clare and Bridget founded orders. Catherine was a vocal reformer.[42] All defied expectations that they marry, or remarry, instead pursuing unconventional vocations. Their piety has much in common with that of the Douce saints: they are devoted to the sacraments, particularly the Eucharist; they practice a creative but wholly orthodox Christianity; they are visionaries and zealous ascetics. Catherine of Siena epitomizes the extreme fasting described so eloquently by Caroline Walker Bynum and Rudolph Bell.[43] She and her spiritual sisters all practiced self-injury, whether by wearing hair shirts or by cutting or flagellating themselves. Bridget wore not only "rough & sharp wolen cloth" but "next hir bare skyn a corde of hempe with many knottes harde bounden tohir & lyke wyse about euery of hir legges vnder hir knees"; on Fridays, she "toke wax candellys & made brennyng dropes fall von hir bare flesshe so that the brennynge marks of them contynuelly remained."[44] Extreme as these acts are, they convey the age-old message that one expresses one's love of God most perfectly through suffering. Suffering enables confessors to imitate their beloved savior and join the ranks of the martyrs.

The Middle English lives of modern Continental holy women reprise broader impulses in fifteenth-century hagiography, including an attention to the saints' emotional and spiritual lives, descriptions of the saints' relationships with family members, and the use of hagiography as a vehicle of instruction. Kurtz has described the *vitae* in Douce 114 as "essentially sermons" because the narratives are so heavily "punctuated with admonitory exhortations."[45] Like the translator of the Douce lives, the translator of the *Life of Catherine of Siena* explains to his readers that he has removed "poyntes of diuynyte whiche passeth your vnderstondyng," but what he does translate is nonetheless densely learned.[46] In his preface, he announces that, following Raymond, he will conclude each chapter by recapitulating the points readers should take away from the story. Biography thus serves instruction. Indeed, the author encourages readers to use the table of contents to "fynde what matere in the boke ye desire to here or rede," anticipating that they would be less interested in reading for the story than for what it has to say about "bodily penaunce" ("The lyf of saint Katerin of Senis," bk. 1, chap. 6), "merueylous fastynge" (bk. 2, chap. 5), "grete reuelacions" (bk. 2, chap. 6), and other topics.[47]

THE BOOK OF MARGERY KEMPE

Some of the features of these translated Continental *vitae* also characterize *The Book of Margery Kempe*, the only life that attempts to place an English woman on a par with a Saint Bridget or a Saint Elizabeth. But even though it invokes a continental European-style sanctity, the *Book of Margery Kempe* ultimately celebrates a radically different kind of saint within a radically different and distinctly insular hagiography.

Kempe's *Book* is an extraordinary generic hybrid — part saint's life, part autobiography, part devotional treatise, part social satire.[48] It survives in a single manuscript of circa 1440 that was preserved for centuries in a private collection. Until its discovery in 1936, the public knew only extracts printed by Wynkyn de Worde in 1501 and reprinted by Henry Pepwell in 1521.[49]

The *Book of Margery Kempe* is sui generis in part because, as we have seen, writing lives of contemporary holy women simply "wasn't done" in late medieval England. If we are to believe the prologue, all sorts of "worshipful clerkys," including archbishops, bishops, and doctors of divinity, were impressed with the visions Kempe revealed to them during the 1410s (*Book of Margery Kempe*, 18, 39).[50] Some "worthy and worshipful clerkys" even offered to write "a booke of hyr felyngys and hir revelacyons" (19). God, however, told her that it wasn't time, and twenty years later, when the Deity ordered her to speak, nobody was willing to listen to a woman by then widely regarded as something of a freak (19). A layman, almost certainly her son, traveled from Germany to England to assist her, but his premature death left a partially completed manuscript whose language and handwriting were so garbled that it was barely decipherable. With great difficulty Kempe badgered a local priest into translating her first scribe's work into intelligible English and then carrying on where he had left off. Far from being a chronological account of a holy life relayed by an experienced biographer, *The Book of Margery Kempe* is an assemblage of memories, relayed as Kempe remembered them and as she wished them to be presented (20).[51] Having as her final scribe a skeptic who could barely be induced to write for her in the first place made it unlikely that he would alter the story much to make her a more persuasively conventional saint.

The *Book*'s abnormality is evident from the outset. Instead of proclaiming itself to be the *vita* of a holy woman, it presents itself as a devotional tract recounting Jesus's intervention in the life of a "sinful caytyf," a sort of Everyman:

> Here begynnyth a schort tretys and a comfortabyl for synful wrecchys, wherin thei may have gret solas and comfort to hem and undyrstondyn the hy and unspecabyl mercy of ower sovereyn Savyowr Cryst Jhesu, whos name be worschepd and magnyfyed wythowten ende, that now in ower days to us unworthy deyneth to exercysen hys nobeley and hys goodnesse. Alle the werkys of ower Saviowr ben for ower exampyl and instruccyon, and what grace that he werkyth in any creatur is ower profyth yf lak of charyté be not ower hynderawnce. And therfor, be the leve of ower mercyful Lord Cryst Jhesu, to the magnyfying of hys holy name, Jhesu, this lytyl tretys schal tretyn sumdeel in parcel of hys wonderful werkys, how mercyfully, how benyngly, and how charytefully he meved and stered a synful caytyf unto hys love, whech

synful caytyf many yerys was in wyl and in purpose thorw steryng of the Holy Gost to folwyn oure Savyour, makyng gret behestys of fastyngys wyth many other dedys of penawns. And evyr sche was turned agen abak in tym of temptacyon. (*Book of Margery Kempe*, prologue, p. 17) [52]

It's only thus far into this preamble—more than halfway down the manuscript page—that we learn that Everyman is actually Every-*woman*. But as we read on, what began as a moral exemplum of God's mercy morphs into a highly circumstantial life of a singular woman: a wife, mother of fourteen, erstwhile entrepreneur, pilgrim, and would-be saint. The life, told in two books, begins with the marriage, circa 1393, of twenty-year-old Margery Brunham, referred to throughout as "this creature," to John Kempe, a "worschepful burgeys" of Lynn (*Book of Margery Kempe*, chap. 1, p. 21), and covers about forty years of her adult life before concluding with one of her prayers. We follow her failed attempts at brewing and milling, her religious epiphany, and her travels throughout England and abroad, sobbing uncontrollably and talking of God to whoever will listen. Interwoven into the account of her deeds are her visions of and conversations with Jesus, the saints, and various biblical figures. The "creature" is not named until chapter 45 of book 1, when the bishop says, "Margery . . . I knowe wel inow thu art John of Burnamys dowtyr of Lynne" (p. 112). Only in book 2, chapter 9 is she fully identified as "Mar. Kempe of Lynne" (p. 226).

For all its quirks, Kempe's story has earmarks of a saint's life.[53] She experiences visions and knows "many secret and prevy thyngys" (*Book of Margery Kempe*, prologue, p. 18). Jesus promises that she will not have to endure purgatory; rather, upon her death, "within the twynkelyng of an eye" she will "have the blysse of hevyn" (chap. 5, pp. 30–31; see also chap. 22, p. 63). He performs miracles on her behalf and helps the petitioners for whom she intercedes. Her story, moreover, incorporates tropes from the lives of Continental holy women.[54] She shares her spiritual sisters' devotion to the sacraments and expresses respect for the Church and clergy. Like Elizabeth of Spalbeek, she imagines herself participating in biblical events, albeit without ever losing her identity as Margery Kempe. Like Marie d'Oignies and Christina Mirabilis, she wears white. Like Marie, she weeps copiously and obtains her husband's consent to a chaste marriage. *The Book of Margery Kempe* certifies Kempe's holiness by directly comparing her to Bridget of Sweden, Marie d'Oignies, and Elizabeth of Hungary. In some ways, she surpasses them: her tears and white clothing were more controversial, her husband harder to win over. Jesus rewards her with a Eucharistic vision so extraordinary that even Bridget, he says, "say me nevyr in this wyse" (chap. 20, p. 58).

Kempe, like her Continental counterparts, combines flamboyant practices with indisputable orthodoxy. Under examination, she declares her strict subscription to the tenets of the Church. She manifests her devotion to the sacraments, particularly of penance and the Eucharist, at every turn: "She was schrevyn many tymes and oftyn, and dede hir penawns whatsoevyr hir confessor wold injoyne hir to do, and was governd aftyr the rewelys of the Chirch" (*Book of Margery Kempe*, chap. 4, p. 30). She urges others to confess their sins and do satisfaction (chap. 12). She attends Mass and communicates weekly (chaps. 26, 32, 51). The very sight of the Eucharist induces uncontrollable weeping (chap. 72). Anxious and upset when, during one of her trips, she "myth not be schrevyn ne howselyd," she experiences a miracle allowing her to communicate perfectly with a German priest, though the priest spoke no English and she spoke no German (chaps. 32–33, p. 86). "I am wel plesyd wyth the inasmeche as thu belevyst in alle the saramentys of Holy Chirche and in al feyth that longith therto," God tells Kempe. That this woman, certified by Jesus himself as a faithful daughter of Holy Church, is repeatedly accused of lollardy and threatened with death is an indictment of the hysteria of her accusers and of a conservative orthodoxy that labels as heresy any departure from its norms of religious practice.

Kempe professes a respect for the clergy so profound that even the Virgin Mary is taken aback. When she asks Kempe whom she wishes to have beside her when she achieves her place of honor in in heaven, the Virgin naturally expects her to wish to honor her husband or father, but Kempe instead names her confessor (*Book of Margery Kempe*, chap. 8). Kempe relies on the clergy for Communion, for confession, and for spiritual solace. She consults them about scripture and doctrine, and she enlists them to read to her. She attends sermons regularly and signals her appreciation through her roaring—an endorsement the preachers do not always appreciate. At the same time, she, like her Continental counterparts, asserts an independence from the clergy. She assumes a public role, traveling through England, speaking "redyly and pregnawntly" about God, whether they like it or not (chap. 15, p. 47). She does not hesitate to expose and rebuke clerical laxity, and she flouts orders that contravene God's. Indeed, as much as she professes to revere her confessors, she also disobeys them, Janette Dillon observes, "more frequently and openly" than any other late medieval visionary.[55] Though she denies preaching, her public teaching and her dispensing of spiritual advice encroach on clerical prerogatives.

The officers of the institutional Church and even the sacraments they provide do not wholly satisfy her spiritual needs. Penance doesn't always bring relief from temptation: "Sche was schrevyn and dede al that sche myth, but sche fonde no relesyng tyl sche was ner at dispeyr" (*Book of Margery Kempe*, chap. 21, p. 59; chap. 59, p. 143). A personal relationship with Jesus is required for that. The intensity of that relationship at times suggests that the clergy is expendable. When no priest is available, Jesus sends John the Evangelist to confess her (chap. 32). When she cannot understand sermons spoken in German, Jesus tells her, "I schal preche the and teche the myself" (chap. 41, p. 102). "Ther is no clerk in al this world that can ... leryn the bettyr than I can do, he says" (p. 153). "I am abovyn thy gostly fadyr," he insists (bk. 2, chap. 2, p. 212). After praising her because she "stondist undyr obedyens of Holy Cherch" and "wylt obey thi confessor and folwyn hys cownsel, which throw auctorité of Holy Cherch hath asoyled the of thi synnes," Jesus reminds her, "I am above al Holy Cherch" (chap. 29, p. 79). Note that Kempe always expresses appropriate respect for the clergy—"this lyfe schuldist thu schewyn to religiows men and to preistys," she protests—rather, it is *Jesus* who complains that what "I lofe best thei lofe not," pointing out that "undyr the abyte of holynes is curyd meche wykkydnes" (chap. 64, p. 154).

Even as *The Book of Margery Kempe* appropriates hagiographical conventions and pursues goals similar to the lives of Continental holy women, it also departs radically from established ways of representing a holy life, both traditional and modern. It does not claim, for example, that Kempe was holy from childhood or that she dreaded losing her virginity. To the contrary, Kempe recalls being "unkind" and "veyne" in her youth and taking "gret delectacyon" in sex (chap. 17, p. 50; chap. 3, p. 26). Her husband's body inspired "ful many delectably thowtys, fleschly lustys, and inordinate lovys" (chap. 76, p. 173). Kempe lacks the moral stamina of those female saints who are routinely threatened but not tempted. She agrees to an adulterous liaison (chap. 4, p. 29), and fantasizes about naked priests (chap. 59). What's more, she's somewhat of a coward. When accused of heresy in Canterbury and threatened with death, she "stod style, tremelyng and whakyng ful sor in hir flesch" (chap. 13, p. 42). Accused again at York, "hir flesch tremelyd and whakyd wondirly that sche was fayn to puttyn hir handys undyr hir clothis that it schulde not ben aspyed" (chap. 52, pp. 124–25). Even imagined pain is too much for her to bear:

> Sche ymagyned in hirself what deth sche mygth deyn for Crystys sake. Hyr thowt sche wold a be slayn for Goddys lofe, but dred for the poynt of deth, and therfor sche ymagyned hyrself the most soft deth, as hir thowt, for dred of inpacyens, that was to be bowndyn hyr hed and hir fet to a stokke and hir hed to be smet of wyth a scharp ex for Goddys lofe. (*Book of Margery Kempe*, chap. 14, p. 43)

What is remarkable is not so much that she experiences fear and temptation but that she admits to those emotions, to such a degree that her *vita* is more about "frelté" and "compassyon" than about perfection (chap. 72, p. 166). A holy life, it shows, includes "synnes," "labowrys," and "vexacyons," along with "contemplacyons" and "revelacyons" (chap. 69, p. 163).

The Book of Margery Kempe rejects the asceticism that put confessors on a par with early Christian martyrs. Though, as we have seen, Kempe hates to even think of suffering, Jesus tells her in no uncertain terms that suffering is unnecessary:

> I thank the, dowtyr, that thow woldyst for my lofe, for, as oftyn as thow thynkyst so, thow schalt have the same mede in hevyn as thow thu suffredyst the same deth. And yet schal no man sle the, ne fyer bren the, ne watyr drynch the, ne wynd deryn the. (*Book of Margery Kempe*, chap. 14, p. 43)

Instead of dying for him, she should weep for him, "terys of compunccyon, devocyon, and compassion" (chap. 14, p. 43). Nor need she fast, a practice "good for yong begynnars" (chap. 36, p. 94). When Jesus does order her to abstain, it is a temporary measure designed to provide a bargaining chip she can use to get her husband to agree to a chaste marriage: she will resume eating if he will give up sex (chap. 11, p. 38). Whereas Continental mystics subsisted on the Eucharist, abhorring bodily food, Kempe loves nothing better than "etyng of flesch" (chap. 5, p. 31). Instead of fasting for his love, Jesus tells her to eat for his love so that she has the strength to weep for his love (chap. 66). And she does. References to food and drink abound. When Kempe is reunited with one of her spiritual advisors, they celebrate with "a dyner of gret joy and gladnes," "sawcyd and sawryd wyth talys of Holy Scriptur" (chap. 70, p. 164).

Asceticism simply doesn't pay off, the *Book* shows. Following her religious epiphany, Kempe fasts, holds vigils, and dons a hair shirt (*Book of Margery Kempe*, chap. 3, p. 27). But instead of providing spiritual comfort, these "dedys of penawns" (prologue, p. 17) lead her to smugly reflect that "sche lovyd God mor than he hir" (chap. 4, p. 28). To punish her "presumpcyon" (chap. 4, p. 28), Jesus sends her three years of temptations she can hardly bear before ordering her to desist from self-harm: "dowtyr, thu has an hayr upon thi bakke. I wyl thu do it away, and I schal give the an hayr in thin hert that schal lyke me mych bettyr than alle the hayres in the world" (chap. 5, p. 31). The *Book* associates the sort of bodily self-harm that is routinely practiced by Bridget and her ilk with despair and depravity. When Kempe loses her mind, she rends her flesh; the vision of Jesus that restores her to her senses puts an end to such carryings-on (chap. 1, pp. 22–23). According to Jesus, listening to him speak in her soul pleases him far more than "weryng of the haburjon or of the hayr or fastyng of bred and watyr" (chap. 35, p. 94).

The *Book* is remarkable in its promotion of what I have called a "virtual holiness," wherein the desire to do something is as worthy as the act itself.[56] We have already seen that, in Jesus's eyes, wishing to suffer is good as suffering. But virtual martyrdom is just the beginning. Being a "mayden in thi sowle" is as good as being an intact virgin (*Book of Margery Kempe*, chap. 22, p. 62). Honoring "holy placys" in word or thought is as efficacious as visiting them (chap. 30, p. 82). Desiring to found abbeys and subsidize services is as good as laying out the funds (chap. 84). In fact, imagining good deeds of any kind is as good as performing them: "Dowtyr, thow schalt han as gret mede and as gret reward wyth me in hevyn for thi good servyse and the good dedys that thu hast don in thi mynde and meditacyon as yyf thu haddyst don tho same dedys wyth thy bodily wittys wythowtyn forth" (chap. 84, p. 192). When Kempe laments that the writing of her *Book* has distracted her from her prayers, Jesus assures her that "as many bedys as thu woldist seyin I accepte hem as thow thu seydist hem" (chap. 88, p. 203).

The *Book* has much in common with the hagiography of Capgrave, Lydgate, Bokenham, and their contemporaries. Downplaying pain and suffering is consonant with the tendency of fifteenth-century hagiographers to de-emphasize grisly tortures. As Katherine J. Lewis points out, the legend of Katherine of Alexandria, "the most popular virgin-martyr," was "by far the least gory of all the Middle English virgin martyr legends."[57] As we saw in chapters 2 and 3, English authors of virgin martyr legends generally were playing down not only suffering but virginity, too, to dwell on their protagonists' emotional, spiritual, and intellectual lives and to showcase their imitable virtues. Margery Kempe fits right in with Capgrave's Katherine and Bokenham's Barbara, not to mention the many lives of holy wives, such as Paula or Monica.

Kempe embodies the more spiritually and intellectually engaged paradigm of holiness being promoted by Capgrave, Bokenham, and their peers. She is "wel lernyd in the lawe of God" (*Book of Margery Kempe*, chap. 17, p. 51), having been taught by a "doctor of divinité" and "a bachelor of lawe canon, a wel labowrd man in scriptur" (chap. 69, p. 162). She knows the revelations of Bridget, the writings of Walter Hilton, and the *Stimulus Amorys* and *Incendium Amoris* of Richard Rolle (chaps. 17 and 58). She "hungryd ryth sor aftyr Goddys word" and was fortunate to have a spiritual advisor who comforted her "wyth redyng of Holy Scriptur" (chap. 58, p. 140). She diligently attends sermons. As we have seen, she imparts the knowledge she gained to others, speaking of the gospel and of other religious matters to religious and lay audiences. Relaying both what she learns and what she teaches, the *Book* is a "teaching hagiography": "Be this boke many a man schal be turnyd to me and belevyn therin," Jesus affirms (chap. 88, p. 203).

The *Book* dramatizes the conflict between the open-minded clergy who teach, support, and encourage Kempe and her reactionary detractors. When her enemies complained that her spiritual advisor, a Carmelite with unimpeachable scholarly credentials, "enformyd hir in qwestyons of Scriptur whan sche wolde any askyn him," his superior, Thomas Netter, admonished him "be vertu of obediens that he schulde no mor spekyn wyth hir ne enformyn hir in no textys of Scriptur," much to his distress, her dismay, and Jesus's disgust (*Book of Margery Kempe*, chap. 69, p. 162). Clergy who give Kempe a chance benefit from contact with her. Her hunger for edifying reading causes a "good doctor" to read more than he would have done were it not for her, resulting in a "gret encres of hys cunning and of hys meryte" (chap. 58, p. 141). The skeptical vicar of St. Stephen's in Norwich finds that he can easily spend an hour or two talking about God with a woman: "Benedicité," he'd exclaimed, when told that Kempe wanted to speak with him, "what cowd a woman ocupyn an owyer er tweyn owyrs in the lofe of owyr Lord?" (chap. 17, p. 50); Archbishop Arundel sat talking with Kempe in his garden "tyl sterrys apperyd in the firmament" (chap. 16, p. 49). Sarah Rees Jones has proposed that *The Book of Margery Kempe* was written to demonstrate how members of the clergy can productively interact with lay enthusiasts.[58] One need not accept Jones's claim that the *Book* is a male-authored text whose true subject is not Kempe but the Church to agree that it promotes an orthodoxy attuned to the needs of a spiritually precocious and intellectually demanding laity.

The *Book* shows how a woman who refuses to "don as other women don" renegotiates her relationships with the major men in her life—spiritual advisors, her earthly husband, and her heavenly spouse (*Book of Margery Kempe*, chap. 53, p. 129). We have seen how she asserts both her reliance on and her independence from her confessors and other members of the clergy. She obtains a marriage in which her husband supports her vocation and benefits from his association with her.[59] Though hurt by her priorities—"Ye arn no good wife," he protests when she declares she would not have sex with him even to save his life—her husband agrees to accompany her on her peregrinations within England (chap. 10, p. 36), and was "evyr" "redy whan alle other fayled" (chap. 15, pp. 45–46): "he was evyr a good man and an esy man to hir. Thow that he sumtyme for veyn dred lete hir alone for a tyme, yet he resortyd evyrmor ageyn to her, and had compassion of hir, and spak for hir as he durst for dred of the pepyl" (chap. 15, p. 45). When Kempe is frightened or in trouble, she looks for him before she thinks of Jesus. John can protect her in ways that even Jesus can't. When threatened with rape, she reminds would-be assailants that "sche was a mannys wife" (chap. 54, p. 132). As for her heavenly bridegroom, she remonstrates with him just as she does with her husband and her spiritual advisors. Though he is less accommodating than they—at times punishing her temerity by withdrawing his affection or by sending her temptations—he also helps her to achieve goals that are important to her, if not necessarily to him, such as her chaste marriage. He applauds the imaginative holiness that she is prepared to offer him.

Holiness, the *Book* shows, involves compromise. Iterating a major theme of fifteenth-century hagiography, it celebrates a woman who pursues an extraordinary spiritual agenda without abandoning her worldly responsibilities. She spends time conversing with Jesus *unless* "sche wer ocupiid wyth seke folke er ellys wer lettyd wyth other needful occupasyon as was necessary unto hir evyn crystyn" (*Book of Margery Kempe*, chap. 87, p. 202). When John falls and needs her constant care, Jesus assures her that "thu schalt have as meche mede for to kepyn hym and helpyn hym in hys need at hom as yyf thu wer in chirche to makyn thi preyerys" (chap. 76, p. 173).

The *Book* evolves into something wholly unlike the "schort" and "comfortabyl" treatise that its preface promises. Kempe is too distinctive to be Everyman—or Everywoman. And yet, the *Book* never wholly abandons the universalizing impulse of its preface. Most obviously, it recounts the story of "this creature" rather than of "Margery" or "I." Kempe's own view of sainthood is, moreover, democratic. When a man entreats her, "Damsel, yf evyr thu be seynt in hevyn, prey for me," she replies, "Sir, I hope ye schal be a seynt yowrselfe and every man that schal come to hevyn" (*Book of Margery Kempe*, chap. 53, p. 130).

The extracts, which were perhaps made shortly after the full text of her *Book* was completed and first printed under the title "A shorte treatyse of contemplacyon taught by our lorde Ihesu cryste, or taken out of the boke of Margerie kempe of lynn," do transform the *Book* into a "short tretys and a comfortabyl" and in so doing explain how "every man" can become a "seynt in hevyn."[60] They have not been much studied.[61] Scholars of the *Book* are generally disappointed with their subordination of Kempe's voice to Jesus's and the removal of the what to us are the most fascinating components of her story: where she went, what she did, whom she talked to, what others thought of her, and what she thought of others, of Jesus, and of herself. The material world Kempe inhabited is replaced with one that strikes readers as "reductive and anodyne," the "product of censorship"; in lieu of radicalism readers encounter an unobjectionable piety.[62]

To my mind, however, the extracts actually distill the *Book*'s radicalism by making its essential features more readily apparent and hence easier for anybody to appropriate. Holiness, the extracts insist, relies on feats of the mind rather than of the body: pilgrimages and fasting can be replaced by "good wylles & good desyres" (Meech, *Book of Margery Kempe*, 355). They show Kempe transforming the material world through thought as she perceives the Savior in a beaten horse or an injured man. They preserve Jesus's criticism of "relygyous men" and "prestes" for being less receptive to his will than Kempe (357). The extracts' endorsement of lay piety and their messages about how best to please God would have been infinitely more empowering to a fifteenth-century readership than the experiences of a singular woman or a vivid rendering of the material reality they experienced on a day-to-day basis.[63]

The *Book* was not the only text to undergo such a distillation. Henry Pepwell reprinted the extracts in an anthology that also included a condensed version of the life of Catherine of Siena: "Here followeth Divers Doctrines Devout and Fruitful, Taken out of the Life of that Glorious Virgin and Spouse of Our Lord, Saint Katherin of Seenes."[64] The abridgment of Catherine's life was created through roughly the same editorial principals that produced *The Book of Margery Kempe*.[65] The events of Catherine's life were edited out, leaving only advice on leading a holy life that was given to her by Jesus or that was given by her to others.

The extracts concerning these holy moderns, Catherine and Margery, complement each other on certain points: both stress the importance of compassion and patience; both explain how the ordinary Christian can lead a life pleasing to God; both close the chasm between saints and the rank-and-file faithful. On one major point, however, they differ: the value of pain. Though particular acts of self-harm are not detailed, the Catherine extracts insist on the importance of suffering for Jesus's love.[66] Jesus tells Catherine, "the more pain ye suffer for My love, the more like ye be to Me" (Gardner, *Cell of Self-Knowledge*, 40). Enduring pain on earth allows one to "escape endless pains" (43). Like one of Jacobus de Voragine's virgin martyrs, Catherine not only tolerates but relishes "intolerable pains": "I have chosen pain for my refreshing, and therefore it is not hard to me to suffer them, but rather delectable for the love of my Savior, as long as it pleaseth His Majesty that I shall suffer them" (44). The emphasis on bodily harm, of course, is true to the complete life, which emphasizes Catherine's heroic asceticism and calls her a "glorious vyrgyn and Martyr."[67] It is significant, I think, that the Margery Kempe extracts directly follow Catherine's. The first point Jesus addresses with Margery is the relationship between suffering and holiness: Margery wants to die for the love of Jesus, and Jesus tells her that thinking of him pleases him more than suffering for him. The "great fasters" and "great doers of penance" think that they are pursuing the "best life," but they are mistaken (Gardner, *Cell of Self-Knowledge*, 52); their feats are for beginners. In light of Jesus's instructions to Margery, Pepwell's readers might heave a sigh of relief and conclude that the pain they were being enjoined to suffer isn't bodily pain after all but rather the kind of mental anguish Margery experiences by empathizing with Christ. The Continental model of sanctity based on extreme asceticism gives way to something more "comfortable," something more genuinely insular.

In her stimulating monograph, *Margery Kempe and the Lonely Reader*, Rebecca Krug proposes that Margery Kempe, dissatisfied with the devotional literature available to her, created the book that she wished she had, a book that expressed her understanding of "the nature of spiritual joy and comfort."[68] I propose that Margery engaged similarly with the tradition of life-writing. The available models did not speak to her understanding of a holy life, so she created a form of sacred biography that did. In doing so, she creatively appropriated existing models. Lives of Continental holy women such as Marie d'Oignies would have showed her that "modern" women, including wives, were fitting subjects of sacred biography, that one did not need to be a late antique desert mother or virgin martyr to have a story worth telling. They supplied some useful tropes. Contemporary renderings of desert mothers and virgin martyrs, for their part, would have showed her that blessedness does not require perfection. But the idea that sanctity likewise does not require extreme suffering or deprivation was largely Margery's own contribution to the tradition of sacred biography. As a *vita*, *The Book of Margery Kempe* may have resonated with contemporary readers as profoundly as Krug proposes it resonated as a book of consolation. I would like to think so; however, with little evidence of wide distribution or of imitators, it may also have been as anomalous as it today appears. The extracts offered by Wynkyn de Worde and Henry Pepwell show that Margery Kempe was still being read decades later, though they distill her *Book* to something less singular, more open to interpretation, and perhaps more appealing.

CHAPTER FIVE

Golden Legends and Foxe's *Acts and Monuments*

Rethinking the Hagiographical Anthology

Jacobus de Voragine was by far the most influential hagiographer of the late Middle Ages.[1] We have seen in previous chapters how many Middle English hagiographers used chapters from his *Legenda aurea* as their principal source, even if they modified his narratives significantly. In England, the first full-scale translations of the *Legenda aurea* were not undertaken until the fifteenth century, which produced three English "Golden Legends."[2] The first, known as the *Gilte Legende*, was completed in 1438 by a hagiographer who identifies himself only as a "synfulle wrecche" writing for the benefit of "symple lettrid men and women."[3] The second, dating from the middle of the fifteenth century, was the work of Osbern Bokenham, England's most prolific hagiographer, writing "at the instaunce of my specialle frendis."[4] The third, William Caxton's *Legenda aurea sanctorum, sive Lombardica historia*, first published in 1483 and reprinted regularly into the 1520s, was undertaken to provide salutary reading for lay men and women.

It is in some ways surprising that the first complete translations of the *Legenda aurea* should appear during a century when new paradigms of sainthood were supplanting the models promoted by Jacobus. Against the family-oriented, world-affirming hagiography of the day, with its celebration of Christian intellectualism, Jacobus's legends seem a blast from the past. Do the Middle English golden legendaries represent a backlash against more capacious definitions of sainthood? Probably not. Caxton, more keen on promoting brisk sales than any religious ideology, is an unlikely agent for such a backlash. As for Bokenham, we have witnessed his enthusiastic promotion of the period's new approach to sanctity. Instead, I will argue, these three English "Golden Legends" *both* attest to the stature and sustained influence of Jacobus's *Legenda aurea* as a hagiographical classic *and* signal a resistance to its vision. Thus, although each of the three is usually faithful to Jacobus's *Legenda aurea* when translating from it, each also engages in far more than mere translation. To varying degrees, each Middle English hagiographer replaces or supplements Jacobus's hagiographies with texts that are inimical to his austere and antiworldly model of sainthood. After examining these fifteenth-century legendaries, I will turn to the sixteenth-century anthology that explicitly claims to repudiate the approach to sanctity embodied in the *Legenda aurea*, John Foxe's *Acts and Monuments*. Surprisingly enough, I will argue, a similar process of revision and preservation characterizes his own legendary, which, like its Middle English predecessors (though in different ways), is less revolutionary than revisionary.

1438 *Gilte Legende*, and the "Additional Lives"

We know next to nothing about the "synfulle wrecche" (we'll call him the "Wretch") who undertook the translation of the *Legenda aurea* in the 1430s. We do know (because he tells us in a colophon) that he was not working directly from Jacobus's Latin text but rather from a French translation of it. Scholars have identified that French source as Jean de Vignay's *Légende dorée*, a close translation of the *Legenda aurea* produced during the third quarter of the fourteenth century.[5] The anonymous hagiographer's purpose is wholly unexceptional: "to excite and stere simple lettrid men and women to encrese in virtue bi the often redinge and hiring of this boke. For bi hiring mannes bileuinge is mooste stablid and istrengthid" (Hamer, *Gilte Legende*, 1:3). His translation is conservative, and he adds only a few chapters to his original, mostly chapters dealing feasts of the Church, but also the lives of three saints: Katherine, Alban, and Malchus.

These three lives are very much in tune with broader fifteenth-century trends. The Wretch's life of Katherine is a version of the 1420 prose life we considered in chapter 3, and his "Alban" has much in common with Lydgate's. Both Katherine's and Alban's stories are embedded within sharply defined historical moments. Both texts are invested in British history, which they link with the history of the Roman Empire. At the same time, they also show a distinctly inward orientation with their attention to spirituality and to their protagonists' conversions. Both register emotional turmoil. Katherine hates offending her mother and her friends as she pursues a truth she intuits but does not know. Alban, initially skeptical of Christianity, struggles to overcome his prejudices and fears.

Most remarkable, however, is the "Life of Malchus," the only Middle English saint's life told in the first person. The Wretch's source is Jerome's Latin *Life of Malchus*, composed circa 391.[6] Jerome claims in that *vita* to have met Malchus during the 370s, when the latter was an old man cohabitating with an elderly woman. Surprised, he asked Malchus about his unusual living arrangement and claims to report Malchus's story just as Malchus relayed it to him. And as Jerome reported it to his fourth-century readers, the Wretch relays it more than a millennium later, one saint's story nested within another's, the only such hagiography in Middle English.

Malchus, an only child, flees home because his father wants him to marry and he wants to be a monk. The runaway joins an abbey at Maronias, about thirty miles outside Antioch, but after spending some years there, he longs for home—he's heard his father has died and he plans to comfort his mother and to use his inheritance for charitable works and his own upkeep. Over the vigorous opposition of his abbot, he sets out on his journey but is captured and enslaved by Saracens. The Saracens force him to marry a fellow prisoner, but the couple agrees to live together chastely. Eventually they escape and return to Maronias.

Jerome's is the only surviving record of Malchus's life and may have been pure invention.[7] The cohabitation of holy men and women was controversial in Jerome's day, and, as we would expect, hetero-spiritual couples, that is, friends united in their pursuit of God, were rarely the subject of hagiography. Jerome had come under attack for his friendship with the widow Paula, and the life may, as Christa Gray suggests, have been written as an apology for his own lifestyle, providing "a venerable precedent for the type of chaste-yet-intimate relationship for which he saw himself vilified."[8] In any case, it is an idiosyncratic saint's life.

Though technically the life of a desert father, it is closer to Greek romance than to the more conventional lives of Anthony, Paul, or Hilarion.[9] Its medley of genres—including comedy—makes it something of a literary tour de force, "an exotic, thrilling, and beautifully presented piece of literature which is essentially Christian despite its debts to Classical culture."[10] Malchus is, as Gray puts it, "an unlikely hero for a holy man's biography"; indeed, his presentation is parodic at points.[11] To this most unconventional life, however, Jerome appended a conventional moral, admonishing virgins "to guard their virginity" and exhorting his readers to "tell the story to future generations, so that they may know that amid swords, deserts, and wild beasts chastity is never taken captive, and that a man who is devoted to Christ may die but cannot be defeated."[12] Contradicting his earlier assertion that Malchus and the old woman were cohabitating in Maronias, he concludes by having Malchus claim, "I returned myself to the monks; the woman I handed over to the virgins, loving her as a sister but not entrusting myself to her as a sister."[13]

Malchus's story was told twice in Anglo-Saxon England. Aldhelm abbreviated it (drastically) for his prose *De virginitate* (ca. 675), removing all reference to Malchus's spiritual marriage and transforming him into a virgin martyr who "preferred to die transfixed cruelly by the sword rather than to defend his life by profaning the laws of chastity, fearing in no way the danger to his soul if the status of his virginity were preserved intact."[14] A complete translation of Jerome's original into Old English was also undertaken during the heyday of the monastic reform movement in the tenth century. Perhaps, as Peter Dendle proposes, the story was valued as a warning of what mishaps may befall the monk who disobeys his abbot.[15] It is no wonder that Jacobus de Voragine, wholly uninterested in eliciting chuckles, did not include Malchus's life in his *Legenda aurea*. Nor is it to be found in any of the manuscripts of the *South English Legendary*, whose compilers seem to have largely shared Jacobus's vision of sainthood. The offbeat life of a desert father, however, was very much in keeping with the more capacious tastes in hagiography that had evolved in fifteenth-century England. In Englishing it for his readers, the Wretch extracts from it a moral congenial to a devout lay audience, namely, that they should "wel laboure" to keep "holy scripture" in mind and "to folue the werkes therof" (Hamer, *Gilte Legende*, 1:347). Malchus, indeed, embodies a biblically authorized, creative alternative to Jacobus's model of sanctity.

Malchus is a prime example of the more vulnerable, less conventionally heroic saints whose stories were much in vogue in fifteenth-century England. Stubborn and headstrong, he disobeys not only his biological father but also his spiritual father. Unlike Jacobus's martyrs and confessors, Malchus fears bodily harm and is anxious to avoid it: he travels west to avoid the "periles" of "wicked people" in Egypt. His account of escaping from the Saracens is a litany of his dreads, both real and imagined: he dreads being overtaken and killed by his angry master; he dreads the serpents, scorpions, and other venomous beasts he might encounter while hiding in a cave; he dreads the lioness who kills his master and his servant; he dreads the night. Malchus describes himself as a man caught between dreads and incapacitated by them. As his enemies search the cave he's hiding in, dread at once tempts him to surrender and keeps him from doing so: "We entered into the caue for the ouer gret drede that we hadde of oure maister whanne we herde hym, for moche more greued vs the dethe that we abode though we hadde suffered it. I hadde so gret drede that though I wolde haue spoke I myght not, for though my lorde had called me I myght not one worde haue ansuered hym" (Hamer, *Gilte Legende*, 1:353). Much like Margery Kempe, Malchus at no point expresses the pious confidence that God will protect him from danger. In fact, when he considers whether he ought to rely on God's help or commit suicide, he attempts suicide (1:351).

Unlike the saints of the *Legenda aurea*, Malchus is willing to compromise. He serves his Saracen masters faithfully, reminding himself of the "words of the apostell that saiethe that a man shulde as truly serue his lorde as God in rightwisnesse" (Hamer, *Gilte Legende*, 1:350). He convinces himself that by following the examples of the Old Testament patriarchs, he has remained true to his faith: "Ther as I was in [the waste] desert with my bestis I recorded witheinne myselff how Iacob and Moyses were kepers of bestes in desert. I ete none other mete but melke and softe praiers towards oure Lorde and saide suche psalms as I hadde lerned in the abbey, and in this lyff I delited me gretly sith I myght none otherwise do" (1:350). When his master rewards his good service by offering him a wife, he attempts to decline: "I tolde hym that I hadde liued chastely al my liff and purposed for to so forthe" (1:350).[16] But when the Saracen remonstrates with his sword, he quickly gives in: "I was in the gret desert and was sore aferde to lese my liff and tolde hym that I wolde do alle his wille" (1:351). Though Malchus has just married to avoid death, in the privacy of the bridal bower he bewails the prospect of losing his virginity, avers that death would be preferable, and puts his own sword to his breast. Whether feigned or sincere, the performance pays off: his wife protests that she will not be responsible for his death and suggests that they simply not consummate the marriage.

Despite his compromises, Malchus thrives spiritually, navigates numerous perils, and lives with his wife to a ripe old age, respected and admired by everyone who meets him. The Wretch omits Jerome's assertion that Malchus and his wife parted ways once they returned to Maronias, having Malchus tell Jerome, "we haue euer continued oure lyues sithe we come togedre in chastite" (Hamer, *Gilte Legende*, 1:355). He thus unequivocally affirms the spiritual partnership that obtains within marriage—a theme that, along with his promotion of a scripturally based life, is eminently appropriate for a lay audience.

The *Gilte Legende* survives roughly complete in seven manuscripts. An eighth manuscript preserves the first half of it. Three of these manuscripts have been substantially embellished, mostly with lives of British Isles saints: Winifred, Erkenwald, Edmund of Abingdon, Bridget of Ireland, Edward the Martyr, Frideswide, Edmund the Martyr, Augustine of Canterbury, Oswald, Dunstan, Aldhelm, Kenelm, Cuthbert, and Brendan. Many of the additional lives are relatively brief prose renderings of narratives found in the *South English Legendary*; some, however, are historically and psychologically rich narratives in the spirit of "Malchus," "Alban," and "Katherine."[17]

The life of Edward the Confessor, found in one of the three elaborated manuscripts, is a case in point. It begins with an extended description of the turbulent state of England prior to the Confessor's ascension to the throne, and of the messy path that led to his coronation. Edward, much like the *Gilte Legende*'s Katherine of Alexandria, is torn between his spiritual aspirations and his secular responsibilities. When his subjects urge him to marry, he agonizes about what course to take: "He was than gretely astonyed, dredyng to lese the tresoure of his virgynite, the which was kepte in a bretelle and a fulle frayle vesselle. And what that he shulde do or saye he wyste not, for if he shulde obstinately denye it he drad leste his avowe in chastite shulde be opynly knowen, and if he consented thereto he drad to lese his chastite" (Hamer and Russell, *Supplementary Lives*, 9).[18] Ultimately, he bows to pressure and entrusts his virginity to God, who provides a bride willing to embrace a chaste marriage. As king, he is shown "in jugement fulle discrete" (7), discharging his duties conscientiously, listening to counsel, and, where necessary, compromising his religious pursuits for the good of his people. Thanks to his judicious governance and God's favor, England enjoyed peace.

The life of Edmund of Abingdon also caters to modern tastes. In keeping with the fifteenth-century interest in devout women, it devotes considerable attention to the pious practices of Edmund's mother, Mabel (saying nothing about his father). We learn of how she raised her two sons to be devout, hair shirt–wearing young men. Her influence, indeed, extends beyond the grave: Edmund chooses to study divinity because she appeared to him in a dream and instructed him to do so. As in so many fifteenth-century *vitae*, education is a recurring theme of Edmund's life: the training he receives as a student at Oxford, the erudition he acquires through diligent study, and the knowledge he imparts through his teaching and preaching. The lives of Jerome and Augustine of Canterbury added to the *Gilte Legende* similarly focus on the saints as intellectuals and proselytes who battle error and ignorance through education.[19]

Two of the embellished manuscripts of the *Gilte Legende* substitute for the Wretch's faithful translation of Jacobus's life of Thomas Becket a far longer and more complex biography. Like the life of Edmund of Abingdon, this life devotes considerable attention to Thomas's mother, depicted as a resourceful, determined, intrepid, and intelligent Muslim, whose qualities the saint inherited. The treatment of Thomas's career in this "new" *vita* is not only longer than Jacobus's but more complex politically and morally. Where Jacobus represented the struggle between Thomas and King Henry as a simple conflict between Church and state, right and wrong, the Wretch offers a more evenhanded and detailed treatment, acknowledging that Thomas was pitted against not only the English king but also against the English bishops. He charts the deterioration of a healthy friendship between Thomas and the king, and he portrays Thomas not as an unyielding champion of God but as a pragmatist who at times compromises. Jacobus concludes by relaying the grisly retribution God wreaks on Thomas's murderers: "Some of them gnawed their fingers to bits, others became slavering idiots; some were stricken with paralysis, still others went mad and perished miserably."[20] The reviser, more interested in relaying a moral lesson than a spectacular retribution, has them realize their enormous mistake and dread God's just vengeance (he does not say what became of them).

Bokenham and Caxton

Bokenham and Caxton were far more radical in their "translations" of the *Legenda aurea*. Unfortunately, as discussed in chapter 2, the single surviving manuscript of Bokenham's translation is incomplete. Its 175 surviving chapters, each on a saint or major Church festival, are arranged, conventionally enough, according to the liturgical calendar; however, its strange amalgam of prose and verse is decidedly unconventional, as is much of its content.

Bokenham had already written numerous verse saints' lives when he undertook his *Legenda aurea* project, probably in the mid-1450s. Those verse legends, as I have discussed in chapter 2, suggest that he did not find Jacobus's approach altogether congenial. It is hardly surprising, then, that though Bokenham's Abbotsford legendary is recognizably derived from Jacobus's *Legenda aurea*, it is no straightforward Englishing. Thirteen of Bokenham's own, previously written verse lives, with references to friends and patrons scrupulously excised, replace translations from Jacobus to produce a hybrid prose/verse legendary that is, to the best of my knowledge, unique among medieval legendaries. Bokenham apparently did not have the leisure to recast all of Jacobus's legends: some he translated fairly faithfully, others, Simon Horobin observes, he tweaked in ways that model a "core set of sound moral and social values."[21] He used whatever more liberal adaptations of Jacobus's legends he already had to hand, even if the verse clashed with the prose. Moreover, Bokenham supplemented Jacobus's *Legenda aurea* with prose lives of at least forty saints.

Most of Bokenham's added lives fall into one or more of three overlapping categories: British saints, female saints, and educators.[22] I have already discussed in previous chapters his varied representation of holy women, from devout matrons to zealous virgin preachers, and his predilection for Anglo-Saxon missionaries, scholars, and reformers. The addition of these lives alters the character of the *Legenda aurea* found in Jacobus. Indeed, Bokenham does not appear to have thought of his collection as a translation of the *Legenda aurea* so much as a new work based on Jacobus's: in one of his later writings, he refers to it as "the englische boke the whiche y haue compiled of legenda aurea and of oþer famous legends."[23]

Caxton goes a step further by claiming that the legends he adds are his collection's raison d'être. He initially states that he will be translating the *Legenda aurea* because, just as gold is more noble than other metals, "thys legende [is] holden moost noble aboue al other werkys."[24] He then addresses those who might wonder why he's translating anew a work that has already been translated into English by explaining that he has on hand three legendaries with somewhat different contents — one in French, another in Latin, and a third in English — that he proposes to combine into one. The result is the most comprehensive *Golden Legend* in Middle English, but it is not a *Legenda aurea* that Jacobus de Voragine would have recognized. Of Caxton's 250 chapters, about 70 not are not found in Jacobus's collection, and more than 40 are not found in either of the prior Middle English translations. Like Bokenham, Caxton includes lives of many learned Anglo-Saxons; in addition to lives of the missionaries and teachers celebrated in Bede's *Ecclesiastical History*, he provides the only surviving Middle English life of Bede himself. Perhaps most surprisingly, Caxton includes the "lives" of thirteen Old Testament figures whose stories are translated from scripture with little embellishment.[25]

Caxton's added lives are consistent with the predilection for history that he shared with his readership and with what we know of the piety of the London bourgeoisie and upper classes. Few of them are martyrs, and instead of describing dramatic confrontations and grisly mutilations, Caxton celebrates the sober and imitable piety of good folk. In lieu of social, political, and religious radicals, he proffers as exemplars saints who respect authority and who achieve respect themselves through labor and intelligence. In legend after legend, Caxton expounds his protagonists' virtues of charity, discipline, compassion, studiousness, patience, humility, and social responsibility. Miracles are comparatively scarce, and they occur usually to manifest the saints' compassion for others through cures, exorcisms, or rescues rather than to display a privilege or prerogative designed to chastise, frighten, or intimidate.

A case in point is Caxton's "signature" life, that of the Roche, which he explicitly bills as *his* translation. Roche, an obedient and affectionate son, lives modestly and devotes his life to good works, particularly among the sick, whom he serves with dedication and patience—not only curing their maladies but also comforting and counseling them. Though he heals others, he is himself not immune from pain, and Caxton presents him not only as an intercessor who might protect readers from the plague but also as an exemplar whose patient suffering transmutes illness into a form of penitence.

Caxton's other French saints exhibit a similarly accessible piety based on compassion for others. Saint Ives, we read, was "euer redy to oryson or predycacion or ellys he was studyeng in the holy scryptures or doyng werkys of charyte and pyte" (Caxton, *Legenda aurea sanctorum*, 427). Just as Ives lives his life according to "the doctryne of the apostles," Genevieve, knowing that virginity alone does not make one holy, seeks to live hers according to the precepts outlined in scripture. Initiative—particularly the zeal to learn—enables Saint Turien to rise from a shepherd in the bishop's household to become an archbishop. Saint Rigobert, archbishop of Rheims, is humble, prudent, self-disciplined, and devoted to the needs of his flock: "By the multyplycacion also of hys good doctrynes many one ledde a lyf of holy conuersacyon ... thus he gaue hym selfe to alle folke / trauayllyng alweye for theyr saluacyon" (425). Though a recluse, Fiacre harbors poor wayfarers who travel past his cell. Arnold, another recluse, gives up his cherished life of solitude to become a bishop. The few martyrs Caxton adds to his collection embody the same virtues: French shoemakers and Christian proselytes Crispin and Crispinian eschew profit to work *pro bono*; indeed, they are arrested as they are repairing the shoes of poor people. The rare postmortem miracles Caxton includes—like those performed by Saint Landry—tend to illustrate the saints' compassion for others rather than to reinforce their singularity.

Caxton's most frequent embellishments occur within lives of saints with British connections. For example, he concludes his life of Saint George by explaining the martyr's importance as England's patron saint, whose name roused English soldiers to battle, whose chivalry inspired the Order of the Garter, and whose heart rests at Windsor Castle in a college endowed in his honor, which also houses a bit of his head. The heart, Caxton adds, a "grete and a precious relyque" (*Legenda aurea sanctorum*, 157), was a gift to King Henry V from Emperor Sigismund of Germany, a brother of the Order of the Garter. For Jacobus's life of Katherine, Caxton, like the Wretch, substitutes a version of the 1420 prose life of Katherine, whose prologue links Katherine to kings of England. For Jacobus's life of Thomas Becket, he substitutes an abbreviated version of the life that was added to the *Gilte Legende*, which preserves the earlier English life's representation of the complex politics that lead to Thomas's martyrdom.

The illustrations Caxton included in his 1487 edition of *Legenda aurea sanctorum* are heavily slanted towards British and biblical saints. Twenty-eight of the seventy-five miniatures depict biblical saints—Old Testament "saints," the apostles, and the Evangelists. The scriptural orientation of the legendary is underscored by the scenes from the Bible or the apocryphal gospels: the Nativity, visitation of the Three Kings, Conception of Mary, Purification of Mary, the Annunciation, Death of John the Baptist, Assumption of Mary, and Birth of Mary. The second largest category of saints are British natives, missionaries to Britain, and saints otherwise associated with Britain (Gregory the Great, Katherine of Alexandria, and George).

Caxton reinforces through his images the bourgeois piety evinced in his additions and revisions to Jacobus's *Legenda aurea*. Whereas illustrated manuscripts of the *Legenda aurea* and Jean de Vignay's French translation tend to depict lurid acts of violence, Caxton is prone to represent the saints and martyrs as respectable denizens of the world, whom he commemorates with portraits rather than with sensationalized scenes.[26] The violent ends of martyrs are discreetly signaled through the emblems they bear; the main impression is of decorum and devotion. The saints, in short, were reassuringly like the men and women who perused the book.

In her groundbreaking monograph *The Legenda Aurea: A Reexamination of Its Paradoxical History*, Sherry Reames surveyed the manifold criticisms leveled against Jacobus de Voragine's magnum opus during the sixteenth century, particularly by Catholic reformers distressed that it offered "exaggerated and unbelievable pictures of human conduct instead of edifying ones."[27] She wondered whether at least some of Jacobus's medieval translators might have worked to mitigate his harsh view of sanctity and "to add explicit lessons or stories designed to edify a lay audience."[28] As I hope to have shown, fifteenth-century English translators did exactly that. These translators appear to have "Englished" Jacobus's legendary not because they found his understanding of sainthood congenial, but only because the *Legenda aurea* was comprehensive and had acquired the authority of a classic. As for why fifteenth-century writers wished to produce English legendaries at all, we need only recall that period's taste for encyclopedic productions as evinced in undertakings ranging from John Lydgate's *Troy Book* and *Fall of Princes* to Thomas Malory's *Morte Darthur*. Jacobus's *Legenda aurea* provided an authoritative foundation that was adapted to later tastes and values, at first modestly and tentatively, in the *Gilte Legende*, but more confidently and freely by the hands of Bokenham and Caxton. Like a parish church that, though sturdy, no longer suited contemporary needs and tastes, Jacobus's *Legenda aurea* underwent a stunning process of alteration, partial demolition, and accretion, evolving into a hybrid that could retain its name and history while boasting modern conveniences.

From Golden Legend to Leaden Legend: John Foxe's *Acts and Monuments*

If the medieval English *Golden Legends* renovated the metaphorical church, John Foxe undertook to raze it in his *Acts and Monuments*, the most renowned English legendary of any period. The first edition appeared in 1563, a large codex of 1,800 pages, which covered the history of the Church from circa 1000 to the ascension of Elizabeth.[29] In 1570 a revised and expanded edition of 2,300 pages was published, "so thoroughly rewritten as to constitute a separate work."[30] Among other material, the edition added a substantial history of the early Church, which celebrated many of the martyrs whose lives had been recounted in Jacobus's *Legenda aurea* and its translations. The *Acts and Monuments* underwent two further editions under Foxe's direction in 1576 and 1583. Because this vast undertaking was the product of a team of researchers and writers, Foxe was not, as Thomas S. Freeman points out, its author in the usual sense of having written it all himself, but rather in the looser sense of having shaped it and controlled its messages: "[Foxe] could be compared to the conductor of a large orchestra, where the musicians have each written their own scores, and the conductor has then orchestrated them into one harmonious composition. . . . the themes of the text are presented with complete assurance. It says exactly what Foxe wishes it to say, and absolutely nothing else."[31]

Foxe may have intended his work "to be owned and read by individuals," but it was too expensive for most budgets.[32] It was, however, readily accessible in churches; indeed, in 1571 the Privy Council mandated that it should be "set up in every cathedral church, and in the homes of chapter clergy."[33]

John King says that Foxe "designed" his work "to supplant medieval hagiographies, which celebrated the alleged ability of the saints to work miracles, cures and magical feats."[34] Foxe complained that "þe stories of Sainctes haue bene poudered and sawsed wyth dyuers vntrue additions and fabulous inuentions of men, who eyther of a superstitious deuotion, or of a subtill practise, haue so mingle mangled their stories & liues, þat almost nothyng remaineth in them simple & vncorrupte" (Foxe, *Acts and Monuments*, 145).[35] The so-called *Legenda aurea* was for Foxe not golden but leaden, the nadir of medieval hagiography.[36] Foxe promised to draw his information from "auncient autors," rather than from medieval sources that "are wont to paynt out the liues and histories of good men, with fayned additions of foreged miracles" (75). Yet his representation of saints has more in common with Jacobus's legendary than he admits, and his revisionary legendary is not unlike the Middle English adaptations of the *Legenda aurea*.

The chief way in which the lives contained in Foxe's *Acts and Monuments* resemble the hagiography of fifteenth-century England is their attention to intellectual and family life.[37] These themes are abundantly illustrated in the best-known sections of the *Acts and Monuments*, those dealing with the Tudor martyrs. Foxe typically begins his lives of Tudor martyrs with some reference to their education. Many of his protagonists are Cambridge- or Oxford-trained theologians whose scholarly habits Foxe describes at length. But Foxe is also concerned with the intellectual lives of humbler students of scripture, as a few examples will show. There is blind old Joan Waste, "herselfe vnlearned" but inspired by the preaching of "diuers learned men," who saves her meager earnings to buy a New Testament so that others can read to her every day.[38] So "greate" was her "desire . . . to vnderstande and haue printed in her memory and saiynges of holy Scriptures" that she learned whole chapters by heart and used them to teach others and to defend her faith against inquisitors. Raulins White the fisherman was likewise "altogether vnlearned, & withall very simple" (*Acts and Monuments*, 1765), but he satisfied his own "great desire" for knowledge by sending his son to school and having him read to him every night. Thanks to his "great industry and indeuour in holy Scripture," his "singulare gift of memory," and his son's ongoing assistance, "he became in that countrey both a notable and open professour of the truth." And Foxe holds up the town of Hadley, Suffolk, as a model community, for there, thanks to the preaching of Master Thomas Bilney, not only men, but women, children, and servants became so well-versed in scripture "that the whole towne seemed rather an Vniuersitie of the learned, then a towne of Clothmakyng, or laboryng people" (1732).

Knowledge and intellectual curiosity are good, Foxe insists, because they lead people to the truth, transforming Julius Palmer, for example, from an "obstinate Papist" to "an earnest Gospeller" (*Acts and Monuments*, 2157). Conversions such as Palmer's threaten the Catholic state, which retaliates by attempting to prohibit the pursuit and dissemination of knowledge. William Hunter was arrested after a priest saw him reading scripture in English. Edmund Allen the miller got in trouble for publicly "reading . . . the scriptures and interpreting them" (2205). The Marian persecutions were for Foxe nothing less than an assault on scripture, vividly demonstrated when Hunter's adversary, frustrated at being out-argued, "tooke vp the Byble and turned the leaues, and then flong it downe againe in . . . a fury" (1753). Foxe writes that the state actively pursued teachers of scripture in the hope "that the people being terrified with example of these great learned men condemned, neuer would ne durst once route against their violent religion" (1744).

Closely related in the *Acts and Monuments* to the theme of Christian intellectual life is that of family. Repeatedly Foxe shows families nurturing an educated, scripture-based Christianity that is then shared with the broader community. Raulins White, the illiterate fisherman taught by his son, is of course a case in point. John Bradford is a more typical example: "His parentes did bryng him vp in learnyng frō his infancy, vntill he attayned such knowledge in the Latin toung, and skil in writyng, that he was able to gayne his own liuing in some honest condition" (*Acts and Monuments*, 1818). Even where there is not a narrative connection, learning and family appear to be closely connected in Foxe's mind and are often mentioned in the same paragraph, or even sentence: Bishop Hooper went to Zurich, where he "married his wife and applied very studiously to the Hebrue tounge" (1943). Though Foxe insists that love of God must come before love of family, he most typically shows family members nurturing each other's faith and encouraging each other in their final hours. He movingly portrays the love among siblings, between parents and children, and between spouses. And he shows family members worrying about each other's material, and also spiritual, welfare. In anticipation of his seizure, Thomas Watts, the draper, was careful to provide for his family: he "sold and made away his cloth in his Shop, and disposed his thynges beyng set in order to his wife and children" (1808).

Foxe takes pains to distinguish laudable chastity from dubious career virginity, and his accounts of Tudor martyrs include long and detailed defenses of marriage. Indeed, some invert the popular medieval genre of the virgin martyr legend by celebrating clergymen persecuted for being married. When Bishop Hooper appears before his inquisitors, their first question is whether he is married. "Yea, my Lord, &, tyl death vnmary me" (*Acts and Monuments*, 1717), he replies. His marital state appears to eclipse other concerns in the minds of his accusers: "They bade the Notaries write that he was maryed, and sayd, that he would not go from his wife, and that he beleued not the corporall presence in the sacrament, wherefore he was woorthy to be depriued from hys bishoprike" (1718). Marriage also figures prominently in Foxe's account of Rowland Taylor, who boasts repeatedly of his wife and his nine children: "I am maried in deede, and I haue had nine children in holy Matrimony, I thanke God: and this I am sure of, that your procedinges now . . . agaynst Priests mariages is þe mayntenance of the doctrine of deuils, agaynst naturall law, Ciuill law, Canon law, generall Councels, Canons of the Apostles, auncient doctors, & Gods lawes" (1736). On the eve of his execution, Rowland tells one of his sons, "Flie from whoredome, and hate all filthy liuing, remembring that I thy father doe dye in the defence of holy mariage" (1739). Just before his death, he iterates this point, summoning his son and saying to the bystanders, "Good people, this is mine own sonne, begotten of my body in lawfull matrimony: and God bee blessed for lawfull matrimony" (1740). In a variant on a common virgin martyr theme, Taylor declares that Christ is "more faythfull and fauourable" than any human husband, but he nonetheless urges his wife to remarry after his death (1739).

In the second edition of his *Acts and Monuments*, published in 1570, Foxe adds to his account of Protestant martyrs a history of the early Church, which links the modern martyrs with the heroes of old.

In it, he carefully anticipates the themes of family and teaching that he will develop in later books on the Tudor martyrs. His principal source, Eusebius, supplies a great deal of material about early Christian thinkers and writers, some of which also speaks to the importance of family. The Church Father Origen offers an early example of Christian intellectualism nourished within the family: "His father . . . brought him vpon from his youth most studiouslye in all good literature, but especiallye in the reading and exercise of holye scripture"; and much to his father's delight, Origen "would moue questions to his father, of the meaning of this place, or that place of the scripture" (*Acts and Monuments*, 92).

As he does in his accounts of religious persecution under Mary Tudor, Foxe emphasizes the anti-intellectual impulses that propel the mass killings of Christians. Diocletian orders the public burning of Bibles. Maximinus strategically seeks "the teachers and leaders of the church, thinking therby the sooner to vanquishe the reste, if the captaynes and guydes of them were remoued out of the waye" (*Acts and Monuments*, 8). Likewise, Licinius "slew those that were the worthiest men amongest the Doctors and Prelates." (135). This nefarious Licinius, who "though[t] no vice woorse became a prince, then learning, because he himself was vnlearned" (135), stands in striking contrast to the "bountiful & gracious" Constantine, who has "a desire to nourish learning & good artes, & did often times vse to reade, write, & study himselfe" (152).

Foxe offers numerous examples of families—siblings, spouses, parents, and children—who suffer together under the Roman persecutions. Moreover, following in the footsteps of fifteenth-century revisionary hagiographers such as Lydgate and Bokenham, he uses virgin martyrs to convey paradigms of familial piety. Saint Cecilia is a case in point. In Jacobus's account, in the earliest recorded account of her life, and in many others, including Chaucer's, Cecilia rebuffs her bridegroom on their wedding night, warning that an angel will strike him dead if he so much as touches her. With the help of miraculous signs, she converts him, his brother, and many others to Christianity, and they all die for their faith. Foxe, in the tradition of Bokenham, offers Cecilia as a model wife and teacher who makes converts through "reasons and godly exhortations" rather than through "straunge miracles" (*Acts and Monuments*, 98). He omits altogether the story of how she avoids the marriage debt—a startling omission, but one that had a precedent in the account of Cecilia that John Capgrave provides in his *Solace of Pilgrims*.³⁹ Like Foxe, Capgrave praised Cecilia for converting her husband and many others and for being "hardy on to þe deth," while omitting the well-known account of her chaste marriage and of the miracles associated with her martyrdom.⁴⁰ In a manner of speaking, Capgrave out-Foxes Foxe by celebrating Cecilia as a reader of scripture.

Foxe likewise appropriates the story of the virgin martyr Eugenia, who, as legend has it, disguises herself as a man and joins a monastery in order to escape marriage and to learn more about Christianity. Her life, Foxe admits, is "a long history full of straunge and prodigious miracles." But certain facets of that "history" are amenable to his promotion of Christian family and intellectual life, and those are the facets he relays to his Protestant readers. Eugenia is "diligently brought vp by her parents in the study of science & learning." She disguises herself as a man in order to study "more boldlye" with a Christian *bishop* (not the *abbot* of his source) in "a societie of Christians" (Foxe very much doubts it was a monastery). Foxe's Eugenia has no aversion to marriage per se, though he allows that her desire to escape an *inappropriate* marriage (to a pagan, that is) *may* have factored into her decision to leave home. In recounting her eventual conversion of her family, Foxe makes Eugenia's father into something of a Raulins White prototype, who educated the child, who in turn educates him: "Philippus the father of her by nature, nowe by grace was begotten of his owne daughter to a more perfect lyfe" (*Acts and Monuments*, 117).

We find many other virgin martyrs in Foxe's *Acts and Monuments*. To make these saints amenable to his project of promoting a family-oriented piety, Foxe, following the practice of fifteenth-century hagiographers, consistently tones down or omits their commitment to celibacy, even when it is attested in an eminently reliable (that is, ancient) source. For example, where Eusebius writes of Potamiaena's "endless . . . struggle . . . in defense of her chastity and virginity," Foxe more ambiguously says that "she could not be remoued from her profession" (*Acts and Monuments*, 93).⁴¹ Foxe's Saint Agnes, "young & not maryable" (144), is persecuted simply for her faith and not because she rejects a well-connected suitor. Foxe edits out stories of dysfunctional families—recounting, for example, Saint Barbara's great suffering, but omitting mention of her father's role in bringing it about.

Foxe's celebration of family and his promotion of an informed, educated Christianity is very much in keeping with trends evident since the early fifteenth century—yet, as Alice Dailey has shown, Foxe also draws on modes of narrating saints' lives that were characteristic of Jacobus de Voragine's *Legenda aurea*, modes that, I have argued, fifteenth-century hagiographers were less inclined to use. Foxe's martyrs, Dailey observes, demonstrate the "invulnerability" that is "a hallmark of *The Golden Legend*."[42] His legends dramatize a struggle between good and evil that is quintessentially Jacobian, with guilelessly innocent martyrs facing a "caricatured representation of consummate evil."[43] The illustrations reinforce these themes, representing intrepid martyrs, serene in their torment.[44] Dailey argues that by adhering to a Jacobian mode of representing martyrdom Foxe made his protagonists "legible" as martyrs to his sixteenth-century readers: "One of the central arguments of the English Reformation was that the Protestant church was not invented by Martin Luther and John Calvin but claims a continuous history all the way back to the apostles. And one of the most effective ways of solidifying this argument was by consciously connecting Reformers' executions with established notions of what constitutes a legible martyr's death."[45] I agree, but with a caveat. Dailey and others view Jacobus's *Legenda aurea* as *representative* of "medieval martyrological structures and topoi."[46] This view is understandable, given its broad circulation both in Latin and in translation. In fact, however, the *Legend aurea* offered just one configuration of those structures and topoi, one that, albeit influential, had encountered much pushback, *even in translations of the Legenda aurea*. Foxe appropriated Jacobus's diametric opposition between good and evil, right and wrong, not because it was *the* way of representing martyrs, but because it better suited Foxe's political agenda of demonizing Catholics than the morally complex and nuanced accounts being told during the fifteenth century. Foxe was researching and writing about martyrdom during the reign of Mary I, which saw "the most concentrated persecution of religious dissidents in English history"; Mary I died in 1558, just five years before he published the first edition of his *Acts and Monuments*, and during the decades when his magnum opus was printed and reprinted "there seemed to be a real possibility that the Reformation might be defeated."[47] Foxe aimed, among other things, to make that eventuality as terrifying as possible for his Protestant readers.

Foxe's relationship to Catholic hagiographical antecedents is more troubled than he pretends. Though he boasts of his scrupulous scholarship, he celebrates saints such as Katherine and Barbara whose very existence is attested by *no* ancient authors. He cites the story of Katherine of Alexandria to illustrate medieval hagiographers' "mingle mangling" of the truth (*Acts and Monuments*, 145). Foxe claims to "nothing doubt" that "in her lyfe was great holines, in her knowledge excellencie, in her death constancie"; however, the story of "good Katherine" that has come down to us is full with "straunge fictions." Foxe's disdain for the "incredible" and "impudent" stories that have been told about the saint is hardly surprising, but what is surprising is his detailed recital of them:

> As where Petrus de Natalibus, writyng of her conuersion declareth, howe that Katherine sleepyng before a certayne picture or table of the crucifixe, Christe with his mother Mary appeared vnto her: And when Mary had offred her to Christ to be his wife, he first refused her for her blacknes. The next tyme, she beyng baptised, Mary appearing agayne, offred her to mary with Christ, who then beyng liked, was espoused to him and maried, hauing a golden ring the same tyme put on her finger in her slepe, &c. (145)

The claim that Katherine was imprisoned "semeth heterto not muche to digres from truth"; other facets of Katherine's legend, less colorful than the story of her mystical marriage, he breezes through without addressing their plausibility one way or another: her encounter with Maxentius, her conversation with an angel, her debate with the fifty philosophers, her conversion of the emperor's wife and kinsman, and her torture and execution. His narration of her debate with the philosophers takes the form of refusing to narrate: "this also I omit concerning the .50. Philosophers, whom she in disputation conuicted, and conuerted vnto our religion, and dyedmartyrs [*sic*] for the same" (145).

Foxe's treatment of the Eustace legend is similarly vexed. Eustace's legend, which, like Katherine's, has no early witnesses, reads much like a romance: the saint is converted when, during a hunting expedition, the crucified Christ appears to him between the antlers of a stag.[48] Shortly thereafter, plague and rapine impoverish him; shipmen abduct his wife and wild animals seize his children. After many adventures, he is reunited with his family, but the next day the Roman emperor, discovering that Eustace and his family are Christians, executes them all. Foxe strips the legend of its romance elements to provide an unobjectionable account of the martyr's death:

> There was one Eustachius, a Captaine, whom Traianus in tyme past had sent out to warre agaynst the Barbarians. After he had by Gods grace valiauntly subdued hys enemies, and now was returnyng home with victory: Hadrian for ioy meetyng him in his iourney, to bring him home with triumphe, by the way first would do sacrifice to Apollo, for the victory gotten, willyng also Eustachius to do the same with him. But when Eustachius could be no meanes thereto be inforced, beyng brought to Rome, there with hys wife and children suffered Martyrdome, vnder the foresayd Hadrian. (*Acts and Monuments*, 79)

But he can't resist telling readers about what he left out, dedicating about as many words to the spurious incidents as he did to the plausible core:

> It were a long processe here to recite all the miracles contained and read in this story of this Eustachius concernyng his conuersion, and death. How the crucifixe appeared to him betwene the hornes of an harte. Of the sauyng of his wife from the shipmen. Of one of his sonnes saued from the Lyon, the other saued from the Wolfe. Of their miraculous preseruation from the wild beastes, from the tormentes of fire, mentioned in Bergomensis, and Vincentius & other. All which as I finde them in no auncient recordes, so I leaue them to their authors and compilers of the Legendes. (79)

The same method informs his chapter on Eugenia. As we have seen, Foxe transforms "long history full of straunge and prodigious miracles" into one that promotes Christian family and intellectual life (*Acts and Monuments*, 117). But he also tells readers what he will not tell them:

> Here by the wai I omit the myracles of the foresayd Helenus (bishop as the story sayth of Hierapolis) howe he caried burnyng coales in hys lap, and how he aduentred him selfe to go in the burning fire, to refell wicked Zereas a Pagane, remayning in the same

vnburned. Here also I omyt the careful search of her parentes for her, and of the answer of the Pythonysse againe vnto them, that she was taken vp to the heauen among the Goddesses. I omyt moreouer the myracles done by the sayde Eugenia, in healing the diseases and sicknesses of suche as came to her. &c. (117)

What is interesting is that when Caxton revised Eugenia's legend he silently omitted the very incidents that Foxe talks about omitting. He also omitted Eugenia's aversion to marriage and radically abridged Jacobus's account of how a woman attempts to seduce "Brother Eugenius" and accuses him of rape when she fails. Caxton's Eugenia, like Foxe's, is an exemplar of faith, perseverance, and filial piety rather than of defiance and celibacy. But in producing a simple story of faith and perseverance without the sensational, Caxton has again out-Foxed Foxe.

In their views of sainthood, the medieval translators of Jacobus's *Legenda aurea* are much like Foxe, its disparager. Foxe, as we see, is not as averse as he claims to wonder-laden medieval legends. Like Bokenham, Caxton, and the Wretch, he reforms but does not reject altogether the tradition of hagiography that Jacobus embodied. I have tried to point to some of the complications in Foxe's relationship to medieval hagiography. Foxe presents himself as working against that tradition, and in many ways he is, but the very real tensions obscure important affinities. Foxe did not have much to say about saints, such as Katherine and Barbara, who most interested his fifteenth-century predecessors; in cases such as Audrey, he did not even approve of them. But he couldn't resist including them, and their trademark miracles, even when his ancient authorities didn't attest to their existence. He shared with fifteenth-century hagiographers an understanding of holiness founded on intellectualism and a respect for secular institutions such as family. And in his treatment of the early martyrs, he shared their method of reforming saints rather than discarding them altogether — even though, with his genuine concern for authority, he works by elision alone and not by embellishment.

What do the affinities between Foxe and the late medieval hagiographical tradition tell us? I am not at all arguing that Foxe read Bokenham, Lydgate, Capgrave, or any of the many anonymous hagiographers I have discussed in this book. The only medieval English hagiography he almost certainly knew is Caxton's *Legenda aurea sanctorum*. But these writers both reflected and helped shape the intellectual climate that preceded the Reformation. They exemplify a strain of orthodox resistance to the narrow and repressive policies of conservatives within the English Church hierarchy; though they loathe Wycliffe and the lollards, whom Foxe would later celebrate, they sympathize with the ideal of an informed faith and deprecate the preference for persecution and censorship over disputation and education that produced trials and executions rather than conversions. Understanding the richness of fifteenth-century orthodoxy helps us better understand the foundations not only of Foxe's hagiography but of Reformation piety more generally.

AFTERWORD

Afterlives

In the preceding chapters, I have described a major shift in the portrayal of saints in fifteenth-century England. Middle English lives of the late thirteenth and fourteenth centuries, from the *South English Legendary* to Chaucer's Second Nun's Tale, were very much in the tradition of Jacobus de Voragine's *Legenda aurea*, representing the saints as embodiments of perfection and workers of miracles, persons far superior to the rank-and-file faithful. Without jettisoning miracles, hagiographers of the fifteenth century highlighted the blessed qualities that their readers could aspire to emulate. Many of the protagonists of fifteenth-century lives were vulnerable to fear and temptation. They grappled with moral dilemmas and had to reconcile their secular responsibilities with their pursuit of heaven. In richly contextualized narratives, fifteenth-century hagiographers imagined not only their protagonists' inner struggles but also the social and political circumstances that induced those struggles. Though socially conservative in their celebration of marriage and family, fifteenth-century lives endorsed transgressive behavior if it was required to nurture an informed, intellectualized faith. Christian intellectualism, indeed, is the sine qua non of much fifteenth-century hagiography. It is enshrined in the new lives of Church Fathers that were being written but also in the lives of female teachers, preachers, and scholars, from Katherine of Alexandria to Catherine of Siena.

Here I want to take an exploratory look at the "afterlife" of the trends I have been tracing. What I have encountered in the hagiography of the Renaissance convinces me that both the approaches to writing the lives of the saints and the ideals embodied in fifteenth-century hagiography persisted into the early sixteenth century and underwent a renaissance of their own during the first half of the seventeenth century.

Epic Hagiography, circa 1515

Of course, it is hardly surprising that those features should be conspicuously present in saints' lives composed during the early sixteenth century, a period that is reasonably claimed as part of the "long fifteenth century." That continuity is abundantly evident in the hagiography of Alexander Barclay and Henry Bradshaw, both Benedictines self-consciously following in the footsteps of their famous Benedictine predecessor John Lydgate. Shortly before his death in 1513, Bradshaw, a monk at the Abbey of St. Werburge in Chester, completed a life of his abbey's patroness, a seventh-century abbess of Ely, which Richard Pynson published in 1521.[1] Circa 1515, Barclay, then a monk of Ely, published his *Life of St. George*, dedicated to Thomas Howard, Duke of Norfolk. Unfolding in thousands of lines assembled into rhyme royal stanzas, both of these lives are manifestly "epic."[2]

Exemplarity figures prominently in both. Barclay trusts that George's example will turn "englysshe youth" from "thriftless game" to pursuits that enhance "a common welth" and their "soules helth" (Barclay, *Life of St. George*, lines 22–29).[3] The saint accordingly embodies everything a sixteenth-century youth should aspire to. Tall and muscular, with a ruddy complexion and fine golden hair that tumbles over his shoulders, he excels in sports from swordsmanship to swimming. He possesses the skills needed to be a successful courtier along with the moral fiber of a saint. Bradshaw, though he claims to have written the life of Werburge for "marchaunt men hauyng litell lernyng" (Bradshaw, *Life of Saint Werburge of Chester*, line 2016), avers that everyone will profit from knowing her life; he touts her, particularly, as an "example" for women—queens, duchesses, ladies, widows, religious, and virgins "of hie or low degree" (1999).[4] "Fayre and amiable," discreet and gracious, she is a paragon of gentility (708–49). Even when she disagrees with her parents, she cherishes and respects them, following their counsel insofar as possible and striving to please them (701–7). As a princess, she makes time to worship, study, and pray (750–56). As an abbess, she rules with fairness and perspicuity.

Like so many fifteenth-century lives, Bradshaw's *Werburge* shows a particular interest in family relations, which is conveyed as much through its structure as its story. Embedded within Werburge's life are the lives of her parents, her siblings, and members of her extended family; their stories complement hers by reinforcing certain themes and complicating others. Werburge's family members face many of the same challenges and moral dilemmas that she does but sometimes deal with them differently. They exhibit many of her virtues but also model qualities that Werburge, as a professed virgin, cannot—for example, being a good sovereign, parent, and spouse. Thus the lives of Werburge's mother and grandmother demonstrate that living in "loue and amyte" with one's spouse and producing "a noble yssue" are as worthy as the perpetual virginity that not every holy man or woman can, or should, aspire to (*Werburge*, lines 338–39).

Both *George* and *Werburge* recount political struggles. Bradshaw describes warfare, treason, and disputes over succession. He shows how otherwise judicious and honorable men can succumb to temptation or to bad advice. Werburge's grandfather Penda, as Bradshaw tells the story, supported the conversion of his people to Christianity; however, "by the temptacyon of our ghostly enemy" (*Werburge*, line 470), he died fighting in an unjust battle. Werburge's father, King Wulfer, is a princely paragon, "flourynge in manheed wysedome and policy," who

> Excelled the peres of this realme, certayne,
> In person fortitude and proued chyualry;
> Lyberall to his seruauntes gentyll in company,
> Gracyous to the poore and a sure protectour,
> A founder of chyrches and a good benefactour.
> (568–74)

Yet he falls under the influence of an ambitious steward, who secures his consent to wed Werburge. Werburge, her mother, and her brothers, astonished that the king could even contemplate marrying a princess to a steward, derail that plan. Foiled in his effort to marry into the royal family, the steward convinces the king that his sons are plotting treason, causing Wulfer, in "hastynesse and cruell fury" (1223), to kill them both, an act he immediately regrets. Wulfer's example demonstrates that rulers make mistakes, sometimes terrible mistakes; however, it also demonstrates that they can redeem themselves in the eyes of God and of the world by taking responsibility, confessing, and performing penance.

Barclay's representation of the events leading up to George's fight with the dragon endows *George* with the moral and political complexity of Lydgate's lives of Alban and Edmund. Threatened with the dragon, Barclay's king and parliament conclude that the best course of action is to agree to sacrifice two humans daily to the beast, drawing lots to determine who is to die. When the lot falls upon the king's daughter, however, the monarch balks. Surely, he protests, he cannot not be expected to sacrifice his beloved only child. Barclay presents his audience with competing political views, that "a kynge in mercy may be aboue his lawes" (610) and that "the kynge himself his lawes shuld abyde" (*Life of St. George*, line 612); however, he ultimately supports a socially conservative message consistent with Lydgate's. All people are not equal: George arrives in time to save the princess rather than one of the many commoners who died before her. His daughter's close call teaches the king proper respect for authority. The unruliness of the commons, who remonstrated with their sovereign, he learns, mirrors his own inadvertent unruliness: the king's paganism is an affront to God, who sent the dragon to punish his false faith (1016–43). Once the king and his people have accepted Christianity, a proper order can be restored and the king and commons can prosper under the auspices of the Almighty (1146, 1176).

George underscores the importance of unity and obedience in his lengthy parting speech to king, queen, and commons. The commons he exhorts to

> obey your kynge and lorde
> Obserue vnto hym loue and fydelyte
> Auoyde Rebellyon for certaynely discorde
> Is rote and mother of carefull pouerte
> Kepe eche to other loue and fydelyte
> Expell enuy and slouth moste chefe of all
> Where slouth hath place there welth is faynt and small.
> (*Life of St. George*, lines 1261–67)

He goes on to dilate on the virtues of "concorde and vnyte" (1277) and of "stedfast faythfulnes" (1281). Thrift, moderation, and compassion should guide the citizens. As for their king, his life should be "clennest from offence" (1305) because he is not only the governor but the model for his people. The clergy, too, should remember that their lives and also their words "techyth other the way to paradyce" (1322). Christianity, as George presents it, requires that "eche man" should "lyue and do / After the degree whiche he is callyd to" (1301–2). Religion is one with social and political behavior: if "your lyfe agre with your byleue," then "welth shall folowe ease and tranquylyte" (1324–25).

Both Werburge and George are shown to be effective teachers, and their lives edify on various levels. Bradshaw describes in detail how Werburge orders her private devotional life and how she governs her convent (*Life of Saint Werburge of Chester*, lines 2493–2590); he also relays the dying abbess's teachings on life and death. George models Christian chivalry and lay intellectualism. Following his conversion, he studies "the doctrine / Of christe" (*Life of St. George*, lines 239–40) and later expounds it to others. Through George's exhortations, Barclay educates his readers on subjects ranging from spiritual baptism to the responsibilities of a Christian prince.

Barclay's representation of lay learning is consonant with fifteenth-century lives from Lydgate's "George" to the lives of the beguines. Like Marie d'Oignies, Margery Kempe, Digby's Mary Magdalene, and so many of Bokenham's saints, George, a layman, performs the traditionally clerical function of teaching religion. After telling the citizens "what ryte of seruyce that they shuld exercise" (Barclay, *Life of St. George*, line 1127), he "ordeyned mynystres ... by whose example and lyfe of holynes / Lay men might lerne" (1390–91) and leaves instructions for these newly minted clergy "in wrytyng playne and clere" (1140). The radicalism of a layman ordaining and training clergy is balanced, however, by Barclay's description of George's obedience to proper clerical authority: after leaving Salena, George sojourns with the Carmelites, who inculcate the disdain for worldly life that will enable him to confront the pagan oppressors and to endure martyrdom.

A Seventeenth-Century "Renaissance"

Later in the sixteenth century, lives of early Christian saints and of medieval holy people were eclipsed by lives of contemporary martyrs,

Protestant or Catholic. However, the values enshrined in hagiography from Lydgate to Barclay were integral to the English culture of reform, with its emphasis on "Scripture, godly living, [and] a true and lively faith."[5] Those values flourished well after the lives that helped promote them were being published and read. They inform, as I argued in chapter 5, Foxe's "reformed" paradigm of sanctity. They also inform the reformed Catholic hagiography of the early seventeenth century, whose hagiographers were largely as eager as Foxe to dissociate themselves from a "medieval" tradition perceived to favor wonders over the Word of God.

After a hiatus of almost a century, what I will call "traditional hagiography," namely, the writing of lives of late antique and medieval saints, underwent a renaissance among Catholics during the first half of the seventeenth century, producing narratives strongly in the tradition of those written in fifteenth- and early sixteenth-century England. Hagiographers of the seventeenth century shared their predecessors' fascination with British saints, particularly the denizens of preconquest Britain. Because women figured prominently in the literary culture of the seventeenth century—as they had in the fifteenth—it is not surprising that they were well represented in hagiography: J. T. Rhodes observes that nearly half of the printed lives published for Catholics during the seventeenth century "were about women saints and the majority of dedications were addressed to women."[6] We encounter many of the same saints and types of saints that first appeared in the fifteenth century: theologians, late antique matrons, desert mothers and fathers (including the tremulous Malchus), and late medieval holy people. Seventeenth-century hagiography privileges family life, study, and social responsibility and often embeds accounts of individual lives within lavish political and historical contexts. A strong humanizing impulse is evident in lives that capture the saints' vulnerability and delineate their emotions, intellectualism, and spirituality.

Exemplarity appears to have governed Catholic hagiographers' selection of saints to write about and their treatment of the saints' lives. As John Falconer put it in the preface to his *Life of Saint Catherine of Sweden* (1634), "the fruit of reading Saintes Liues, is chiefly indeed an imitation of their Vertues," emphasizing that Catherine's "were both eminent and very imitable."[7] Henry Hawkins, among the period's most prolific hagiographers, likewise emphasized imitability. He proposed the life of Saint Aldegond as "a liuely imitable patterne... to either Sex" and translated a collection of lives of male confessors whose "Examples," "not so miraculous, or stupendious, as virtuous," were "not vneasy to bee imitated."[8] "My scope and intention," he declares in his life of Malachy, is "to demonstrate those thinges which in his life are most imitable."[9]

Hawkins's collection, *Fuga saeculi. Or the holy hatred of the world* (1632), translated from a tract by Giovanni Pietro Maffei, consists of seventeen lives of holy men, fifteen prelates and two kings. The prelates include renowned scholars and theologians, such as Thomas Aquinas and Anselm of Canterbury. Perhaps sensitive to the accusation that Catholics are indifferent to scripture, Hawkins takes every opportunity to present his protagonists as devout scholars of the Bible whose teachings were grounded in "the authorityes of the sacred scriptures" (*Fuga saeculi*, 213).

Effective teaching is a recurring theme. Hawkins uses Malachy's good example to criticize those who "vndertake to teach the same which they haue not learned, and go gathering and multiplying Scholers without euer hauing been at school" (*Fuga saeculi*, 5); poor teachers "seeme to know well the Syllables of sacred Sentence, but not awhit the sense therof" (5, 7). A good teacher knows how to pitch his message. Bishop Hugh's lessons "were efficacious and liuely, and fitly accommodated to each condition and quality of persons" (276). Anthony of Padua "wanted not iudgment to discerne the difference of his Auditours, nor skill and practize to deale with the rich, with the poore, with the noble and ignoble, according to the capacity, and nature, and state of ech one" (296). A true teacher genuinely cares about the well-being of his flock: even as an old man, Malachy never gave up his "ancient vse to go on foote, to preach himselfe in person," a "truly Euangelicall" habit that ought to be practiced by more teachers (36). Abbot Pachomius taught those who have no pastors and are "consequently depriued of the word of God, and the holy Communion" (132).

Hawkins presents Bernard of Clairvaux as an object lesson on the importance of teaching well. Though a great scholar, he induced in his pupils "a certaine sadness and timidity," particularly among the "yonger" members of his audiences (*Fuga saeculi*, 211). He often "soared so high" that his auditors would "loose the sight of him" and "insteed of being fed and refreshed would come to be dry and arid"

(211). "He required so curious & exact perfection of all" that instead of inspiring "hope of gaining it" his auditors "came to loose the desire & will of procuring it" (211). The learned abbot and visionary had to "learne to compassionate the weake, to temper himselfe to the capacity of the rude, and to condescend to ech what he might well do with the safety of Monasticall discipline" (211). Once he realized that, he was a new man, attending to both the spiritual and bodily needs of each person with "extraordinary tenderness and solicitude" (212).

Portraits of devout readers and scholars abound. Young Anselm, a "feruent louer of liberall arts, without sparing eyther day or night employed himselfe with singular industry, to enrich his breast with sundry knowledges of high & extraordinary things, in giuing eare to the doctor, in turning of books, in gathering notes, in framing Epitomes, in rehearsing of thinges heard, and expounding others" (*Fuga saeculi*, 312). Otho, bishop of Bamberg, "was busyed at his book," where he "attended to the study of humanity, and to some part of Philosophy" (170). When the abbot Pachomius "read or recited any things of the sacred scripture, he posted not in hast, as many are wont, but tasting and ruminating on the sentences, & precepts, one by one" in order to "deriue profit from them, and to serue the Highest with fit attention" (74). Descriptions of the saints' reading practices are sometimes lengthy. Bernard, for example,

> fayled not to read, and read ouer agayne whole bookes at tymes, and in the very reading was accustomed with particuler delight and profit of spirit, to stick vpon the text and words of the sacred Scripture, with leasure ruminating vpon them, and therewith deducing rare and strange conceipts, and therewith afterwardes helping himselfe with that copy, elegancy, and dexterity, as his diuine treatises & discourses shew. And notwithstanding with much humility also, he would consider the studyes and interpretations of the Fathers and Catholique doctors. (201)

Hawkins's scholars are not all prelates. King Stephen strove to educate himself so that he could implement "iustice, as well towards God as to mortals," which he understood to be "the nerues, and sinews of empire" (265). Unsure of "his owne knowledge," he would "ordinarily recurre partly to the documents of diuine scriptures, wherin day and night, he made himself very conuersant, and partly to the counsayle of prudent and learned men" (265).

Hawkins celebrates saints devoted not just to God but to the public good. All his saints, as he writes in his introduction, led their lives "so much in Solitude, as in Community," and were wholly invested in the welfare of their communities. King Stephen brought his faith to "publique meetings," where he would speak "with merueilous efficacy" of Christian virtues (*Fuga saeculi*, 263). He was assiduous in dispensing peace and pursuing justice (265). King Edward was a "Pastour of his people" (292). Bishop Otho—"pious and learned," "wise and discreet"—"negotiated affaires of no small importance" with "learning and integrity" (171). Abbot Bernard "was none of those, who vnder pretext of contemplation, eschew trauayle, or els for priuate gust, forgo the publique good" (200); he undertook "so great variety of vniuersall businesses . . . without neglecting euer the custody of his hart" (251). Laurence Justinian, patriarch of Venice, "goouerned his House, and the Citty, with singular fruit and edification of all" (372). "Whether he studied, or wrote, or made his prayer," he was never too busy to tend to those who called upon him (379).

Though the anthology deals overwhelmingly with celibate men, it does not neglect family life. Many of the lives describe the roles that parents—especially mothers—play in the education and spiritual development of the saints. Bishop Andrew's "faythfull parents trained" him in "learning" and "manners" (*Fuga saeculi*, 346). Fulgentius, bishop of Ruspa, was educated by his mother; Malachy's mother taught him "the feare of God" (3) to complement the lessons in grammar he learned in school. The influence of his mother, Aletta, guided Bernard even after her death (193). Bernard "aboue all . . . obeyed his Elders with great reuerence," evincing a respect characteristic of Hawkins's saints (190). Those elders model behavior appropriate to the laity. Bernard's mother was a "matrone surely most noble, truly pious, and worthy to be imitated of all those who in coniugall state, hauing the body in power of the husband, with the soule do seeke to serue and please Christ only" (191). Wives and husbands, such as Edward the Confessor and Edith, are praised for being partners in holiness.

Humanizing the saints meant conveying their mental anguish. Edward the Confessor agonizes when forced to choose between his responsibility to marry and his desire to remain chaste and between his responsibility to attend to "the quiet of the Kingdome, and necesityes of his Subiects" and a vow he made to undertake a pilgrimage to Rome (*Fuga saeculi*, 293). When Anthony of Padua was a youth, "he felt himselfe not a little to be allured by sensuality, with enticements of flatteryes" (246). Young Hugh, future bishop of Lincoln, is beset by "sharpe prickes of conscience, and scuples felt he in himself" as he was "molested day and night by the concupisiple part" (258).

Hawkins's anthology of men's lives has its counterpart in an anonymous anthology of female saints' lives preserved in British Library, MS Stowe 53.[10] The anthology, written circa 1610, contains thirty-two lives of Anglo-Saxon, Welsh, and Irish saints; a life of Queen Margaret of Scotland; a life of the thirteenth-century German visionary Mechtild; and seven lives of early Christian saints composed by Church Fathers. As its editor, Carl Horstmann, points out, it is the first English-language anthology of female saints since Thomas Burgh assembled Bokenham's female saints' lives into Arundel 327 in 1447 (Horstmann, *Lives of Women Saints*, vi). Like Bokenham, the anonymous seventeenth-century hagiographer conveys a spectrum of female sanctity that focused on exemplarity.

The heroines of Stowe 53 include nuns, wives, widows, matrons, and pilgrims. We observe their interaction with friends, family members, clergy, subordinates, and petitioners. We see them raising their children, governing their households or convents, studying, teaching, advising, traveling, making their wills, pursuing lawsuits, and coping with bereavement and other misfortunes. As they go about their lives, they model the qualities to be cultivated by a pious gentleperson, including self-control, judgment, studiousness, patience, prudence, decorum, charity, industriousness, and compassion. Lessons on matters such as childrearing are often expounded at length, as in this description of Macrina's education:

> Her mother was verie carefull to haue her well instructed, but would not permitt her to learne Poets, and such authors as vsuallie children are taught: For she thought it vnseemelie, yea filthie to haue a yong mayd defiled with the discourses of furious tragedies, or wanton comedies, or like argument or like Authors. Wherefore she caused some choice partes of holie scriptures, as of the wisedome of Salomon, and such like, which informeth to virtue and good life, to be

read vnto her. She was taught the psalmes also, a parcel whereof euerie day at sett times she had to recite. For whether she arose out of her bed or did goe to her booke or come thence; whether she went to the table, or came from the table, whether to her rest or to her prayers euermore she was rehearsing some psalms. She being thus bred, and her hands excellentlie exercised and taught to spinne, knitte and manage wooll, she was now twelue yeares olde. (Horstmann, *Lives of Women Saints*, 191)

Perhaps because confessors are more readily imitable than martyrs, only eight chapters are devoted to those who died for their faith (Ursula, Dympna, Inthware, Winifred, Ositha, Maxentia, Agnes, Julitta). Instead of lamenting women's suffering, the author prefers to show them overcoming their adversaries through eloquence, diplomacy, and wisdom. With her "virtue and patience," "faith and pietie," Ethelburga transforms her father from "a most cruell persecuter" into "a professor of Christ" (*Lives of Women Saints*, 52). Eanswide persuades her father to support her vocation by "forceible reason" and "wise discourse" (51). The author celebrates what men and women are able to achieve together. An Iberian king and queen, converted through the teaching of a (female) Christian captive, together convert their realm, the king preaching to the men, the queen to the women (187). Ermenilde and her husband, Wulfere, likewise partner to bring their people "to the knowledge and fauour of Christ" (59). Margaret of Scotland takes an active role in governing, and her husband "moste gladlie did ... obey and yield vnto her in all things" (110). Nonna was not just her husband's "helper," but in spiritual matters his "captaine and leader" (175). In addition to showcasing loving and productive marriages, legend after legend praises healthy relationships between the saints and their parents, siblings, and children. Christianity begins at home.

The legendary celebrates women "excellentlie learned in the liberall sciences" (*Lives of Women Saints*, 52), women who spend their time "conuersing with god" or listening to "his talke, by holie reading and secret inspiration" (29), women who do not let a day pass "without learning some thing of the holy scriptures" (25). These women learn, teach, advise, and mentor. Yet they also succeed in balancing their spiritual and intellectual pursuits with their mundane obligations. Nonna, for example, is "so industrious and good a housewife" that one might mistake her for one who had no inkling of "what belonged to pietyie and deuotion"; yet she is also "so whollie addicted . . . to God and diuine matters" that one might suppose "she had no medling with housholde business" (175–76). The examples of women like Nonna encourage readers to lead lives that blend piety with pragmatism, and they promote respect for the intelligence and self-discipline of those who are able to achieve that mixed life.

The qualities showcased in the legendaries I have discussed are abundantly illustrated in other contemporaneous anthologies of saints' lives and also in freestanding narratives, a few examples of which I will touch on. Though the capacious orthodoxy that had prevailed in Catholic thought during the first half of the sixteenth century was giving way, during the last quarter of that century, to a dogmatism less concerned with educating than with producing conformity,[11] we still find in Catholic hagiography of the early seventeenth century a contrarian celebration of understanding, education, and compromise—just as there had been in the fifteenth century.

Robert Howard's verse life of Mary of Egypt, published in 1640, is manifestly antihierarchical. In its concluding section, Zozilmas, a priest, has wandered into the desert, hoping to encounter "some saint-like father . . . who may instruct him in the way of grace."[12] Instead of encountering a "father," he finds Mary, a penitent, who has not seen or heard a human being for the past forty-seven years. The two become friends: they confide in each other, crave each other's blessing, encourage each other, and comfort each other. Though Zozilmas is a priest and Mary a former prostitute, he considers her his superior, and vice versa. He can consecrate the Eucharist, but she instructs him and makes him think more deeply about life and about sin. Hierarchy becomes moot as the friends strive to out-humble each other.

John Falconer's *Winifred* (1635) praises the appropriate deference of the laity to the clergy. When the priest Beuno requests land upon which to build a church, Winifred's wealthy father immediately agrees; he and his wife become Beuno's "deuout Auditours and obedient children."[13] Moreover, they put Beuno in charge of their beloved daughter's education, freely permitting her "punctuall obedience to him" (*Winifred*, 31). Winifred, however, is no passive receptacle of clerical instruction. Falconer shows her actively *choosing* a religious vocation. Stirred by "a restles and most amorous desire," she "applied herselfe to learne" from Beuno, taking in his "pious speaches, and deuout instructions" as she further "sought more and more to illuminate her soule by heauenly documents, & practicall lessons, for the direction of herselfe, & others in a spirituall and Religious life" (24) She proves such an "apt scholler" that Beuno appoints her his successor, informing her parents that it is time for him to move on but that they have in their daughter a "mistresse" fully "able to guide them in their Redeemers seruice" (66–67). Beuno's confidence is not misplaced: a woman of "discret thoughts" with "powerfull authority in commanding her subiects" (95), she ends up "wisely and maturely" governing a large convent of nuns.

Henry Hawkins uses Elizabeth of Hungary to promote discretion and compromise, qualities congenial to Catholic readers, such as his dedicatee Lady Mary Tenham, who were striving to live respectably in Caroline England without renouncing their faith.[14] From childhood, Elizabeth avoided ostentatious piety. When young, she challenged her friends to races, betting she could beat them to the church; in later years, she played cards with her ladies, but gave her winnings to charity. As a wife, she learned to "dissemble her abstinence" and was willing to give "satisfaction to the world" (*History of S. Elizabeth*, 82, 72). She dressed humbly "in the absence of her lord," but upon his return, "she put on againe more fitting cloathes, to giue content to her husband, and the rest of the court" (72). During her widowhood, she moderated her spirituality to "accommodate her children and family the better" (193). At the same time, in widowhood she struggled to preserve "the liberty of my free will" against schemers and to be "mistresse of myself" (218). Elizabeth may not have been "a Doctor of the Church," but she possessed the "spirit of the Doctors" insofar as she "laboured to catechize the children and the ignorant, and was a light of instruction to her mayds" (406).

Eschewing the emphasis on "total obedience to one's confessor"[15] that characterized much literature following Council of Trent (1545–63), Hawkins plays down the relationship between Elizabeth of Hungary and her domineering confessor, Conrad, focusing instead on Elizabeth's relationship with her husband, Louis, a relationship based on compromise and mutual respect. "There neuer was a creature caryed herself more euen betweene her heuenly and earthly spouse than Elizabeth did" (*History of S. Elizabeth*, 84): "by experience shee found that the sweet conuersation of the one diminished not the others. . . . It was an admirable thing how from her husband she could presently compose her self to prayer, and from her prayer how amiable and gracioius shee would be to her husband" (401). Elizabeth and Louis support each other's goals and aspirations, even if they disagree: Louis wishes Elizabeth would moderate her asceticism; she dreads the thought of him going on crusade. Their "harts during life seemed all as one" (402), and she was brokenhearted when he died. Similar themes of partnership between spouses, between women and clergymen, and between family members are found in Binet's joint life of Elzear Sabran and his wife, Delphine, (1638) and in Falconer's life of Catherine of Sweden (1634), which recounts the pursuit of holiness that Catherine undertakes in the company of her mother, Bridget. Lives emphasizing partnership, mutual respect, scholarship, and teaching suggest that in the seventeenth century, as in the fifteenth, hagiography pushed back against impulses towards repression.

Renaissance hagiography was not, of course, identical to fifteenth-century hagiography. In some respects, hagiographers of the sixteenth and seventeenth centuries were pushing to the next level impulses evident at the close of the Middle Ages. The exemplarity implicit in most fifteenth-century hagiography became explicit in Renaissance lives. Indeed, authors such as John Falconer *theorized* exemplarity, often at great length. The lives I have examined from the early sixteenth and seventeenth centuries indicate that the Middle Ages bequeathed to the Renaissance an approach to writing lives that is capacious and complex. Inwardly oriented, it explores the moral struggles that produce virtue. Yet it also looks outward at the worldly dynamics—historical, political, religious, social, and familial—that produce those moral struggles. Without repudiating virginity or suppressing miracles, it underscores the saints' love of family along with their devotion to Christ, and it lauds their sense of responsibility towards others. It celebrates a thirst for knowledge that goes hand in hand with a zeal to teach. Against those who favored persecution, the example of many a saint protested that knowledge is the basis of faith and education the most effective instrument of reform.

NOTES

INTRODUCTION

1. Studies of exemplarity in fifteenth-century hagiography, with particular attention to female saints, include Sanok, *Her Life Historical*; Winstead, *Virgin Martyrs*, 112–80; and Horobin, "Politics, Patronage, and Piety."

2. On Capgrave's narrative voice, see Winstead, "John Capgrave and the Chaucer Tradition."

3. See the discussion of autohagiography in Kieckhefer, *Unquiet Souls*, 6–8. I review the controversy over the *Book of Margery Kempe* as autobiography in Winstead, "Medieval Life-Writing and the Strange Case of Margery Kempe."

4. For editions of the collections of beguines and scholars, respectively, see Brown, *Three Women of Liège*, and Waters, *Virgins and Scholars*. The "family-oriented" collection I am thinking of is British Library MS Arundel 20, whose lives of Christine, Katherine, and Dorothy all take particular interest in parent–child relationships.

5. On that process of displacement, see Crane, "Anglo-Norman Cultures."

6. I examine a number of these richly contextualized sacred biographies in Winstead, *Oxford History of Life-Writing: The Middle Ages*; for more on hagiography in the French of England, see Wogan-Browne, *Saints' Lives*.

7. I discuss the narrators employed by Garnier and Capgrave in Winstead, *Oxford History of Life-Writing*, 28–31 and 173–75. See also Winstead, "John Capgrave and the Chaucer Tradition."

8. Garnier addresses Becket's sister, while Paris dedicates his life of Edmund to Isabella, Countess of Arundel. Crane discusses the importance of female authors and patrons in "sustain[ing] the precocity of Anglo-Norman literary production" in Crane, "Anglo-Norman Cultures," 45. For more on women's roles as patrons of French-language hagiography, see Wogan-Browne, *Saints' Lives*.

9. Lydgate dedicated his life of Margaret to Anne Mortimer. The countesses of Oxford and Eu were the patrons of Osbern Bokenham's lives of Elizabeth of Hungary and Mary Magdalene, respectively. Symon Wynter wrote his life of Jerome for Margaret of Clarence. On women's participation in literary culture, see Sanok, *Her Life Historical*; Meale, *Women and Literature*; and Hill, *Women and Religion*.

10. See note 9, above, for the lives of Mary Magdalene and Jerome; Capgrave composed his life of Augustine at the request of an unnamed gentlewoman.

11. Capgrave's life of Augustine and Wynter's life of Jerome.

12. Horobin, "Politics, Patronage, and Piety."

13. Armstrong, "Piety of Cicely, Duchess of York," 141.

14. Strohm, "Walking Fire."

15. See the field-shaking study of Watson, "Censorship and Cultural Change."

16. Copeland, *Pedagogy, Intellectuals, and Dissent*, 123.

17. Watson, "Censorship and Cultural Change," 826.

18. Cole, *Literature and Heresy*, xvi.

19. Kerby-Fulton, *Books under Suspicion*, 16; Catto, "After Arundel." The essays collected by Gillespie and Ghosh, *After Arundel*, convey a sense of the richness of religious writings after Arundel. See also Gayk, *Image, Text, and Religious Reform*. Unless otherwise indicated, emphasis within quotations is always the quoted author's.

20. Gillespie, "Chichile's Church."

21. See the discussion of fifteenth-century "ecclesiastical humanism" in Cole, "Heresy and Humanism," 422.

22. McSheffrey, "Heresy, Orthodoxy and English Vernacular Religion," 57.

23. Michael G. Sargent discusses "clashing texts . . . made to be neighbours in a codex" and "textual mixes" in Sargent, "Censorship or Cultural Change?," 84, 87. Lollards, McSheffrey shows, "read and profited from" writings "originally aimed at an orthodox audience," including devotional treatises and saints' lives (McSheffrey, "Heresy, Orthodoxy and English Vernacular Religion," 49). On the endurance of some of these theologically complex manuscripts into the sixteenth century, see Connolly, *Sixteenth-Century Readers, Fifteenth-Century Books*.

24. Watson, "'A clerke schulde have it of kinde for to kepe counsel,'" 587.

25. Tanner, *Heresy Trials in the Diocese of Norwich, 1428–31*.

26. Shannon McSheffrey argues that the problem for authorities wasn't the possession of heterodox tracts so much as lollards' use of even orthodox writings to bypass clerical authority—with the right books, who needs a priest? (see McSheffrey, "Heresy, Orthodoxy and English Vernacular Religion," 64–65). See also McSheffrey and Tanner, *Lollards of Coventry, 1486–1522*; appendix 2 (343–44) lists the books cited in the prosecution records.

27. For an overview of Pecock's writings and career, see Scase, *Reginald Pecock*; on Pecock's educational program, see Campbell, *The Call to Read*.

28. Somerset, *Feeling Like Saints*, 182.

29. Ibid., 137.

30. For valuable overviews of the various European traditions, see Minnis and Voaden, *Medieval Holy Women*.

31. Mulder-Bakker, *Lives of the Anchoresses*.

32. Lucy Wooding discusses the values that united Catholic and Protestant reformers until the later part of the sixteenth century in Wooding, *Rethinking Catholicism in Reformation England*. On the "fiercely contested" role of the saints in Reformation England, see Peters, *Patterns of Piety*, 207–45.

33. De Hamel, *A History of Illuminated Manuscripts*, 159. See also Harthan, *Books of Hours*; and Duffy, *Marking the Hours*.

34. This Book of Hours was produced in Flanders at the end of the fifteenth century, probably for a member of the English Bourchier family, whose heraldic knot forms part of the manuscript's original decoration. For more on the manuscript's provenance, see "MS. 349" in *The Catalogue, The Queen's College, University of Oxford*, https://www.queens.ox.ac.uk/sites/www.queens.ox.ac.uk/files/349.pdf.

35. Blanton, *Signs of Devotion*; Good, *Cult of St. George*; Brown, *Fruit of the Orchard*.

36. Recent appropriations of medieval saints' lives include Holman, *A Stolen Tongue*; Potter, *Lucy's Eyes and Margaret's Dragon*; and Setterfield, *Once Upon a River*, which uses the legend of Saint Margaret of Antioch to construct one of its protagonists.

37. Important revisionary work includes Simpson, *Reform and Cultural Revolution*; Peters *Patterns of Piety*; and N. Warren, *The Embodied Word*.

ONE   New Directions: The Hagiography of John Lydgate

1. Though Lydgate has undergone a massive reappraisal, the most thorough account of his career remains Pearsall, *John Lydgate*. See also Ebin, *John Lydgate*.

2. For discussions of Lydgate as a court poet and his much debated Lancastrian politics, see Nall, *Reading and War in Fifteenth-Century England*; Simpson, "John Lydgate"; Cole, *Literature and Heresy in the Age of Chaucer*, 131–52; Meyer-Lee, *Poets and Power*; Nolan, *John Lydgate and the Making of Public Culture*; Perkins, "Representing Advice in Lydgate"; Straker, "Propaganda, Intentionality, and the Lancastrian Lydgate"; Strohm, *England's Empty Throne*, 173–95; and Green, *Poets and Princepleasers*.

3. Quoted in Pearsall, *John Lydgate*, 30.

4. John Lydgate, *Life of Our Lady*, 240.

5. Jeremy Catto, "Religious Change under Henry V," 106.

6. For discussions of Henry's strategies, see the essays in Harris, *Henry V*, and Lewis, *Kingship and Masculinity in Late Medieval England*, 65–138.

7. On the influence of Henry V on Lydgate's ideals of kingship in that work, see Winstead, *John Capgrave's Fifteenth Century*, esp. 134–35.

8. Nolan, *John Lydgate*, 19. Though Nolan was referring specifically to Lydgate's secular writings, the sense of loss she observes can also be found in his hagiography, especially in Lydgate, *Lives of Saints Edmund and Fremund.*

9. See note 2, above.

10. See my discussion of the politics of this very odd "hagiography" in Winstead, "John Lydgate's 'Mumming at Windsor.'"

11. For a discussion of the *Testament* as hagiography, see Nisse, "'Was it not Routhe to Se?': Lydgate and the Styles of Martyrdom."

12. I discuss Lydgate's place within the "Chaucer-Lydgate" tradition of hagiography in Winstead, "Lydgate's Lives of Saints Edmund and Alban: Martyrdom and 'Prudent Pollicie.'"

13. Bale, "John Lydgate's Religious Poetry," 82.

14. For Margaret and Petronilla, see Winstead, *Virgin Martyrs*, 112–46; for Edmund, see Winstead, *John Capgrave's Fifteenth Century*, 116–37.

15. Lydgate, *Minor Poems of John Lydgate*, 145. All parenthetical references to this life are line numbers in this edition. Jennifer Floyd has persuasively argued that the life was inscribed on the tapestry itself in Floyd, "Saint George and the 'Steyned Halle.'"

16. Good, *The Cult of Saint George*; Riches, *St. George*; and Bengtson, "Saint George."

17. Brie, *The Brut or The Chronicles of England*, 2:555.

18. Bengtson, "Saint George," 326.

19. Jacobus de Voragine, *The Golden Legend*, 1:238–42. All page references will be to this translation.

20. He is ambiguous about the king's role in the pact: the *people* say, "you yourself issued this decree," but the *narrator* says that the *townspeople* "held a council" and arrived at the solution of a sacrifice determined by lottery from which "no one was exempt" (*Golden Legend*, 1:238). Other hagiographers clear up this ambiguity, in so doing justifying the people's anger.

21. On Jacobus's relentless antiworldliness, see Reames, *The Legenda aurea*. On Jacobus's thought and oeuvre, see Epstein, *Talents of Jacopo da Varagine*.

22. All line references are to "Legend of St. Gyle," in Lydgate, *The Minor Poems of John Lydgate*, 1:161–71.

23. For a list of lives of Giles, see D'Evelyn and Foster, "Saints' Legends." Giles is also included in Bokenham, *Legenda aurea*, fol. 178v–179. The contents of this manuscript, which is part of the Abbotsford Special Collections, housed at the Faculty of Advocates Library in Edinburgh, may be viewed at http://lib1.advocates.org.uk/legenda/#/1/. Simon Horobin is preparing an edition.

24. "Michael," line 4; "To St. Katherine, St. Margaret, and St. Mary Magdalene," 19; "Prayers to Ten Saints," 18.

25. Lydgate summarizes, for example, the passion of Robert of Bury and the practices and virtues of Thomas Becket; six of the eight lines devoted to Katherine of Alexandra in "Prayers to Ten Saints" recount details from her life (138–39, 140–43, 122–23).

26. For Jacobus's "Giles," see Jacobus, *Golden Legend*, 2:147–49. Quotations and pages numbers refer to this translation.

27. Lydgate, *Minor Poems of John Lydgate*, 2:193.
28. See Whatley, "John Lydgate's *Saint Austin at Compton*." See also the introduction to "Giles" in Whatley, Thompson, and Upchurch, eds., *Saints' Lives in Middle English Collections*, 213–51. I will be using this edition for quotations and line references.
29. Whatley provides an edition of this exemplum in Whatley, "John Lydgate's *Saint Austin at Compton*."
30. Whatley, "John Lydgate's *Saint Austin at Compton*," 224 (my translation).
31. For Chaucer's General Prologue portrait of the Parson, see Chaucer, *Riverside Chaucer*, 31–32. Line references and quotations are to this edition.
32. On the controversies surrounding tithing, see Robertson, "Tithe-Heresy."
33. Anne Hudson notes that many Wycliffite texts "regard tithes as legitimate payment for work done"; much criticism of tithes sprang from the resentment against the inflexible demands that unworthy priests imposed on poor parishioners (Hudson, *Premature Reformation*, 342).
34. Of course, from a theological standpoint, the lord *must* repent in order to be saved. However, Lydgate strategically defers showing him as a "penaunt" ("Austin," 302) until after he has engaged his readers' sympathies against the lord and for the priest. Only when Austin hands the priest the scourge, does the lord ask forgiveness; thereupon, he takes his scourging "with meeknesse, / Hopyng that Jhesus shuld his soule save" (331–34).
35. For the first discussion of *Edmund and Fremund* (I often shorten this title to *Edmund*) as political commentary and advice literature, see Winstead, "Lydgate's Lives of Saints Edmund and Alban," whose points are revised somewhat and elaborated in Winstead, *John Capgrave's Fifteenth Century*, 118–37; Other discussions of *Edmund*'s political themes include Camp, *Anglo-Saxon Saints' Lives as History Writing*, 173–209; Sisk, "Lydgate's Problematic Commission"; Lewis, "Edmund of East Anglia"; and Somerset, "'Hard is with Seyntis for to make Affray.'"
36. Sanok, *New Legends of England*, 173–202. Ganim discusses the "poetics of exemption" that informs Lydgate's writing, with particular attention to *Edmund*, in Ganim, "Lydgate, Location, and the Poetics of Exemption." Sanok maintains that *Edmund*'s "most urgent concern" is "the exemption of Benedictine monasteries from ecclesiastical and secular jurisdictions" (*New Legends of England*, 184), while Ganim sees a balance between the narrative's "defense of monastic privilege and exemption" and its "concern to educate the king" ("Lydgate, Location, and the Poetics of Exemption,"167), a view more congenial with my own.
37. Lydgate, *Saint Alban and Saint Amphibalus*, 198. I am using this edition for all subsequent citations of book and line numbers.
38. Howlett, "Studies in the Works of John Whethamstede," 6.
39. Ibid., 181, 199.
40. Ibid., 181, 191.
41. Ibid., 99.

42. Sanok, *New Legends of England*, 185; see 192–97 for her discussion of Lydgate's use of *Alban and Amphibalus* to address themes of jurisdiction and monastic privilege.

43. Lydgate, "George," line 197, "Margaret," line 118.

44. Lydgate, *Lives of Ss Edmund and Fremund*, l. 1045.

45. Cole, *Literature and Heresy*, 131–52 (quote on "aggressive orthodoxy" at 135). Gayk, "Images of Pity."

TWO Osbern Bokenham's Holy Women

1. Bokenham, *Legendys of Hooly Wummen*. For "Margaret," see pp. 1–38, lines 1–1400. I have used this edition for quotations and parenthetical line references for all of Bokenham's Arundel lives.

2. Edwards, "The Transmission and Audience of Osbern Bokenham's *Legendys of Hooly Wummen*."

3. Bokenham, *Legendys of Hooly Wummen*, p. 289.

4. Simon Horobin, who identified the collection as Bokenham's, is preparing an edition of this manuscript for the Early English Text Society. For more information about this collection, see the following articles by Horobin: "The Angle of Oblivioun"; "A Manuscript Found in Abbotsford House and the Lost Legendary of Osbern Bokenham"; and "Politics, Patronage, and Piety in the Work of Osbern Bokenham." In this last article, Horobin argues that Bokenham's audience surely extended beyond the East Anglian readers attested in the Arundel manuscript. He hypothesizes that the intended recipient of the manuscript was Cecily Neville, Duchess of York. For more on Bokenham's patrons, with an emphasis on his Yorkist connections, see Camp, "Bokenham and the House of York Revisited."

5. Spencer discusses Bokenham's authorizing strategies in Spencer, *Language, Lineage and Location in the Works of Osbern Bokenham*.

6. Bokenham, *Legendys of Hooly Wummen*, p. 289.

7. For discussions of Bokenham and his patrons, see Gibson, "Saint Anne and the Religion of Childbed"; Delany, *Impolitic Bodies*; and Horobin, "Politics, Patronage, and Piety in the Work of Osbern Bokenham." Moore situates Bokenham within the broader East Anglian patronage networks in Moore, "Patrons of Letters in Norfolk and Suffolk, c. 1450."

8. See Gibson, "Saint Anne and the Religion of Childbed."

9. On this point, see also Spencer, *Language, Lineage and Location*, 30–32.

10. Winstead, *Virgin Martyrs*, 112–46.

11. "Elizabeth," in Jacobus de Voragine, *Golden Legend*, 2:302–18. All quotations and parenthetical page references are to this translation.

12. Reames has explored this orientation in Reames, *The Legenda aurea*. A very different, far less severe, portrait of a happily married Elizabeth emerges from the testimony of her friends and acquaintances for her canonization procedure, as Petrakopoulos, "Sanctity and Motherhood: Elizabeth of Thuringia," shows.

13. For the development of Anne's cult in England, with an emphasis on East Anglia, see Gibson, "Saint Anne and the Religion of Childbed"; and Hill, *Women and Religion in Late Medieval Norwich*, 17–60. For the broader cult, see Ashley and Sheingorn, *Interpreting Cultural Symbols*; and Welsh, *The Cult of St. Anne*.

14. For the N-Town play's "Joachim and Anna," see Spector, *The N-Town Play*, 71–81. Citations and parenthetical line references are to this edition of the play.

15. Gibson, "The Religion of Childbed," 101. For an edition of the entire book, see Louis, *Commonplace Book of Robert Reynes of Acle*; for "Anne," see 196–228.

16. On this psychologically dense narrative, see also Sanok, *Her Life Historical*, 71–73.

17. Louis, *Commonplace Book of Robert Reynes of Acle*, p. 210, line 198.

18. Sanok, *Her Life Historical*, 73. In the only other Middle English "Anne" to relay Anne's prayer, Anne wholly identifies herself with her husband, alluding to the painful Temple episode as a time when "our ennemys sayde / Offrand to þe we suld non make" and pointing to God's intervention "for our sake" (Parker, *Life of Saint Anne*, p. 9, lines 332–36). Thereafter husband and wife, speaking in unison, commit Mary to God's service.

19. We find a visually distanced Joachim (and other fathers) in contemporary Continental representations of the holy kinship. See Sheingorn, "Appropriating the Holy Kinship."

20. Bokenham, "*Mappula Angliae*," 6.

21. For an overview of this book, its contents, history, possible readers, and some of its major themes, see Horobin, "Politics, Patronage, and Piety." On his discovery of the manuscript, see Horobin, "A Manuscript Found in Abbotsford House and the Lost Legendary of Osbern Bokenham."

22. On this point, see also Winstead, "Osbern Bokenham's 'englische boke.'"

23. For "Paula," see Bokenham, Abbotsford legendary, fols. 49v–50v; for "Monica," fols. 101v–102r.

24. Love, *Nicholas Love's Mirror of the Blessed Life of Jesus Christ*, 21.

25. Kempe, *The Book of Margery Kempe*, ed. Staley, chap. 28, p. 75.

26. For Audrey's cult in England, see Blanton, *Signs of Devotion*; and Camp, *Anglo-Saxon Saints' Lives as History Writing*, 64–101; Camp discusses Bokenham's treatment of Audrey on 77–85.

27. See Catherine Sanok's astute reading of Bokenham's emphasis on compassion, community, and companionship in his Winifred's story in Sanok, *New Legends of England*, 100–116.

28. Bokenham, *Legendys of Hooly Wummen*, lines 8277–78. His other two Valentines are Faith and Cecilia.

29. See Baudouin de Gaiffier, "La Légende Latine de Sainte Barbe par Jean de Wackerzeele"; and van Dijk, *Een rij van spiegels* (van Dijk summarizes her study in English on pp. 236–47).

30. Bokenham is here closely following Jacobus. The anonymous translator of this life in the 1438 *Gilte Legende* modifies Jacobus to mitigate the implicit

criticism of Mary Magdalene, saying that Mary "wolde do no suche seruice for her thought herselff not sufficiaunt to do seruice to so gret an oste" (Hamer, *Gilte Legende*, 2:514).

31. Bokenham follows Jacobus here, but the author of the *Gilte Legende*'s "Martha" transforms Marcella into a man, "Marcell"! See *Gilte Legende*, 2:517.

32. Jacobus de Voragine, *The Golden Legend*, 1:268–69.

33. Coens, "Une 'passio S. Apolloniae' inédite."

THREE Holy Educators and "Teaching Hagiographies"

1. See Keiser, "Patronage and Piety in Fifteenth-Century England."

2. See "Jerome," in Waters, *Virgins and Scholars*, 178–82, for the prologue.

3. Capgrave, *Life of Saint Augustine*, 15. On Capgrave's use of Augustine's life to promote Christian intellectualism, see Winstead, *John Capgrave's Fifteenth Century*, 18–50.

4. For the first freestanding life of John the Evangelist, see "Of Sayne Johne þe euangelist," in Horstmann, *Altenglische Legenden*, 466–71. The conjoined lives of the Baptist and Evangelist have been edited by Waters, *Virgins and Scholars*, 68–177.

5. Duffy notes the popularity of the "Four Latin Doctors" Ambrose, Augustine, Gregory, and Jerome, along with the apostles, or the "founders" of Christianity in Duffy, *Stripping of the Altars*, 155–60. See also Hill, *Women and Religion in Late Medieval Norwich*, 78–83.

6. John Capgrave, *Solace of Pilgrimes*, 109–10. I discuss Capgrave's anomalous portrayal of Cecilia in Winstead, *John Capgrave's Fifteenth Century*, 54–60.

7. For all quotes and page references, I am using the edition in Waters, *Virgins and Scholars*.

8. On the origins and development of Katherine's cult, see Walsh, *Cult of St Katherine of Alexandria in Early Medieval Europe*. On Katherine's cult in England, see Lewis, *Cult of Katherine of Alexandria in Late Medieval England*. On various facets of her representation, see Jenkins and Lewis, *Saint Katherine of Alexandria*.

9. For an edition of this Latin life, known as the "Vulgate" version, that circulated in England, see "Passio S. Katerine," in Ardenne and Dobson, *Seinte Katerine*, 132–203.

10. See "Seynt Katerine," in Horstmann, *Altenglische Legenden*, 242–59. This version praises Katherine for having "wyt & wysdom" (line 54), without mentioning her education; the "debate" with the philosophers takes only thirty lines. As I will discuss later in this chapter, Osbern Bokenham's "Katherine," written when he was warier of women's learning, similarly de-emphasized her erudition.

11. Winstead, *John Capgrave's Fifteenth Century*, 68; Lucas *From Author to Audience*, 127–65.

12. Caxton, *Legenda aurea sanctorum*, ccclxxxiiij, ccclxxxx.
13. Wogan-Browne, "Bodies of Belief," 404, 408.
14. Camp, "Augustine the Hermit or Augustine the Canon?" The eight "fraternal" lives within Bokenham's collection are of Augustine of Hippo, Monica, Ambrose, Simplician, Paul the hermit, Anthony, Nicholas of Tolentine, and William of Maleval; four of them (Monica, Simplician, Nicholas, and William) were not "standard" in Jacobus's *Legenda aurea* and were never before translated into Middle English. I thank Camp for providing me with a copy of her paper.
15. These lives are edited, with facing-page translations, by Clare M. Waters, *Virgins and Scholars*. The four lives are now in different collections: the conjoined lives of the Baptist and Evangelist and the life of Jerome are preserved in Cambridge, St John's College, MSS N. 16 and 17; the life of Katherine in Harvard University, Houghton Library, MS Richardson 44. All, however, were written on similarly sized parchment in the same mid-fifteenth-century hand. Waters reviews the evidence that they once formed an anthology, whose probable audience and provenance she discusses in her introduction to Waters, *Virgins and Scholars*.
16. Wogan-Browne, "Bodies of Belief," 408, 415.
17. Dresvina, *A Maid with a Dragon*, 138–39.
18. White, *Tudor Books of Saints and Martyrs*, 33.
19. Dove, *The Earliest Advocates of the English Bible*, xx.
20. For detailed studies of this extraordinary play, its context, and its themes, see Coletti, *Mary Magdalene and the Drama of Saints*; and Findon, *Lady, Hero, Saint*. For quotes and line numbers, I am using *Mary Magdalene*, in Baker, Murphy, and Hall, *Late Medieval Religious Plays of Bodleian MMS. Digby 133 and E. Museo 160*, 24–95.
21. On Capgrave's interest in family life, see Winstead, *John Capgrave's Fifteenth Century*.
22. On the development of the Mary Magdalene legend, see Ludwig, *The Making of the Magdalen*.
23. Jacobus de Voragine, *Golden Legend*, 1:375–76.
24. Douay-Rheims Catholic Bible.
25. *The Conversion of St. Paul*, in Baker, Murphy, and Hall, *Late Medieval Religious Plays*, 1–23, lines 349–52.
26. Simmons, *Lay Folks' Catechism*, 24; the corresponding Latin text is given at the bottom of the page.
27. Weatherly, *Speculum Sacerdotale*, 161.
28. Erbe, *Mirk's Festial*, 167.
29. Augustine, *On the Trinity* 1.3.5, in *Basic Writings of Saint Augustine*, 2:670.
30. See book 1 of Lombard, *The Sentences*, 12.
31. Quoted in Spencer, *English Preaching*, 124.
32. Langland, *Vision of Piers Plowman*, 15.71–72.
33. Ibid., 17.133–253. On this point, see Simpson, *Piers Plowman: An Introduction to the B-Text*, 200–202.

34. Pecock, *Reule of Crysten Religioun*, 93. Page references to this edition will hereafter be cited directly in the text.

35. On Pecock's educational program, see Campbell, *Call to Read*.

36. Mishtooni Bose comments on Pecock's turn to Latin in discussing the Trinity in Bose, "Reginald Pecock's Vernacular Voice."

37. On Capgrave's life and oeuvre, see Colledge, "John Capgrave's Literary Vocation"; Fredeman, "The Life of John Capgrave"; Lucas, *From Author to Audience*, 7–18; Seymour, *John Capgrave*; and Winstead, *John Capgrave's Fifteenth Century*, 1–17.

38. Capgrave, *Life of Saint Katherine*, prologue, line 66. Subsequent line and book references and quotations are to this edition.

39. An analogous combination of theology with affect may be seen in the "Vierges ouvrantes," statues of the Virgin Mary that open on hinges to reveal the Trinity within her womb. See Gibson, *Theater of Devotion*, 144–45, fig. 6.2.

40. Augustine, *On Faith and the Creed*, 348 (*De fide et symbol* 3.4).

41. Lombard, *The Sentences, Mystery of the Trinity*, distinction 5, 1.5.

42. On other facets of Bokenham's apparent intellectual evolution, see Winstead, "Osbern Bokenham's 'englische boke,'" in Gayk and Tonry, *Form and Reform*.

43. Bokenham, *Legendys of Hooly Wummen*. All parenthetical line references and citations use this edition.

44. Price, "Trumping Chaucer."

45. See the *Legendys of Hooly Wummen* anthology in the bibliography, as with "Katherine" above.

46. On Bokenham's East Anglian audience, see Delany, *Impolitic Bodies*; and Moore, "Patrons of Letters in Norfolk and Suffolk."

47. See Winstead, *Chaste Passions*, 181. This account is found in a manuscript of the *South English Legendary*.

48. Wackerzeele, "La Légende Latine de Sainte Barbe par Jean de Wackerzeele"; van Dijk, *Een rij van spiegels* (see 236–47 for an English summary of this study). Van Dijk discusses the English prose life in van Dijk, "Being Saint Barbara in England." Bokenham's "Barbara" is part of his Abbotsford collection.

49. On the movement's commitment to learning and its transmission, see Goudriaan, "Empowerment through Reading, Writing and Example."

50. Van Dijk, *Een rij van spiegels*, 244.

51. Van Dijk discusses the prose life's presentation of Barbara as a conduit for God's power and an embodiment of his will in van Dijk, "Being Saint Barbara," 12–17.

52. An edition of the Middle English prose version can be found in Hamer and Russell, *Supplementary Lives in Some Manuscripts of the Gilte Legende*, 381–470 (quote at 388). The Latin, similarly, presents Barbara's reasoning as divinely inspired: *luce tamen divini spiritus* (London, British Library, MS Harley 3043, 107v).

53. Copeland, *Pedagogy, Intellectuals, and Dissent in the Later Middle Ages*, 123.

54. Simpson, "Reginald Pecock and John Fortescue," 274.
55. Kerby-Fulton, *Books under Suspicion*, 16.

FOUR Holiness and the Modern Woman

1. Paris, *Matthew Paris's English History*, 1:474.
2. The scholarship on the beguines is rich and copious. For a succinct overview, see Simons, "Holy Women of the Low Countries," in Minnis and Voaden, *Medieval Holy Women in the Christian Tradition*. The essays in this volume, with their ample bibliographies, provide a splendid overview of the diversity of women's religious life in Western Europe during the late Middle Ages. See also Miller, *The Beguines of Medieval Paris*; Mulder-Bakker, *Lives of the Anchoresses*; and the essays in Dor, Johnson, and Wogan-Browne, *New Trends in Feminine Spirituality*. Many beguine lives have been translated into English as part of the Medieval Women: Texts and Context series published by Brepols; these volumes include extended introductions, critical essays, and bibliographies.
3. Simons, *Cities of Ladies*. According to Simons, the largest court beguinages housed more than a thousand women.
4. Simons, "Holy Women of the Low Countries," 626.
5. Goudriaan, "Empowerment through Reading, Writing and Example."
6. Matter, "Italian Holy Women"; Ronald E. Surtz, "Iberian Holy Women."
7. The essays in Minnis and Voaden, *Medieval Holy Women*, abundantly document their lives and writings.
8. Simons, "Holy Women of the Low Countries," 636.
9. See Coakley, *Women, Men, and Spiritual Power*.
10. Van Engen, "Communal Life: The Sister-Books"; and Lewis, *By Women, For Women, About Women*.
11. Blumenfeld-Kosinski, "Holy Women in France," 242–454. On the hagiography of battered wives, see Sahlin, "Holy Women of Scandinavia," 690–94.
12. Bartlett, "Holy Women in the British Isles."
13. Gilchrist, *Gender and Material Culture*, 170–87. A. Warren, *Anchorites and Their Patrons*. Warren breaks down the anchoritic population by century and gender (see table 1, p. 20).
14. Warren lists these guides as appendix 2 of A. Warren, *Anchorites and Their Patrons*.
15. I am not including in this reckoning the autobiographical *Book of Margery Kempe*. I discuss this life in the context of the paucity of (auto)biographies of late medieval Englishwomen in Winstead, *The Oxford History of Life Writing*, 56–64.
16. On Capgrave's use of the trefoil as a *nota bene* mark, see Lucas, *From Author to Audience*, 48–68.

17. Capgrave, *Abbreuiacion of Cronicles*, 159. Capgrave's source for this information is unknown.
18. Bynum, *Holy Feast and Holy Fast*; and Bell, *Holy Anorexia*.
19. Capgrave, *Abbreuiacion of Cronicles*, 130–31.
20. Winstead, *John Capgrave's Fifteenth Century*, 88–115.
21. Camp, "Osbern Bokenham and the House of York Revisited," 331.
22. Bokenham, "*Mappula Angliae*," 11.
23. Bokenham, "Dialogue at the Grave," 63–69.
24. Camp, "Osbern Bokenham and the House of York Revisited," 351.
25. "Orders and Rules of the Princess Cecill." See the discussion of the context and dating of this account in Armstrong, "The Piety of Cicely, Duchess of York."
26. Armstrong, "The Piety of Cicely, Duchess of York," 141.
27. Folkerts, "The Manuscript Transmission of the *Vita Mariae Oigniacensis*." Brown lists manuscripts "found in England" that contain the Latin *vitae* of Elizabeth of Spalbeek, Christina Mirabilis, and Marie d'Oignies in her introduction to Brown, *Three Women of Liège*, 13.
28. For more on Clare and the hagiography that grew up about her, see Mooney, *Clare of Assisi and the Thirteenth-Century Church*.
29. The life takes up 179 double-columned pages in de Worde's edition, 388 pages in its 1886 edition by Carl Horstmann, "The lyf of saint Katerin of Senis." See the study of the reception of Catherine of Siena in late medieval and early modern England in Brown, *Fruit of the Orchard*.
30. On the dissemination of the writings of Continental mystics in England, see Barry Windeatt, "1412–1534: Texts."
31. These lives have been edited by Brown, *Three Women of Liège*. For the information that follows I am indebted to Brown's introduction.
32. Brown, *Three Women*, 16.
33. Ibid., 17.
34. On the distinctive features of these lives, see the critical essays in Brown, *Three Women of Liège*. See also Macmillan, "Phenomenal Pain."
35. See Kerby-Fulton's discussion of the repressive measures taken against the beguines in Kerby-Fulton, *Books under Suspicion*, 251.
36. Kurtz, "Mary of Oignies, Christine the Marvelous, and Medieval Heresy." Brown discusses at far greater length the radicalism and orthodoxy of these lives in Brown, "Gender, Confession, and Authority"; see also Brown's introduction and interpretive essays in Brown, *Three Women of Liège*.
37. Elliott, *Proving Women*, 48.
38. Brown, *Fruit of the Orchard*, 29–57.
39. Ibid., 54.
40. Ibid., 53.
41. Ibid., 41.
42. See Luongo, *Saintly Politics of Catherine of Siena*.
43. Bynum, *Holy Feast*; and Bell, *Holy Anorexia*.
44. Bridget of Sweden, *Liber Celestis*, 1.
45. Kurtz, "Mary of Oignies," 194.

46. Horstmann, "Lyf of Saint Katerin of Senis," 33–112, 265–314, 353–91. For a detailed discussion of this translation, see Brown, *Fruit of the Orchard*, 140–58.

47. Horstmann, "Lyf of Saint Katherin of Senis," 34.

48. For an overview of Kempe criticism, see Watt, "Margery Kempe." On the *Book* as social criticism, see Staley, *Margery Kempe's Dissenting Fictions.*

49. Foster, "'A Shorte Treatyse of Contemplacyon': The Book of Margery Kempe in Its Early Print Contexts."

50. For all quotations and page references, I am using Staley, *The Book of Margery Kempe*.

51. At only one point does the narrative lapse into the first person (*The Book of Margery Kempe*, chap. 14, p. 47), and the relative importance of Margery and her scribe in the shaping of the *Book* has been hotly debated. I find no reason to doubt that Kempe dictated the *Book* and closely supervised its production, as indicated in the prologue and chapter 88.

52. Compare this beginning to the beginnings of the other lives of other modern European saints translated into English: "Here bigynneth the lyfe of seint Elizabeth of Spalbeck" (Brown, *Three Women of Liège*, 28); "Here beginneth the prolog in the lyfe of Seinte Cristin the meruelouse" (ibid., 51); "Here bigynneth the lyfe of Seint Mary of Oegines" (ibid., 86); "Here begynneth the lyfe of seynt Birgette" (Blunt, *Myroure of Oure Ladye*, xlvii); "here begynneth the lyf of saint Katherin of Senis" (Horstmann, "The lyf of saint Katerin of Senis," 33); and "*The proloug into seynt Elyzabeth Lyf*" (Bokenham, *Legendys of Hooly Wummen*, 257). Instead of being identified as a "seinte," Margery is a "synful caytyf" (*Book of Margery Kempe*, 17).

53. Lewis, "Margery Kempe and Saint Making."

54. See Dillon, "Holy Women and Their Confessors"; Dickman, "Margery Kempe and the Continental Tradition of the Pious Woman"; and Stargardt, "The Beguines of Belgium, the Dominican Nuns of Germany, and Margery Kempe." For more specialized studies, see Cleve, "Margery Kempe: A Scandinavian Influence on Medieval England"; and the following essays in McEntire, *Margery Kempe*: Hopenwasser, "Margery Kempe, St. Bridget, and Marguerite d'Oingt"; Barratt, "Margery Kempe and the King's Daughter of Hungary"; and Holloway, "Bride, Margery, Julian, and Alice." Most provocatively—but, to my mind persuasively—Alicia Spencer-Hall construes Kempe's relationship to and appropriation of Marie, Bridget, and other Continental luminaries as that of fan to celebrity; see Spencer-Hall, *Medieval Saints and Modern Screens*, 167–82.

55. Dillon, "Holy Women and Their Confessors," 134.

56. I first discussed Margery's virtual piety in Winstead, "Medieval Life-Writing and the Strange Case of Margery Kempe," reprinted with a few modifications in Winstead, *The Oxford History of Life-Writing*, 69–79.

57. Lewis, "Lete me suffer," 71.

58. Jones, "'*A peler of Holy Cherch*,'" 382.

59. Contrast the Kempes' marriage with the abusive relationships rife in Continental hagiography, which are compellingly analyzed in Nienhuis and Kienzle, *Saintly Women*.

60. See Foster's discussion of the possible origin of the extracts in the mid-fifteenth century in Foster, "'A Shorte Treatyse of Contemplacyon.'"

61. For an edition of the extracts, see appendix 2 of Meech, *The Book of Margery Kempe*, 353–57. All quotations are from this edition.

62. Foster, "'A Shorte Treatyse of Contemplacyon,'" 100. In this essay, Foster reviews the negative responses to the extracts and offers a much-needed corrective interpretation, pointing out that "the expurgating of controversial elements that makes the treatise so problematic to modern scholarship is also what preserved at least a semblance of Margery's message in a time of religious debate and transition" (112).

63. In this respect, I differ somewhat from Rebecca Krug, who finds that de Worde's tract "undoes the work" that Kempe's *Book* does (Krug, *Margery Kempe and the Lonely Reader*, 134). Although I wholly agree that certain important facets of Kempe's work are lost in the anthology, other important facets are not only preserved but underscored.

64. For this anthology, see Gardner, *The Cell of Self-Knowledge*. For quotes and page references, I am using Gardner's edition. See Brown's discussion of the Catherine extracts in Brown, *Fruit of the Orchard*, 164–70; as my discussion will make clear, I disagree that, in the printed extracts, "Catherine becomes indistinguishable from the equally altered Margery Kempe" (ibid., 170), but I do agree that there are significant similarities in the two women's representation.

65. On this point, see Foster, "'A Shorte Treatyse of Contemplacyon.'"

66. On the extracts' omission of specific ascetic acts, see Foster, "'A Shorte Treatyse of Contemplacyon,'"110; and Brown, *Fruit of the Orchard*, 151.

67. Horstmann, "Lyf of Saint Katerin of Senis," 391.

68. Krug, *Margery Kempe and the Lonely Reader*, 7.

FIVE   Golden Legends and Foxe's *Acts and Monuments*: Rethinking the Hagiographical Anthology

1. On Jacobus's career, thought, and influence see Reames, *The Legenda aurea*; and Epstein, *Talents of Jacopo da Varagine*.

2. Scotland's first extended legendary, undertaken in the late fourteenth century or early fifteenth century, was based principally on Jacobus's *Legenda aurea*. See the fascinating study by von Contzen, *Scottish Legendary*. The *Scottish Legendary*'s anonymous author, like the English editor/authors to be considered in this chapter, adapted Jacobus's legends in ways that humanized the saints.

3. Hamer, *Gilte Legende*, 3.

4. Bokenham, "*Mappula Angliae*," 6. As I have been doing previously, I refer to Bokenham's collection as the Abbotsford legendary.

5. On the Middle English hagiographer's debt to the *Légende dorée* and his departures from it, see Hamer, *Gilte Legende*, 1:xi. For all quotations and parenthetical citations, I am using Hamer's edition.

6. Christa Gray provides extensive commentary on this work in her edition and translation of Jerome's *Vita Malchi*; see Jerome, *Vita Malchi: Introduction, Text, Translation, and Commentary*.

7. Gray, introduction to Jerome, *Vita Malchi*, 7.

8. Ibid., 14.

9. For the work's affinity with other lives of desert fathers, and with a host of other literary genres, including romance, see Gray, introduction to Jerome, *Vita Malchi*, 14–42. See also Virginia Burrus's discussion of the life's unusual qualities in the context of Jerome's richly experimental hagiography in Burrus, *Sex Lives of the Saints*, 18–52.

10. Gray, introduction to Jerome, *Vita Malchi*, 14.

11. Ibid., 3. Gray discusses the *vita*'s comic features and its debt to Roman comedy in Gray, "The Monk and the Ridiculous."

12. Jerome, *Vita Malchi*, 93.

13. Ibid., 91.

14. Aldhelm, *Prose Works*, 91.

15. For a discussion of the Old English "Malchus," with an edition and translation into Modern English, see Dendle, "The Old English 'Life of Malchus' and Two Vernacular Tales from the *Vitas Patrum*." Dendle considers its congeniality to the reformers' goals on 507.

16. The Middle English hagiographer augments the parallel between Malchus's situation and that of a conventional virgin martyr. In Jerome's account, Malchus refuses to marry on the grounds that the woman is already married.

17. See the discussion of these British lives and their relationship with the *South English Legendary* in Sanok, *New Legends of England*, 133–72.

18. Here and elsewhere I am using Hamer and Russell, *Supplementary Lives in Some Manuscripts of the Gilte Legende*.

19. "Jerome" is Symon Wynter's version. See my discussion of that text in chapter 3 herein.

20. Jacobus de Voragine, *Golden Legend*, 1:62.

21. Horobin, "Politics, Patronage, and Piety in the Work of Osbern Bokenham."

22. See the provocative discussion of Bokenham's British saints in Sanok, *New Legends of England*, 145–51.

23. Bokenham, "*Mappula Angliae*," 6.

24. Caxton, *Legenda aurea sanctorum*, 2. All quotes will be from this edition.

25. White comments on the anomaly of these biblical "lives" in White, *Tudor Books of Saints and Martyrs*, 33.

26. See, for example, San Marino, Huntington Library MS 3027, a richly illuminated manuscript produced at the end of the thirteenth century and the analysis in Easton, "Pain, Torture, and Death."

27. Reames, *The Legenda aurea*, 52.

28. Ibid., 208.

29. For a detailed discussion of the four editions produced by Foxe, and of Foxe's two prior Latin martyrologies, see Freeman, "The Life of John Foxe."

For an overview of these and subsequent editions, see Loades, "Introduction: John Foxe and the Editors." For scholarly editions of Foxe's four versions, see Foxe, *The Unabridged Acts and Monuments Online*.

30. Freeman, "The Life of John Foxe."
31. Ibid.
32. Felch, "Shaping the Reader in the *Acts and Monuments*," 59.
33. Loades, "Introduction: John Foxe and the Editors," 4.
34. King, "Fiction and Fact in Foxe's *Book of Martyrs*," 15.
35. For all quotations and parenthetical references, I am using John Foxe, *Unabridged Acts and Monuments Online* (1570 edition, unless otherwise indicated).
36. Foxe, *The Unabridged Acts and Monuments Online* (1563 edition), 9–10.
37. See Felch's interpretation of the *Acts and Monuments* as "a manual on how to read" in Felch, "Shaping the Reader in the *Acts and Monuments*."
38. Foxe, *The Unabridged Acts and Monuments Online* (1576 edition), 1872.
39. See my discussion of this episode in Winstead, *John Capgrave's Fifteenth Century*, 54–60.
40. Capgrave, *Solace of Pilgrims*, 110.
41. Eusebius, *History of the Church*, bk. 4.1, p. 184.
42. Dailey, *The English Martyr*, 57. Rhodes similarly observes a "recognizable continuity" between the martyrs of the Jacobus de Voragine's *Legenda aurea* and the lives of sixteenth- and seventeenth-century martyrs in Rhodes, "English Books of Martyrs and Saints of the Late Sixteenth and Early Seventeenth Centuries," 9. See also Matthew Woodcock, "Crossovers and Afterlife." Woodcock notes how Foxe employs the "diametric, binary struggle of good versus evil—and good *over* evil—employed in medieval martyrology" (155). Nancy Warren also discusses Foxe's debt to the medieval tradition he disparages in N. Warren, *Embodied Word* (211–20), calling his *Acts and Monuments* "perhaps the most Catholic of Protestant polemical works" (215).
43. Dailey, *The English Martyr*, 80.
44. The illustrations of martyrs in *Acts and Monuments* are quite unlike the illustrations in fifteenth-century English legendaries, Caxton's *Legenda aurea sanctorum* and the Tanner *South English Legendary*, which play down violence; they more nearly resemble the iconography of San Marino, Huntington Library, HM 3027, an illustrated *Legenda aurea* dating from the late thirteenth century. For a detailed discussion of Foxe's iconography, see Aston and Ingram, "The Iconography of the *Acts and Monuments*." On the iconography of HM 3027, see Easton, "Pain, Torture, and Death in the Huntington Library *Legenda aurea*."
45. Dailey, *The English Martyr*, 87.
46. Ibid., 14. See also Lupton's use of Jacobus's "massively influential compendium of saints' lives" as a "thesaurus of hagiographic exempla" (42) in Lupton, *Afterlives of the Saints*, 40–70. It is all too common to lump together "the *Legenda aurea* and other medieval hagiographies," as Freeman does (see Freeman,

"Imitatio Christi with a Vengeance," 36). This conflation leads Freeman and others to attribute to the sixteenth century developments, such as the reaction against "prodigious marvels," that in fact occurred a good century earlier.

47. Monta, *Martyrdom and Literature in Early Modern England*, 1; Loades, introduction to *John Foxe and the English Reformation*, 4.

48. For Jacobus de Voragine's version, see Jacobus, *Golden Legend*, 2:266–71.

AFTERWORD Afterlives

1. Camp contextualizes this life and discusses Bradshaw's political and historical agendas in Camp, *Anglo-Saxon Saints' Lives as History Writing in Late Medieval England*, 102–32; see also Sanok, *Her Life Historical*, 83–115.

2. On the self-conscious literariness of Barclay's *Life of St. George* and other hagiographies of the early sixteenth century, see Henry, "Humanist Hagiography."

3. For all quotations and line references, I am using Nelson's edition of *The Life of St. George*.

4. For all quotations and line references, I am using Horstmann's edition of *The Life of Saint Werburge of Chester*.

5. Wooding, *Rethinking Catholicism in Reformation England*, 116.

6. Rhodes, "English Books of Martyrs and Saints of the Late Sixteenth and Early Seventeenth Centuries," 19. On the contribution of Catholic women to the literature of early modern England, see Lay, *Beyond the Cloister*. See also N. Warren, *The Embodied Word*.

7. Falconer, *Life of Saint Catherine of Sweden*, 5.

8. Hawkins is reflecting on his newly completed *Admirable Life of S. Aldegond* (1632) in the preface to his *History of S. Elizabeth, Daughter of the King of Hungary* (1632). His collection is Hawkins, *Fuga saeculi. Or the Holy Hatred of the World* (1632).

9. Hawkins, *Fuga saeculi*, 36.

10. For all quotations and page references, I am using Horstmann, *Lives of Women Saints of our Contrie of England*. Horstmann identifies the manuscript as British Library MS Stowe 949, but its current BL designation is Stowe 53.

11. Wooding, *Rethinking Catholicism*, discusses this process.

12. Howard, *A sacred poem describing the miraculous life and death of the glorious conuert S. Marie of Ægipt*, 11.

13. Falconer, *The admirable life of Saint Wenefride virgin, martyr, abbesse*, 16.

14. Hawkins, *History of S. Elizabeth*.

15. Rhodes, "English Books of Martyrs," 15.

BIBLIOGRAPHY

PRIMARY SOURCES

Aldhelm. *The Prose Works.* Translated by Michael Lapidge and Michael Herren. Cambridge: D. S. Brewer, 1979.
Augustine of Hippo. *Basic Writings of Saint Augustine.* 2 vols. Edited by Whitney Oates. New York: Random House, 1947.
——. *On Faith and the Creed.* Translated by S. D. Salmond. Edinburgh: T&T Clark, 1892.
Baker, Donald C., John L. Murphy, and Louis B. Hall Jr., eds. *The Late Medieval Religious Plays of Bodleian MSS. Digby 133 and E Museo 160.* EETS OS 283. Oxford: Oxford University Press, 1982.
Barclay, Alexander. *The Life of St. George.* Edited by William Nelson. EETS OS 230. London: Oxford University Press, 1955.
Blunt, John Henry, ed. *The Myroure of Oure Ladye.* EETS ES 19. London, 1873. Reprint, Millwood, NY: Kraus, 1981.
Bokenham, Osbern. "Dialogue at the Grave." Edited by Katherine Barnardiston. In *Clare Priory: Seven Centuries of a Suffolk House*, edited by Norman Scarfe, 63–69. Cambridge: W. Heffer, 1962.
——. *Legenda aurea* (Abbotsford Legendary). Ms., Abbotsford Collection, Advocates Library, Edinburgh. http://lib1.advocates.org.uk/legenda/#/1/.
——. *Legendys of Hooly Wummen.* Edited by Mary S. Serjeantson. EETS OS 206. 1938. Reprint, New York: Kraus, 1971.
——. "*Mappula Angliae*, von Osbern Bokenham." Edited by Carl Horstmann. *Englische Studien* 10 (1887): 1–34.
Bradshaw, Henry. *The Life of Saint Werburge of Chester.* Edited by Carl Horstmann. EETS OS 88. 1887. Reprint, Millwood, NY: Kraus, 1988.
Bridget of Sweden. *The Liber Celestis.* Edited by Roger Ellis. EETS OS 291. Oxford: Oxford University Press, 1987.
Brie, Friedrich W. D. *The Brut or The Chronicles of England.* 2 vols. 1906, 1908. Reprint, New York: Kraus, 1987.

Brown, Jennifer N., ed. *Three Women of Liège: A Critical Edition and Commentary on the Middle English Lives of Elizabeth of Spalbeek, Christina Mirabilis, and Marie d'Oignies.* Turnhout: Brepols, 2008.
Capgrave, John. *Abbreuiacion of Cronicles.* Edited by Peter J. Lucas. EETS OS 285. Oxford: Oxford University Press, 1983.
———. *Life of Saint Augustine.* Edited by Cyril Lawrence Smetana. Toronto: Pontifical Institute of Mediaeval Studies, 2001.
———. *The Life of Saint Katherine.* Edited by Karen A. Winstead. Kalamazoo, MI: Medieval Institute, 1999.
———. *Ye Solace of Pilgrimes.* Edited by C. A. Mills. London: Oxford University Press, 1911.
Caxton, William. *Legenda aurea sanctorum, sive Lombardica historia.* London: William Caxton, 1483.
Chaucer, Geoffrey. *The Riverside Chaucer.* 3rd ed. Edited by Larry D. Benson. New York: Houghton Mifflin, 1987.
Dove, Mary, ed. *The Earliest Advocates of the English Bible: The Texts of the Medieval Debate.* Exeter: Exeter University Press, 2010.
Erbe, Theodor, ed. *Mirk's Festial.* EETS ES 96. London: Kegan Paul, Trench, Trübner, & Co., 1905.
Eusebius. *The History of the Church.* Translated by Andrew Louth. 1965. Revised and reprinted, London: Penguin, 1989.
Falconer, John. *The admirable life of Saint Wenefride* (1635). Ilkley: Scolar Press, 1976.
———. *The Life of S. Catherine* (1634). Menston: Scolar Press, 1973.
Foxe, John. *The Unabridged Acts and Monuments Online (TAMO).* HRI Online Publications, Sheffield, 2011. https://www.dhi.ac.uk/foxe/index.php.
Gardner, Edmund G., ed. *The Cell of Self-Knowledge: Seven Early English Mystical Treatises Printed by Henry Pepwell in 1521.* London: Chatto, 1910.
Hamer, Richard, ed. *Gilte Legende.* 2 vols. EETS OS 327–28. Oxford: Oxford University Press, 2006–7.
Hamer, Richard, and Vida Russell, eds. *Supplementary Lives in Some Manuscripts of the Gilte Legende.* EETS OS 315. Oxford: Oxford University Press, 2000.
Hawkins, Henry. *The Admirable Life of S. Aldegond* (1632). Menston: Scolar Press, 1970.
———. *Fuga saeculi. Or the Holy Hatred of the World* (1632). Ilkley: Scolar Press, 1977.
———. *History of S. Elizabeth, Daughter of the King of Hungary* (1632). Ilkley: Scolar Press, 1974.
Horstmann, C., ed. *Altenglische Legenden: Neue Folge.* Heilbronn: Henninger, 1881.
———. *The Lives of Women Saints of our Contrie of England, and Some Other Lives of Holie Women Written by Some of the Auncient Fathers.* EETS OS 86. 1886. Reprint, Millwood, NY: Kraus, 1987.
———. "The lyf of saint Katerin of Senis." *Archiv für das stadium der neueren sprachen und literaturen* 76 (1886): 3–400.

Holman, Sheri. *A Stolen Tongue.* New York: Grove Press, 1997.
Howard, Robert. *A sacred poem describing the miraculous life and death of the glorious conuert S. Marie of Ægipt.* 1640.
Jacobus de Voragine. *The Golden Legend: Readings on the Saints.* 2 Vols. Translated by William Granger Ryan. Princeton, NJ: Princeton University Press, 1993.
———. *Legenda aurea.* Edited by Theodor Graesse. Lipsiae, 1892. Reprint, Osnabrück: Otto Zeller, 1969.
Jerome. *Vita Malchi: Introduction, Text, Translation, and Commentary.* Edited by Christa Gray. Oxford: Oxford University Press, 2015.
Kempe, Margery. *The Book of Margery Kempe.* Edited by Emily Hope Allen and Sanford Brown Meech. EETS OS 212. Oxford: Oxford University Press, 1940.
———. *The Book of Margery Kempe.* Edited by Lynn Staley. Kalamazoo, MI: Medieval Institute Publications, 1996.
Langland, William. *The Vision of Piers Plowman.* 2nd ed. Edited by A. V. C. Schmidt. London: Dent, 1995.
Lombard, Peter. *The Sentences: The Mystery of the Trinity.* Translated by Giulio Silano. Toronto: Pontifical Institute of Mediaeval Studies, 2007.
Love, Nicholas. *Nicholas Love's Mirror of the Blessed Life of Jesus Christ: A Critical Edition Based on Cambridge University Library Additional MSS 6578 and 6686.* Edited by Michael G. Sargent. New York: Garland, 1992.
Lydgate, John. "The Legend of Seynt Gyle." In *Minor Poems of John Lydgate: The Religious Canon,* 161–73.
———. "The Legend of St. George." In *Minor Poems of John Lydgate: The Religious Canon,* 145–54.
———. *Life of Our Lady.* Edited by Joseph A. Lauritis. Louvain: Editions E. Nauwelaerts, 1961.
———. *Lives of Ss Edmund and Fremund and the Extra Miracles of St Edmund.* Edited by Anthony Bale and A. S. G. Edwards. Heidelberg: Universitätsverlag Winter, 2009.
———. "Lyfe of Seynt Margarete." In *Middle English Lives of Women Saints,* edited by Sherry L. Reames, 147–68. Kalamazoo, MI: Medieval Institute Publications, 2003.
———. *Minor Poems of John Lydgate: The Religious Canon.* Edited by Henry Noble MacCracken. London: Oxford University Press, 1911.
———. "A Prayere to Seynt Michaell." In *Minor Poems of John Lydgate: The Religious Canon,* 133.
———. "A Prayer to St. Leonard." In *Minor Poems of John Lydgate: The Religious Canon,* 135–36.
———. "A Prayer to St. Thomas of Canterbury." In *Minor Poems of John Lydgate: The Religious Canon,* 140–43.
———. "Prayers to Ten Saints." In *Minor Poems of John Lydgate: The Religious Canon,* 120–27.
———. *Saint Albon and Saint Amphibalus.* Edited by George F. Reinecke. New York: Garland Publishing, 1985.

———. "Saint Austin at Compton." In *Saints' Lives in Middle English Collections*, ed. Whatley, 213–51.

———. "To St. Ositha." In *Minor Poems of John Lydgate: The Religious Canon*, 137.

———. "To St. Katherine, St. Margaret, and St. Mary Magdalene." In *Minor Poems of John Lydgate: The Religious Canon*, 134–35.

———. "To St. Robert of Bury." In *Minor Poems of John Lydgate: The Religious Canon*, 138–39.

McSheffrey, Shannon, and Norman Tanner, eds. and trans. *Lollards of Coventry, 1486–1522*. Cambridge: Cambridge University Press, 2003.

"Orders and Rules of the Princess Cecill." In *A Collection of Ordinances and Regulations for the Government of the Royal Household Made in Divers Reigns*, 35–39. London: Society of Antiquaries, 1790.

Paris, Matthew. *Matthew Paris's English History: From the Year 1235 to 1273*. 3 vols. Translated by J. A. Giles. London: H. G. Bohn, 1889.

Parker, Roscoe E., ed. *The Middle English Stanzaic Versions of the Life of Saint Anne*. 1928. Reprint, Millwood NY: Kraus, 1987.

"Passio S. Katerine." In *Seinte Katerine*, edited by S. R. T. O. d'Ardenne and E. J. Dobson, 132–203. EETS SS 7. Oxford: Oxford University Press, 1981.

Pecock, Reginald. *The Reule of Crysten Religioun*. Edited by William Cabell Greet. EETS OS 171. Oxford: Oxford University Press, 1927.

Potter, Giselle. *Lucy's Eyes and Margaret's Dragon: The Lives of the Virgin Saints*. San Francisco, CA: Chronicle Books, 1997.

Reynes, Robert. *The Commonplace Book of Robert Reynes of Acle: An Edition of Tanner MS 407*. Edited by Cameron Louis. New York: Garland, 1980.

Setterfield, Diane. *Once Upon a River*. New York: Simon and Schuster, 2018.

Simmons, Thomas Frederick, ed. *Lay Folks' Catechism*. EETS OS 118. Oxford: Oxford University Press, 1901.

Spector, Stephen, ed. *N-Town Play*. EETS SS 11. Oxford: Oxford University Press, 1991.

Tanner, Norman P., ed. *Heresy Trials in the Diocese of Norwich, 1428–31*. London: Royal Historical Society, 1977.

Wackerzeele, John. "La Légende Latine de Sainte Barbe par Jean de Wackerzeele." Edited by Baudouin de Gaiffier. *Analecta Bollandiana* 77 (1959): 5–41.

Waters, Clare M., ed. *Virgins and Scholars: A Fifteenth-Century Compilation of the Lives of John the Baptist, John the Evangelist, Jerome, and Katherine of Alexandria*. Turnhout: Brepols, 2008.

Weatherly, Edward H. *Speculum Sacerdotale*. EETS OS 200. Oxford: Oxford University Press, 1936.

Whatley, E. Gordon, Anne B. Thompson, and Robert Upchurch, eds. *Saints' Lives in Middle English Collections*. Kalamazoo, MI: Medieval Institute Publications, 2004.

Winstead, Karen A., ed. and trans. *Chaste Passions: Medieval English Virgin Martyr Legends*. Ithaca, NY: Cornell University Press, 2000.

SECONDARY SOURCES

Armstrong, C. A. J. "The Piety of Cicely, Duchess of York." In *England, France, and Burgundy in the Fifteenth Century*, 135–56. London: Hambledon Press, 1983.

Arnold, John, and Katherine J. Lewis, eds. *A Companion to "The Book of Margery Kempe."* Cambridge: D. S. Brewer, 2004.

Aston, Margaret, and Elizabeth Ingram. "The Iconography of the *Acts and Monuments*." In Loades, *John Foxe and the English Reformation*, 52–142.

Bale, Anthony. "John Lydgate's Religious Poetry." In Boffey and Edwards, *A Companion to Fifteenth-Century English Poetry*, 73–85.

Barratt, Alexandra. "Margery Kempe and the King's Daughter of Hungary." In McEntire, *Margery Kempe*, 189–201.

Bartlett, Anne Clark. "Holy Women in the British Isles: A Survey." In Minnis and Voaden, *Medieval Holy Women in the Christian Tradition, c. 1100–c. 1500*, 165–93.

Bell, Rudolph M. *Holy Anorexia*. Chicago: University of Chicago Press, 1985.

Bengtson, Jonathan. "Saint George and the Formation of English Nationalism." *Journal of Medieval & Early Modern Studies* 27, no. 2 (1997): 317–40.

Blanton, Virginia. *Signs of Devotion: The Cult of St. Aethelthryth in Medieval England, 695–1615*. University Park: Pennsylvania State University Press, 2007.

Blumenfeld-Kosinski, Renate. "Holy Women in France: A Survey." In Minnis and Voaden, *Medieval Holy Women*, 241–65.

Blurton, Heather, and Jocelyn Wogan-Browne, eds. *Rethinking the South English Legendaries*. Manchester: Manchester University Press, 2011.

Boffey, Julia, and A. S. G. Edwards, eds. *A Companion to Fifteenth-Century English Poetry*. Cambridge: D. S. Brewer, 2013.

Bose, Mishtooni. "Reginald Pecock's Vernacular Voice." In *Lollards and Their Influence in Late Medieval England*, edited by Fiona Somerset, Jill C. Havens, and Derek G. Pitard, 217–36. Woodbridge, Suffolk: Boydell Press, 2003.

Brown, Jennifer N. *Fruit of the Orchard: Reading Catherine of Siena in Late Medieval and Early Modern England*. Toronto: University of Toronto Press, 2019.

———. "Gender, Confession, and Authority: Oxford, Bodleian Library, MS Douce 114 in the Fifteenth Century." In Gillespie and Ghosh, *After Arundel*, 415–28.

Burrus, Virginia. *The Sex Lives of the Saints: An Erotics of Ancient Hagiography*. Philadelphia: University of Pennsylvania Press, 2004.

Bynum, Caroline Walker. *Holy Feast and Holy Fast: The Religious Significance of Food to Medieval Women*. Berkeley: University of California Press, 1987.

Camp, Cynthia Turner. *Anglo-Saxon Saints' Lives as History Writing in Late Medieval England.* Cambridge: D. S. Brewer, 2015.

———. "Augustine the Hermit or Augustine the Canon? The Fraternal Hagiography of Osbern Bokenham." Paper given at the 47th International Congress on Medieval Studies, Western Michigan University, Kalamazoo, MI, May 11, 2012.

———. "Osbern Bokenham and the House of York Revisited." *Viator* 44, no. 1 (2013): 327–52.

Campbell, Kirsty. *The Call to Read: Reginald Pecock's Books and Textual Communities.* Notre Dame, IN: University of Notre Dame Press, 2010.

Catto, Jeremy. "After Arundel: The Closing or the Opening of the English Mind?" In Gillespie and Ghosh, *After Arundel,* 43–54.

———. "Religious Change under Henry V." In Harriss, *Henry V: The Practice of Kingship,* 97–115.

Coakley, John W. *Women, Men, and Spiritual Power: Female Saints and Their Male Collaborators.* New York: Columbia University Press, 2000.

Coens, Maurice. "Une 'passio S. Apolloniae' inédite suivie d'un miracle en Bourgogne." *Analecta Bollandiana* 70 (1952): 138–59.

Cleve, Gunner. "Margery Kempe: A Scandinavian Influence on Medieval England." In Glasscoe, *The Medieval Mystical Tradition in England,* 163–75.

Cole, Andrew. "Heresy and Humanism." In Strohm, *Oxford Twenty-First Century Approaches to Literature: Middle English,* 421–37.

———. *Literature and Heresy in the Age of Chaucer.* Cambridge: Cambridge University Press, 2008.

Coletti, Theresa. *Mary Magdalene and the Drama of Saints: Theater, Gender, and Religion in Late Medieval England.* Philadelphia: University of Pennsylvania Press, 2004.

Colledge, Edmund. "John Capgrave's Literary Vocation." *Analecta Augustiniana* 40 (1977): 187–95.

Connolly, Margaret. *Sixteenth-Century Readers, Fifteenth-Century Books: Continuities of Reading in the English Reformation.* Cambridge: Cambridge University Press, 2019.

Cooper, Lisa H., and Andrea Denny-Brown. *Lydgate Matters: Poetry and Material Culture in the Fifteenth Century.* New York: Palgrave Macmillan, 2008.

Copeland, Rita. *Pedagogy, Intellectuals, and Dissent in the Later Middle Ages: Lollardy and Ideas of Learning.* Cambridge: Cambridge University Press, 2001.

Crane, Susan. "Anglo-Norman Cultures in England, 1066–1460." In *The Cambridge History of Medieval English Literature,* edited by David Wallace, 35–60. Cambridge: Cambridge University Press, 1999.

Dailey, Alice. *The English Martyr: From Reformation to Revolution.* Notre Dame, IN: University of Notre Dame Press, 2012.

Delany, Sheila. *Impolitic Bodies: Poetry, Saints, and Society in Fifteenth-Century England: The Work of Osbern Bokenham.* New York: Oxford University Press, 1998.

Dendle, Peter J. "The Old English 'Life of Malchus' and Two Vernacular Tales from the *Vitas Patrum* in Ms Cotton Otho C.i" (2 parts). *English Studies* 90, no. 5–6 (2009): 505–17 and 631–52.

D'Evelyn, Charlotte, and Frances A. Foster. "Saints' Legends." In *A Manual of the Writings in Middle English, 1050–1500*, edited by J. Burke Severs, 2:410–39, 553–635. Hamden, CT: Archon Books, 1970.

De Hamel, Christopher. *A History of Illuminated Manuscripts*. Boston: David R. Godine, 1986.

Dickman, Susan. "Margery Kempe and the Continental Tradition of the Pious Woman." In Glasscoe, *The Medieval Mystical Tradition in England*, 150–68.

Dillon, Janette. "Holy Women and Their Confessors or Confessors and Their Holy Women? Margery Kempe and the Continental Tradition." In *Prophets Abroad: The Reception of Continental Holy Women in Late-Medieval England*, edited by Rosalynn Voaden, 114–40. Woodbridge: D. S. Brewer, 1998.

Dolan, Frances E.. "Reading, Work, and Catholic Women's Biographies." *English Literary Renaissance* 33 (2003): 328–57.

Dor, Juliette, Lesley Johnson, and Jocelyn Wogan-Browne, eds. *New Trends in Feminine Spirituality: The Holy Women of Liège and their Impact*. Turnhout: Brepols, 1999.

Dresvina, Juliana. *A Maid with a Dragon: The Cult of St Margaret of Antioch in Medieval England*. Oxford: Oxford University Press, 2016.

Duffy, Eamon. *Marking the Hours: English People and Their Prayers*. New Haven, CT: Yale University Press, 2006.

———. *The Stripping of the Altars: Traditional Religion in England 1400–1580*. New Haven, CT: Yale University Press, 1992. Reprint, 2005.

Easton, Martha. "Pain, Torture, and Death in the Huntington Library *Legenda aurea*." In *Gender and Holiness: Men, Women and Saints in Late Medieval Europe*, edited by Samatha J. E. Riches and Sarah Salih, 49–64. London: Routledge, 2002.

Ebin, Lois A. *John Lydgate*. Boston: Twayne, 1985.

Edwards, A. S. G. "The Transmission and Audience of Osbern Bokenham's *Legendys of Hooly Wummen*." In *Late Medieval Religious Texts and Their Transmission*, edited by Alastair Minnis, 157–67. Cambridge: Brewer, 1994.

Elliott, Dyan. *Proving Woman: Female Spirituality and Inquisitional Culture in the Later Middle Ages*. Princeton, NJ: Princeton University Press, 2004.

Epstein, Steven A. *The Talents of Jacopo da Varagine: A Genoese Mind in Medieval Europe*. Ithaca, NY: Cornell University Press, 2016.

Felch, Susan. "Shaping the Reader in the *Acts and Monuments*." In Loades, *John Foxe and the English Reformation*, 52–65.

Findon, Joanne. *Lady, Hero, Saint: The Digby Play's Mary Magdalene*. Toronto: Pontifical Institute of Mediaeval Studies, 2011.

Floyd, Jennifer. "Saint George and the 'Steyned Halle': Lydgate's Verse for the London Armourers." In Cooper and Denny-Brown, *Lydgate Matters*, 139–64.

Folkerts, Suzan. "The Manuscript Transmission of the *Vita Mariae Oigniacensis* in the Later Middle Ages." In *Mary of Oignies: Mother of Salvation*, edited by Anneke B. Mulder-Bakker, 221–41. Turnhout: Brepols, 2006.
Foster, Allyson. "'A Shorte Treatyse of Contemplacyon': *The Book of Margery Kempe* in its Early Print Contexts." In Arnold and Lewis, *A Companion to "The Book of Margery Kempe,"* 95–112.
Fredeman, Jane. "The Life of John Capgrave, O.E.S.A. (1393–1464)." *Augustiniana* 29 (1979): 197–237.
Freeman, Thomas S. "'Imitatio Christi with a Vengeance': The Politicisation of Martyrdom in Late-Medieval and Early-Modern England." In *Martyrs and Martyrdom in England, c. 1400–1700*, edited by Thomas S. Freeman and Thomas F. Mayer, 35–69. Woodbridge, Suffolk: The Boydell Press, 2007.
———. "John Foxe: A Biography," In *The Unabridged Acts and Monuments Online (TAMO)*. Sheffield: HRI Online Publications, 2011. https://www.dhi.ac.uk/foxe/index.php?realm=more&type=essay.
Freeman, Thomas S., and Thomas F. Mayer, eds. *Martyrs and Martyrdom in England, c. 1400–1700*. Woodbridge, Suffolk: The Boydell Press, 2007.
Ganim, John M. "Lydgate, Location, and the Poetics of Exemption." In Cooper and Denny-Brown, *Lydgate Matters*, 165–83.
Gayk, Shannon. "'Among psalms to fynde a cleer sentence': John Lydgate, Eleanor Hull, and the Art of Vernacular Exegesis." *New Medieval Literatures* 10 (2008): 162–89.
———. *Image, Text, and Religious Reform in Fifteenth-Century England*. Cambridge: Cambridge University Press, 2010.
———. "Images of Pity: The Regulatory Aesthetics of John Lydgate's Religious Lyrics." *Studies in the Age of Chaucer* 28 (2006): 175–203.
Gayk, Shannon, and Kathleen Tonry, eds. *Form and Reform: Reading across the Fifteenth Century*. Columbus: Ohio State University Press, 2011.
Gibson, Gail McMurray. "Saint Anne and the Religion of Childbed: Some East Anglian Texts and Talismans." In *Interpreting Cultural Symbols: Saint Anne in Late Medieval Society*, edited by Kathleen Ashley and Pamela Sheingorn, 95–110. Athens: University of Georgia Press, 1990.
———. *The Theater of Devotion: East Anglian Drama and Society in the Late Middle Ages*. Chicago: University of Chicago Press, 1989.
Gilchrist, Roberta. *Gender and Material Culture: The Archaeology of Religious Women*. London: Routledge, 1994.
Gillespie, Vincent. "Chichile's Church: Vernacular Theology in England after Thomas Arundel." In Gillespie and Ghosh, *After Arundel*, 3–42.
Gillespie, Vincent, and Kantik Ghosh, eds. *After Arundel: Religious Writing in Fifteenth-Century England*. Turnhout: Brepols, 2011.
Glasscoe, Marion, ed. *The Medieval Mystical Tradition in England*. Exeter Symposium 5. Cambridge: D. S. Brewer, 1992.
Good, Jonathan. *The Cult of St. George in Medieval England*. Woodbridge, Suffolk: The Boydell Press, 2009.
Goudriaan, Koen. "Empowerment through Reading, Writing and Example: The *Devotio moderna*." In Rubin and Simons, *The Cambridge History of Christianity: Christianity in Western Europe, c. 1100–c. 1500*, 407–19.

Gray, Christa. "The Monk and the Ridiculous: Comedy in Jerome's *Vita Malchi*." *Studia Patristica* 69 (2013): 115–21.
Green, Richard Firth. *Poets and Princepleasers: Literature and the English Court in the Late Middle Ages*. Toronto: University of Toronto Press, 1980.
Harriss, G. L., ed. *Henry V: The Practice of Kingship*. 1985. Reprint, Stroud, Gloucestershire: Alan Sutton, 1993.
Harthan, John. *Books of Hours and Their Owners*. 1977. Reprint, London: Thames and Hudson, 1988.
Henry, Joni. "Humanist Hagiography in England, c. 1480–c. 1520." *Literature Compass* 10 (2013): 535–43.
Hill, Carole. *Women and Religion in Late Medieval England*. Woodbridge, Suffolk: Boydell Press, 2010.
Holloway, Julia Bolton. "Bride, Margery, Julian, and Alice: Bridget of Sweden's Textual Community in Medieval England." In McEntire, *Margery Kempe*, 203–21.
Hopenwasser, Nanda. "Margery Kempe, St. Bridget, and Marguerite d'Oingt: The Visionary Woman as Shaman." In McEntire, *Margery Kempe*, 165–87.
Horobin, Simon. "The Angle of Oblivioun": A Lost Medieval Manuscript Discovered in Walter Scott's Collection," *Times Literary Supplement*, November 11, 2005, 12–13.
———. "A Manuscript Found in Abbotsford House and the Lost Legendary of Osbern Bokenham." *English Manuscript Studies 1100–1700* 14 (2008): 132–64.
———. "Politics, Patronage, and Piety in the Work of Osbern Bokenham." *Speculum* 82 (2007): 932–49.
Howlett, D. R. "Studies in the Works of John Whethamstede." D. Phil, Oxford University, 1975.
Hudson, Anne. *The Premature Reformation: Wycliffite Texts and Lollard History*. Oxford: Clarendon, 1988.
Jansen, Katherine Ludwig. *The Making of the Magdalen: Preaching and Popular Devotion in the Later Middle Ages*. Princeton, NJ: Princeton University Press, 2000.
Jenkins, Jacqueline, and Katherine J. Lewis, eds. *Saint Katherine of Alexandria: Texts and Contexts in Western Europe*. Turnhout: Brepols, 2003.
Jones, Sarah Rees. "'*A peler of Holy Cherch*': Margery Kempe and the Bishops." In *Medieval Women: Texts and Contexts in Late Medieval Britain*, edited by Jocelyn Wogan-Browne, Rosalynn Voaden, Arlyn Diamond, Ann Hutchison, Carol Meale, and Lesley Johnson, 377–91. Turnhout: Brepols, 2000.
Keiser, George R. "Patronage and Piety in Fifteenth-Century England: Margaret, Duchess of Clarence, Symon Wynter and Beinecke MS 317," *Yale University Library Gazette* 60 (1985): 32–46.
Kerby-Fulton, Kathryn. *Books under Suspicion: Censorship and Tolerance of Revelatory Writing in Late Medieval England*. Notre Dame, IN: University of Notre Dame Press, 2006.

Kieckhefer, Richard. *Unquiet Souls: Fourteenth-Century Saints and Their Religious Milieu*. Chicago: University of Chicago Press, 1984.
King, John. "Fiction and Fact in Foxe's *Book of Martyrs*." In Loades, *John Foxe and the English Reformation*, 12–35.
Krug, Rebecca. *Margery Kempe and the Lonely Reader*. Ithaca, NY: Cornell University Press, 2017.
Kurtz, Patricia Deery. "Mary of Oignies, Christine the Marvelous, and Medieval Heresy." *Mystics Quarterly* 14, no. 4 (1988): 186–96.
Lay, Jenna. *Beyond the Cloister: Catholic Englishwomen and Early Modern Literary Culture*. Philadelphia: University of Pennsylvania Press, 2016.
Lewis, Gertrud Jaron. *By Women, For Women, About Women: The Sister-Books of Fourteenth-Century Germany*. Toronto: Pontifical Institute of Mediaeval Studies, 1996.
Lewis, Katherine J. *The Cult of Katherine of Alexandria in Late Medieval England*. Woodbridge, Suffolk: Boydell Press, 2000.
———. "Edmund of East Anglia, Henry VI and Ideals of Kingly Masculinity." In *Holiness and Masculinity in the Middle Ages*, edited by Patricia H. Cullum and Katherine J. Lewis, 158–73. Cardiff: University of Wales Press, 2004.
———. *Kingship and Masculinity in Late Medieval England*. London: Taylor and Francis, 2013.
———. "'Lete me suffre': Reading the Torture of St Margaret of Antioch in Late Medieval England." In Wogan-Browne et al., *Medieval Women*, 69–82.
———. "Margery Kempe and Saint Making in Later Medieval England." In Arnold and Lewis, *A Companion to "The Book of Margery Kempe,"* 195–215.
Loades, David. "Introduction: John Foxe and the Editors." In Loades, *John Foxe and the English Reformation*, 1–11.
———, ed. *John Foxe and the English Reformation*. Hants: Scolar Press, 1997.
Lucas, Peter J. *From Author to Audience: John Capgrave and Medieval Publication*. Dublin: University College of Dublin Press, 1997.
Luongo, Thomas. *The Saintly Politics of Catherine of Siena*. Ithaca, NY: Cornell University Press, 2006.
Lupton, Julia Reinhard. *Afterlives of the Saints: Hagiography, Typology, and Renaissance Literature*. Stanford, CA: Stanford University Press, 1996.
Macmillan, Sarah. "Phenomenal Pain: Embodying the Passion in the *Life of Elizabeth of Spalbeek*." *Postmedieval: A Journal of Medieval Cultural Studies* 8, no. 1 (2016): 102–19.
Matter, E. Ann. "Italian Holy Women: A Survey." In Minnis and Voaden, *Medieval Holy Women*, 529–55.
McEntire, Sandra J., ed. *Margery Kempe: A Book of Essays*. New York: Garland, 1992.
McSheffrey, Shannon. "Heresy, Orthodoxy and English Vernacular Religion 1480–1525." *Past & Present* 186 (2005): 48–80.
Meale, Carol M. *Women and Literature in Britain, 1150–1500*. Cambridge: Cambridge University Press, 1993.

Meyer-Lee, Robert J. *Poets and Power from Chaucer to Wyatt.* Cambridge: Cambridge University Press, 2007.
Miller, Tanya Stabler. *The Beguines of Medieval Paris: Gender, Patronage, and Spiritual Authority.* Philadelphia: University of Pennsylvania Press, 2014.
Minnis, Alastair, and Rosalynn Voaden, eds. *Medieval Holy Women in the Christian Tradition, c. 1100–c. 1500.* Turnhout: Brepols, 2010.
Monta, Sarah Brietz. *Martyrdom and Literature in Early Modern England.* Cambridge: Cambridge University Press, 2005.
Mooney, Catherine M. *Clare of Assisi and the Thirteenth-Century Church: Religious Women, Rules, and Resistance.* Philadelphia: University of Pennsylvania Press, 2016.
Moore, Samuel K. "Patrons of Letters in Norfolk and Suffolk, c. 1450." *PMLA* 27 (1912): 188–207; and 28 (1913): 79–105.
Mulder-Bakker, Anneke. *Lives of the Anchoresses: The Rise of the Urban Recluse in Medieval Europe.* Translated by Myra Heerspink Scholz. Philadelphia: University of Pennsylvania Press, 2005.
Nall, Catherine. *Reading and War in Fifteenth-Century England: From Lydgate to Malory.* Cambridge: D. S. Brewer, 2012.
Nienhuis, Nancy, and Beverly Mayne Kienzle. *Saintly Women: Medieval Saints, Modern Women, and Intimate Partner Violence.* New York: Routledge, 2017.
Nisse, Ruth. "'Was it not Routhe to Se?': Lydgate and the Styles of Martyrdom." In *John Lydgate: Poetry, Culture, and Lancastrian England*, edited by Larry Scanlon and James Simpson, 279–98. Notre Dame, IN: University of Notre Dame Press, 2006.
Nolan, Maura. *John Lydgate and the Making of Public Culture.* Cambridge: Cambridge University Press, 2005.
Pearsall, Derek. *John Lydgate.* Charlottesville: University Press of Virginia, 1970.
Perkins, Nicholas. "Representing Advice in Lydgate." In *The Lancastrian Court: Proceedings of the 2001 Harlaxton Symposium*, edited by Jenny Stratford, 173–91. Donington: Shaun Tyas, 2003.
Peters, Christine. *Patterns of Piety: Women, Gender and Religion in Late Medieval and Reformation England.* Cambridge: Cambridge University Press, 2003.
Petrakopoulos, Anja. "Sanctity and Motherhood: Elizabeth of Thuringia." In *Sanctity and Motherhood: Essays on Holy Mothers in the Middle Ages*, edited by Anneke B. Mulder-Bakker, 259–96. New York: Garland, 1995.
Price, Paul. "Trumping Chaucer: Bokenham's *Katherine*." *Chaucer Review* 36 (2001): 158–83.
Reames, Sherry L. *The Legenda aurea: A Reexamination of Its Paradoxical History.* Madison: University of Wisconsin Press, 1985.
Riches, Samantha. *St. George: Hero, Martyr and Myth.* Stroud: Sutton, 2000.
Rhodes, J. T. "English Books of Martyrs and Saints of the Late Sixteenth and Early Seventeenth Centuries." *Recusant History* 22 (1994): 7–25.
Robertson, Craig A. "The Tithe-Heresy of Friar William Russell." *Albion* 8 (1976): 1–16.

Rubin, Miri, and Walter Simons, eds. *The Cambridge History of Christianity: Christianity in Western Europe, c. 1100–c. 1500*. Cambridge: Cambridge University Press, 2009.
Sahlin, Claire L. "Holy Women of Scandinavia: A Survey." In Minnis and Voaden, *Medieval Holy Women*, 689–723.
Salih, Sarah, ed. *A Companion to Middle English Hagiography*. Cambridge: D. S. Brewer, 2006.
Sanok, Catherine. *Her Life Historical: Exemplarity and Female Saints' Lives in Late Medieval England*. Philadelphia: University of Pennsylvania Press, 2007.
———. *New Legends of England: Forms of Community in Late Medieval Saints' Lives*. Philadelphia: University of Pennsylvania Press, 2018.
Sargent, Michael G. "Censorship or Cultural Change? Reformation and Renaissance in the Spirituality of Late Medieval England." In Gillespie and Ghosh, *After Arundel*, 55–88.
Scase, Wendy. *Reginald Pecock*. Aldershot: Variorum, 1996.
Seymour, M. C. *John Capgrave*. Brookfield, VT: Variorum, 1996.
Sheingorn, Pamela. "Appropriating the Holy Kinship: Gender and Family History." In Ashley and Sheingorn, *Interpreting Cultural Symbols*, 169–98.
Simons, Walter. *Cities of Ladies: Beguine Communities in the Medieval Low Countries, 1200–1565*. Philadelphia: University of Pennsylvania Press, 2001.
———. "Holy Women of the Low Countries: A Survey." In Minnis and Voaden, *Medieval Holy Women in the Christian Tradition*, 625–62.
Simpson, James. "John Lydgate." In *The Cambridge Companion to Medieval English Literature, 1100–1500*, edited by Larry Scanlon, 205–16. Cambridge: Cambridge University Press, 2009.
———. *The Oxford English Literary History*. Vol. 2, *1350–1547: Reform and Cultural Revolution*. Oxford: Oxford University Press, 2002.
———. *Piers Plowman: An Introduction to the B-Text*. London: Longman, 1990.
———. "Reginald Pecock and John Fortescue." In *A Companion to Middle English Prose*, edited by A. S. G. Edwards, 271–87. Cambridge: D. S. Brewer, 2004.
Sisk, Jennifer. "Lydgate's Problematic Commission: A Legend of St. Edmund for Henry VI." *Journal of English and Germanic Philology* 109 (2010): 349–75.
Somerset, Fiona. *Feeling Like Saints: Lollard Writings after Wyclif*. Ithaca, NY: Cornell University Press, 2014.
———. "'Hard is with Seyntis for to make Affray': Lydgate the 'Poet Propagandist' as Hagiographer." In *John Lydgate: Poetry, Culture, and Lancastrian England*, edited by Larry Scanlon and James Simpson, 258–78. Notre Dame, IN: University of Notre Dame Press, 2006.
Spencer, Alice. *Language, Lineage and Location in the Works of Osbern Bokenham*. Newcastle upon Tyne: Cambridge Scholars Publishing, 2013.
Spencer, H. Leith. *English Preaching in the Late Middle Ages*. Oxford: Clarendon, 1993.

Spencer-Hall, Alicia. *Medieval Saints and Modern Screens: Divine Visions as Cinematic Experience.* Amsterdam: Amsterdam University Press, 2017.

Staley, Lynn. *Margery Kempe's Dissenting Fictions.* University Park: Pennsylvania State University Press, 1994.

Stargardt, Ute. "The Beguines of Belgium, the Dominican Nuns of Germany, and Margery Kempe." In *The Popular Literature of Medieval England*, edited by Thomas J. Hefferman, 277–313. Knoxville: University of Tennessee Press, 1985.

Straker, Scott-Morgan. "Propaganda, Intentionality, and the Lancastrian Lydgate." In *John Lydgate: Poetry, Culture, and Lancastrian England*, edited by Larry Scanlon and James Simpson, 98–128. Notre Dame, IN: University of Notre Dame Press, 2006.

Strohm, Paul. "Walking Fire: Symbolization, Action, and Lollard Burning." In *Theory and the Premodern Text*, 20–32. Minneapolis: University of Minnesota Press, 2000.

———, ed. *Oxford Twenty-First Century Approaches to Literature: Middle English.* Oxford: Oxford University Press, 2009.

Surtz, Ronald E. "Iberian Holy Women: A Survey." In Minnis and Voaden, *Medieval Holy Women*, 499–525.

Van Dijk, Mathilde. "Being Saint Barbara in England: Shifting Patterns of Holiness in the Later Middle Ages." In *Transforming Holiness: Representations of Holiness in English and American Literary Texts*, edited by Irene Visser and Helen Wilcox, 1–19. Leuven: Peeters, 2006.

———. *Een rij van spiegels: De Heilige Barbara van Nicomedia als voorbeeld voor vrouwelijke religieuzen.* Hilersum: Uitgeverij Verloren, 2000.

Van Engen, John. "Communal Life: The Sister-Books." In Minnis and Voaden, *Medieval Holy Women*, 105–31.

Von Contzen, Eva. *The Scottish Legendary: Towards a Poetics of Hagiographic Narration.* Manchester: Manchester University Press, 2016.

Walsh, Christine. *The Cult of St. Katherine of Alexandria in Early Medieval Europe.* Burlington, VT: Ashgate, 2007.

Warren, Ann K. *Anchorites and Their Patrons in Medieval England.* Berkeley: University of California Press, 1985.

Warren, Nancy Bradley. *The Embodied Word: Female Spiritualities, Contested Orthodoxies, and English Religious Cultures, 1350–1700.* Notre Dame, IN: University of Notre Dame Press, 2010.

Watson, Nicholas. "Censorship and Cultural Change in Late-Medieval England: Vernacular Theology, the Oxford Translation Debate, and Arundel's Constitutions of 1409." *Speculum* 70 (1995): 822–64.

———. "'A clerke schulde have it of kinde for to kepe counsel.'" In Gillespie and Ghosh, *After Arundel*, 563–89.

Watt, Diane. "Margery Kempe" (April 26, 2018). *Oxford Bibliographies: British and Irish Literature.* http://oxfordbibliographies.com.

Welsh, Jennifer. *The Cult of St. Anne in Medieval and Early Modern Europe.* New York: Routledge, 2017.

Whatley, E. Gordon, "John Lydgate's *Saint Austin at Compton*: The Poem and Its Sources." In *Anglo-Latin and Its Heritage: Essays in Honour of A. G. Rigg on His 64th Birthday*, edited by Siân Echard and Gernot R. Wieland, 191–227. Publications of the Journal of Medieval Latin 4. Turnhout: Brepols, 2001.

White, Helen C. *Tudor Books of Saints and Martyrs.* Madison: University of Wisconsin Press, 1963.

Windeatt, Barry. "1412–1534: Texts." In *The Cambridge Companion to Medieval English Mysticism*, edited by Samuel Fanous and Vincent Gillespie, 195–224. Cambridge: Cambridge University Press, 2011.

Winstead, Karen A. "John Capgrave and the Chaucer Tradition." *Chaucer Review* 30 (1996): 389–400.

———. *John Capgrave's Fifteenth Century.* Philadelphia: University of Pennsylvania Press, 2007.

———. "John Lydgate's 'Mumming at Windsor': Clothilda, Women's Steadfastness, and Lancastrian Rule." *Chaucer Review* 49, no. 2 (2014): 228–43.

———. "Lydgate's Lives of Saints Edmund and Alban: Martyrdom and 'Prudent Pollicie.'" *Mediaevalia* 17 (1994): 221–41.

———. "Medieval Life-Writing and the Strange Case of Margery Kempe." In Leader, *On Life-Writing*, 142–60. Oxford: Oxford University Press, 2015.

———. "Osbern Bokenham's 'englische boke': Re-forming Holy Women." In *Form and Reform: Reading across the Fifteenth Century*, edited by Shannon Gayk and Kathleen Tonry, 67–87. Columbus: Ohio State University Press, 2011.

———. *The Oxford History of Life-Writing: The Middle Ages.* Oxford: Oxford University Press, 2018.

———. *Virgin Martyrs: Legends of Sainthood in Late Medieval England.* Ithaca, NY: Cornell University Press 1997.

Wogan-Browne, Jocelyn. "Bodies of Belief: MS Bodley 779's *South English Legendary*." In *Rethinking the South English Legendaries*, edited by Heather Blurton and Jocelyn Wogan-Browne, 403–23. Manchester: Manchester University Press, 2011.

———. *Saints' Lives and Women's Literary Culture: Virginity and Its Authorizations.* Oxford: Oxford University Press, 2001.

Wogan-Browne, Jocelyn, Rosalynn Voaden, Arlyn Diamond, Ann Hutchison, Carol Meale, and Lesley Johnson, eds. *Medieval Women: Texts and Contexts in Late Medieval Britain.* Turnhout: Brepols, 2000.

Woodcock, Matthew. "Crossovers and Afterlife." In *A Companion to Middle English Hagiography*, edited by Sarah Salih, 68–156. Cambridge: D. S. Brewer, 2006.

Wooding, Lucy E. C. *Rethinking Catholicism in Reformation England.* Oxford: Clarendon, 2000.

INDEX

Adhelm, 80, 128, 130
Allen, Edmund, 138
Alnwick, William, Bishop of Norwich, 4
Alpais of Cudot, 102
anchoress, 6, 102
Armstrong, C. A. J., 105
Arundel, Thomas, Archbishop of Canterbury, 3–4, 99–100
Augustine of Hippo, 13, 57, 86, 91, 92, 99

Badby, John, 3
Bale, Anthony, 13
Barclay, George
   Life of Saint George, 7, 148–52
Beatas, 102
Beatrijs of Nazareth, 102
Bede, 25, 80, 133
Bedford Hours, 14–15, 19
beguines, 2, 101–2, 106–7
Bell, Rudolph, 103, 110
Berkeley, Elizabeth, 103
Bilney, Thomas, 138
Bokenham, Osbern, 2, 5–6, 41–74, 92–94
  Abbotsford legendary, 3, 55–57, 80, 132–33
  Arundel 327 (*Legendys of Hooly Wummen*), 41, 43–55, 56–57, 71, 156

narrative voice, 41–45
patrons, 41, 44, 55
—Bourchier, Isabel, 43–44
—Burgh, Thomas, 41–43
—Denston, John and Katherine, 44, 54–55
—Elizabeth Vere, Countess of Oxford, 44
prologues, 41–45, 56
publication, 41–43, 55–56
Bokenham, Osbern, works of
  "Agatha," 56
  "Agnes," 56
  "Ambrose," 56, 76
  "Anne," 48–55
  "Apollonia," 56, 71–73, 77
  "Audrey," 56, 60–62
  "Barbara," 56, 65–69
  "Cecilia," 92–94
  "Christine," 56
  "Clare of Assisi," 56, 106
  "David of Wales," 80
  "Dorothy," 56
  "Elizabeth," 46–48, 106
  "Faith," 56
  "John of Beverley," 80
  "Katherine," 92
  Mappula angliae, 55, 104
  "Margaret," 41–43, 56
  "Martha," 69–71
  "Martina," 56

Bokenham, Osbern, works of (cont.)
  "Mary Magdalene," 44, 56
  "Mary of Egypt," 56
  "Monica," 56–60
  "Paula," 56–60
  "Priscilla," 56
  "Ursula," 56
  "Vincent," 56
  "Winifred," 56, 60, 63–65
Books of Hours, 8–9, 71
Bozon, Nicholas, 2, 103
Bradford, John, 138
Bradshaw, Henry
  Life of Saint Werburge, 7, 148–51
Bridget of Sweden, 6, 102, 105, 106, 110, 113–14, 118
Brown, Jennifer N., 106, 107, 110
Burgh, Thomas, 41, 42, 156
Bynum, Caroline Walker, 103, 110

Camp, Cynthia Turner, 9, 81, 104–5
Capgrave, John, 77, 93, 100
  Abbreviation of Chronicles, 103–4
  Life of Saint Augustine, 76
  Life of Saint Katherine, 1, 45, 78–79, 82, 89–92
Catherine of Genoa, 102
Catherine of Siena, 6, 102, 105, 106
  Middle English prose life of, 106, 110–11
  Pepwell's extracts, 121–22
Catto, Jeremy, 4
Caxton, William, 4
  Legenda aurea sanctorum, 7, 79–80, 82, 106, 133–36, 146
censorship, 3–4, 76
Chaucer, Geoffrey, 13, 20, 147
Chichile, Henry, Archbishop of Canterbury, 4, 14
Christina Mirabilis, 6
  Middle English prose life of, 106–10
Christina of Markyate, 102
Clare of Assisi, 56, 106, 110
Cole, Andrew, 4, 39

"Constitutions" of 1409, 3, 39, 76, 99–100
Conversion of Paul (Digby 133), 85
Copeland, Rita, 3
Council of Vienne, 107
Curteys, William, 31, 32

Dailey, Alice, 142
De heretic comburendo, 3
Dendle, Peter, 128
Devotio moderna, 65, 95
Dillon, Janette, 115
Douce 114, Bodleian Library MS, 106–10
Dresvina, Juliana, 82
Duffy, Eamon, 77

Edward III, 14
Elizabeth de Burgh, 102, 106
Elizabeth of Hungary, 6, 46, 106, 110, 114
Elizabeth of Spalbeek, 113
  Middle English prose life of, 106–10
Elliott, Dyan, 107
Eucharist, 83, 89, 103, 107–10, 114, 117, 158
Eusebius, *Ecclesiastical History*, 71

Falconer, John
  Life of Saint Catherine of Sweden, 152
  Life of Saint Winifred, 158–59
Foxe, John
  Acts and Monuments, 7, 126, 136–46, 152
Freeman, Thomas S., 136

Ganim, John, 31
Garnier of Pont-Sainte-Maxence
  Life of Thomas Becket, 2
Gayk, Shannon, 3
Geoffrey, Abbot of St. Albans, 102
Gibson, Gail, 49
Gilte Legende (1438), 125–32
  "Alban," 127
  "Edmund of Abingdon," 131

"Edward the Confessor," 130–31
"Katherine," 79, 127
"Malchus," 127–30
"Thomas Becket," 131–32
Gray, Christa, 127–28

hagiography
   education in, 36–39, 75–100,
     137–38, 147, 153–55, 157, 158–59
   epic, 31, 148
   exemplarity in, 24, 31, 45, 57, 60,
     148, 156–57
   family life in, 2, 42, 60–63, 65–70,
     72–74, 138–40, 149–50, 155,
     156–57, 158–59
   friendship in, 23–24
   intellectualism of, 3, 60 61, 142, 147
   marriage in, 46–62, 119–20, 139–40,
     157–58
   narrative voice, 1–2, 127
   Reformist impulses in, 5, 39, 146–47
   Renaissance, 7–8, 147–60 (*see also*
     Foxe, John)
   "teaching hagiographies," 5, 75–76,
     82–100, 118, 151
   theology in, 3, 6, 75–76, 85–100
Hawkins, Henry
   Fuga Saeculi, 152–56
   History of S. Elizabeth, 159–60
   Life of S. Aldegond, 153
Henry V, 11–12, 14–15
Henry VI, 12, 31
Hildegard of Bingen, 102
Hilton, Walter, 105, 118
Hooper, John, 138–39
Horobin, Simon, 3, 132
Horstmann, Carl, 156
Howard, Robert
   Mary of Egypt, 158
Howlett, D. R., 32
Humphrey, Duke of Gloucester, 32
Hunter, William, 138

Jacobus de Voragine 44–45, 86–87,
   125–26, 142, 145, 147
   Legenda aurea, 2, 3

—"Anne," 48–49
—"Apollonia," 71
—"Elizabeth," 46–47
—English translations of, 5, 7, 80,
   125–36
—"George," 15–19
—"Giles," 21–23
—"Katherine," 79
—"Martha," 70–71
—"Monica," 57
Jacques de Vitry, 106, 107
Jean de Vignay
   Légende dorée, 126
Jerome
   Life of Malchus, 1, 59–60, 127
Jewet Metles, 6, 103
Joan of Acre, 6, 104–5
John of Bedford, 14–15
John of Wackerzele, 65, 95
Jones, Sarah Rees, 119

Kempe, Margery, 59, 105
   Book of Margery Kempe, 2, 103,
     111–23
   printed extracts from, 111, 120–23
Kerby-Fulton, Kathryn, 4, 100
King, John, 137
Krug, Rebecca, 122
Kurtz, Patricia, 107, 111

Langland, William
   Piers Plowman, 87–88
Lateran IV, 107
Lewis, Katherine J., 118
Lollardy, 3, 107, 109, 114, 146
Lombard, Peter, 86, 88, 91
Love, Nicholas
   *Mirror of the Blessed Life of Jesus
     Christ*, 58, 105
Lydgate, John, 2, 5, 11–39, 45, 56, 74,
   148
   audience, 11–12, 19–20
   influence, 11, 39
   Lancastrians and, 5, 11–12, 39
   patrons
   —Curteys, William 31

Lydgate, John (*continued*)
— Henry V, 11–12
— Humphrey, Duke of Gloucester, 32
— Whethamstede, John, 31–32
style, 13–14, 20, 25, 31
Lydgate, John, works of
Alban and Amphibalus, 1, 5, 31–39, 74
"Austin," 1, 5, 25–31
Edmund and Fremund, 1, 12, 13, 31
Fall of Princes, 12, 136
"George," 5, 14–19, 74, 77
"Giles," 1, 5, 19–25
Guy of Warwick, 13
hymns, 12
Life of Our Lady, 11–12
"Margaret," 13
"Mumming at Windsor," 13
Petronilla, 13, 74
prayers, 20–21
Testament, 13
Troy Book, 11, 31, 136

Maconi, Stephen, 106, 110
Malory, Thomas, 136
Margaret, Duchess of Clarence, 75
Marie d'Oignies, 6, 113–14
  Middle English prose life of, 106–10
Mary I, 142
McSheffrey, Shannon, 4
Mechtilde of Hackeborn, 105
Mirk, John, 86

Netter, Thomas, 118
Neville, Anne, 103
Nolan, Maura, 12
N-Town play of Anne, 49–51

Paris, Matthew, 101
Pecock, Reginald, 4, 86–89, 99
penance, 23, 75, 114, 115, 122, 150
Pepwell, Henry, 121–23
Philip of Clairvaux, 106

Pinzochere, 102
Play of Mary Magdalene (Digby 133), 6, 82–85
Poor Clares, 102
Porete, Marguerite, 107
Pynson, Richard, 4, 148

Raymond of Capua, 106, 111
Reames, Sherry, 135
Reformation, 5, 7, 10, 39, 142, 145–46
Reynes, Robert, of Acle, 49
Rhodes, J. T., 152
Rolle, Richard, 118

sacraments, 82, 107, 109–10, 113–15. *See also* Eucharist; penance
saints
  Aldegond, 153
  Anne, 49 (*see also* Bokenham, Osbern; N-Town play of Anne)
  Anthony of Padua, 153
  Augustine of Canterbury, 25 (*see also* Lydgate, John)
  Barbara, 6, 77, 94 (*see also* Bokenham, Osbern)
  — Middle English prose life of, 95–99
  Bernard of Clairvaux, 153–55
  Catherine of Sweden, 152
  Cecilia, 13, 20, 44, 77, 92–94, 100, 140–41
  Crispin and Crispinian, 134
  Edmund of Abingdon, 2, 130–31
  Edward the Confessor, 13, 104, 130, 155–56
  Elizabeth (*see* Bokenham, Osbern)
  Eugenia, 141, 144–45
  Eustace, 143
  Fiacre, 134
  George, 14–15, 105, 134, 148–51 (*see also* Barclay, George; Jacobus de Voragine; Lydgate, John)
  Giles, 19–20
  Jerome, 3 (*see also* Wynter, Simon)
  John the Baptist, 105
  — Middle English prose life of, 81

John the Evangelist
— Middle English prose life of, 77–78, 81
Katherine of Alexandria, 2, 6, 78–80, 118, 130, 135, 143, 147 (*see also* Capgrave, John)
— Middle English prose life of, 78–79, 81
Malachy, 153
Malchus, 128 (*see also Gilte Legende*; Jerome), 152
Mary Magdalene, 3, 76, 82–85, 105
Nonna, 157–58
Pachomius, 153
Petronilla, 8–9
Rigobert, 134
Roche, 133–34
Stephen, 154–55
Thomas Becket, 2, 131, 135
Werburge, 148–51
See also Bridget of Sweden, Catherine of Siena, Christina Mirabilis, Elizabeth of Hungary, Elizabeth of Spalbeek, Marie d'Oignies
Sanok, Catherine, 9, 31, 54, 105
Sawtry, William, 3
scripture, 3, 5, 26, 28, 37, 39, 43, 57, 60, 77, 80–88, 108, 114, 133, 134, 137–41, 152–57
Shirley, John, 14

Simon, Walter, 101
Simpson, James, 99
Somerset, Fiona, 5
South English Legendary, 80, 81, 128, 130, 147
Spalbeek, Elizabeth, 6, 106–10
Speculum Sacerdotale, 86
Stafford, John, Archbishop of Canterbury, 4
Stowe 53, British Library MS (*Lives of Women Saints*), 156–58
Strohm, Paul, 3

Thomas of Cantimpré, 106
tithing, 26–31
Trinity, 6, 75–76, 85–99

Van Dijk, Mathilde, 95
vernacular theology, 4, 108

Waste, Joan, 137
Watson, Nicholas, 3
Whethamstede, John, Abbot of St. Albans, 31–32
White, Raulins, 137–38, 141
Wogan-Browne, Jocelyn, 80, 82
Wycliffism, 3–4
Wynkyn de Worde, 4, 106, 111, 123
Wynter, Simon
Life of Saint Jerome, 7, 75, 76, 81, 82

KAREN A. WINSTEAD
is professor of English at the Ohio State University. She is the author and translator of a number of books, including *The Life of Saint Katherine of Alexandria* by John Capgrave (University of Notre Dame Press, 2011).

www.ingramcontent.com/pod-product-compliance
Lightning Source LLC
Chambersburg PA
CBHW061446300426
44114CB00014B/1856